S0-ABK-820

HEILONGJIANG

○ Ruins of Longquanfu, Capital of Bohai Fiefdom

Lugou Bridge
Beihai and the Round City
White Dagoba and Miaoying Temple
Palace Museum
Ming Mausolea
Altar of Heaven
Ancient Observatory
Summer Palace

Chengde Garden Resort
Puning Temple
Putuozongsheng Temple

INNER MONGOLIA

LIAONING

Northern Mausoleum
Imperial Palace in Shenyang

○ Fengguo Temple

Wanbuhuayan
Sutra Pagoda

Great Wall
at Badaling

Dule Temple
Eastern Qing Mausolea

Shanhai Pass

Yungang Caves
Huayan Temple

BEIJING
Zhoukoudian, the Home of Peking Man

Mausoleum of
Genghis Khan ○

HEBEI

TIANJIN

Sakyamuni Pagoda of Fogong Temple

Nanchan Temple
Temple of Buddha's Light

Longxing Temple

Water City of Penglai

Jin
Temple

Anji Bridge

SHANDONG

SHAANXI

SHANXI

Four Gate Pagoda

Guangsheng
Temple

Yin Ruins

Temple and
Mansion of
Confucius

n Shihuang
Pits

○ Mausoleum of
Yellow Emperor

Yongle
Palace

Youguo
Temple Pagoda

Shaolin Monastery
Songyue Temple Pagoda
Gaocheng Observatory

Longmen Caves
White Horse Temple

HENAN

JIANGSU

ANHUI

Ruins of Zhongdu and Stone Carvings of Imperial Mausoleum

Narrow West Lake

HUBEI

Taihe Palace

Xiao Mausoleum

Taibai Memorial
Hall and Tomb

Hanshan Temple
Tiger Hill Pagoda
Fisherman's Garden

SHANGHAI
Yu Garden

Jade Spring Temple
and its Iron Pagoda

Xingshengjiao Temple Pagoda

g Huan Tower

Chu Town of
Ji'nancheng

West Lake
Six Harmonies Pagoda

Tianyige Library

Baoguo Temple

ulptures on Beishan
culptures on Baoding Mountain

ZHEJIANG

HUNAN

Western Han Tombs
at Mawangdui

JIANGXI

FUJIAN

Ling Canal

Kaiyuan Monastery
Qingjing Mosque

Anping Bridge

TAIWAN

GUANGXI

GUANGDONG

Chikan Building
Temple of Prince Yanping
Anping Castle
Temple of Confucius in Tainan

Chen Family Memorial Hall
Guangxiao Temple

Zhenwu Pavilion

THROUGH THE MOON GATE:
A GUIDE TO CHINA'S HISTORIC MONUMENTS

THROUGH THE MOON GATE

A GUIDE TO CHINA'S HISTORIC MONUMENTS

HONG KONG   OXFORD   NEW YORK
OXFORD UNIVERSITY PRESS
1986

Oxford University Press

Oxford New York Toronto
Delhi Bombay Calcutta Madras Karachi
Petaling Jaya Singapore Hong Kong Tokyo
Nairobi Dar es Salaam Cape Town
Melbourne Auckland

and associated companies in
Beirut Berlin Ibadan Nicosia

Library of Congress Cataloging-in-Publication Data

Through the Moon Gate.

Includes index.
1. Historic sites—China—Guide-books. 2. China—
Description and travel—1976- —Guide-books.
3. Monuments—China—Guide-books. I. Oxford University Press.
DS705.T46 1986 915.1'0458 86-21701
ISBN 0-19-584077-1
ISBN 0-19-584176-X (pbk.)

British Library Cataloguing in Publication Data

Through the Moon Gate: a guide to China's
historic monuments.
1. Historic buildings — China —
Guide-books 2. China — Description
and travel — 1976- — Guide-books
915.1'0458 DS712

ISBN 0-19-584077-1

ISBN 0-19-584176-X Pbk

Edited by the China People's Publishing House of Fine Arts
Printed in Hong Kong by Golden Cup Printing Co. Ltd.
Published by Oxford University Press, Warwick House, Hong Kong

Contents

Acknowledgements ix
Chronology of Chinese Dynasties x
Introduction xi

The City of Beijing 北京市 1
  Zhoukoudian, the Home of Peking Man 周口店 2
  The Lugou Bridge 芦沟桥 4
  Beihai and the Round City 北海及团城 6
  The White Dagoba and the Miaoying Temple 妙应寺白塔 9
  The Palace Museum 故宫 12
  The Ming Mausolea 明十三陵 16
  The Altar of Heaven 天坛 19
  The Ancient Observatory 古观象台 22
  The Great Wall at Badaling 八达岭长城 24
  The Summer Palace 颐和园 26

The City of Tianjin 天津市 32
  The Dule Temple 独乐寺 33

Hebei Province 河北省 37
  The Anji Bridge 安济桥 38
  The Longxing Temple 隆兴寺 39
  The Shanhai Pass 山海关 44
  The Eastern Qing Mausolea 清东陵 46
  The Chengde Garden Resort 避暑山庄 49
  The Puning Temple 普宁寺 52
  The Putuozongsheng Temple 普陀宗乘之庙 55

Shandong Province 山东省 57
  The Four Gate Pagoda 四门塔 58

The Temple and Mansion of Confucius 孔庙及孔府   59
The Water City of Penglai 蓬莱水城及蓬莱阁   65

Jiangsu Province 江苏省   68
The Hanshan Temple 寒山寺   69
The Tiger Hill Pagoda 虎丘塔   71
The Xiao Mausoleum 明孝陵   73
The Fisherman's Garden 网师园   76
The Narrow West Lake 瘦西湖   79

The City of Shanghai 上海市   82
The Xingshengjiao Temple Pagoda 兴圣教寺塔   83
The Yu Garden 豫园   85

Zhejiang Province 浙江省   87
The Baoguo Temple 保国寺   88
The Six Harmonies Pagoda 六和塔   90
The Tianyige Library 天一阁   92
The West Lake 西湖   95

Anhui Province 安徽省   98
The Taibai Memorial Hall and Tomb 太白楼及李白衣冠冢   99
The Ruins of Zhongdu and the Stone Carvings of
  the Imperial Mausoleum 明中都皇城遗址及皇陵石刻   100

Fujian Province 福建省   103
The Kaiyuan Monastery 开元寺   104
The Qingjing Mosque 清净寺   106
The Anping Bridge 安平桥   109

Guangdong Province 广东省   112
The Guangxiao Temple 光孝寺   113
The Chen Family Memorial Hall 陈家祠   115

Guangxi Province 广西省   118
The Ling Canal 灵渠   119
The Zhenwu Pavilion 真武阁   122

Yunnan Province 云南省   124
The Ruins of the Town of Taihe and the Dehua
  Tablet of Nan Zhao 太和城遗址及南诏德化碑   125
The Scripture Pillar of the Ksitigarbha Temple 地藏寺经幢   125
The Golden Hall of the Taihegong Temple 太和宫金殿   128

Sichuan Province 四川省   130
The Du River Dyke 都江堰   131

The Feng Huan Tower 冯焕阙 133
The Great Statue of Maitreya at Leshan 乐山大佛 135
The Buddhist Sculptures on Beishan 北山摩崖造像 137
The Buddhist Sculptures on Baodingshan 宝顶山摩崖造像 139
The Zhuge Liang Memorial Hall 武侯祠 141
Du Fu's Cottage 杜甫草堂 144

Hunan Province 湖南省 148
The Western Han Tombs at Mawangdui 马王堆汉墓 149

Hubei Province 湖北省 153
The Chu Town of Ji'nancheng 楚纪南城 154
The Jade Spring Temple and its Iron Pagoda 玉泉寺及铁塔 155
The Taihe Palace 太和宫 158

Henan Province 河南省 162
The Yin Ruins 殷墟 163
The Longmen Caves 龙门石窟 166
The Shaolin Monastery 少林寺 169
The Songyue Temple Pagoda 嵩岳寺塔 174
The Youguo Temple Pagoda 祐国寺塔 176
The White Horse Temple 白马寺 179
The Gaocheng Observatory 观星台 181

Shanxi Province 山西省 184
The Yungang Caves 云冈石窟 185
The Nanchan Temple 南禅寺 189
The Temple of Buddha's Light 佛光寺 192
The Jin Temple 晋祠 196
The Huayan Temple 华严寺 200
The Sakyamuni Pagoda of the Fogong Temple 佛宫寺释迦塔 203
The Yongle Palace 永乐宫 206
The Guangsheng Temple 广胜寺 210

Shaanxi Province 陕西省 215
The Mausoleum of the Yellow Emperor 黄帝陵 216
The Neolithic Village of Banpo 半坡遗址 218
The Mausoleum of Qin Shihuang and its Auxiliary Pits
   of Pottery Figures 秦始皇陵及兵马俑从葬坑 219
The Mao Mausoleum and the Tomb of Huo Qubing
   茂陵及霍去病墓 223
The Forest of Stelae 西安碑林 226
The Large Wild Goose Pagoda 大雁塔 229
The Small Wild Goose Pagoda 小雁塔 231

The Qian Mausoleum 乾陵 234
The City Walls of Xi'an 西安城墙 236

Liaoning Province 辽宁省 239
The Fengguo Temple 奉国寺 240
The Imperial Palace in Shenyang 沈阳故宫 242
The Northern Mausoleum 北陵 246

Heilongjiang Province 黑龙江省 250
The Ruins of Longquanfu, Capital of the Bohai Fiefdom
渤海上京龙泉府遗址 251

Inner Mongolia 內蒙古 253
The Wanbuhuayan Sutra Pagoda 万部华严经塔 254
The Mausoleum of Genghis Khan 成吉思汗陵 256

Ningxia Province 宁夏省 258
The Haibao Pagoda 海宝塔 259

Gansu Province 甘肃省 262
The Mogao Caves near Dunhuang 莫高窟 263
The Bingling Monastery Caves 炳灵寺石窟 267
The Maijishan Caves 麦积山石窟 269
The Jiayu Pass 嘉峪关 271

Qinghai Province 青海省 275
The Ta'er Lamasery 塔尔寺 276

Xinjiang Province 新疆省 278
The Ancient City of Gaochang 高昌故城 279
The Caves of the Thousand Buddhas at Kezir 克孜尔千佛洞 280

Tibet 西藏
The Dazhao Monastery 大昭寺 284
The Tasilhunpo Temple 扎什伦布寺 285
The Potala Palace 布达拉宫 290

Taiwan 台湾省 294
The Anping Castle 安平古堡 295
The Chikan Building 赤嵌楼 296
The Temple of Prince Yanping 延平郡王祠 297
The Temple of Confucius in Tainan 台南孔庙 298

Glossary 300
Index of Persons 303
Index of Places 306

Acknowledgements

The publisher would like to thank the China People's Publishing House of Fine Arts for editing this book, and would also like to thank the following for their help in its compilation:

Chief compilers: Luo Zhewen, Shen Peng
Associate compilers: Lin Wenbi, Zu Youyi
Consultants: Zhao Bochu, Shao Yu
Authors: Luo Zhewen, Xiao Lin, Ji Feng, Zhang Rong, Guo Zhan, Wu Benhua, Yang En, Xu Dongsheng, Tian Cun, Zhang Xiaoping
Photographers: Luo Zhewen, Di Xianghua, Xiao Shunquan, Xu Zhenshi, Ma Gejun, Yang Limin, Zhou Yi, Mou Hangyuan, Xiong Ruqing, Liu Zhenqing, Jiang Jingyu, Hu Chui, Hu Weibiao, Cheng Jingping, Ye Yongcai, Zhang Yiling, Ren Guoxing, Gu Shengtian, Chen Keyin, Liu Chen, Chen Jinjing, Zhang Hanyi, Shao Huaan, Cao Yuquan, Lan Peijin, Zhou Rende, Zheng Kejun, Wang Xinhui, Guo Yiqing, Xu Bang, Luo Mingyang, An Zheng, Feng Xiaoming, Huang Jianqiu, Xu Yuanrong, Zhang Dezhong, Jin Xuqi, Liu Qi, Wang Pei, Wu Benhua, An Xiaoyuan, Feng Fei, Yan Zhongyi, He Chuan, Zhang Rong, Lei Qibin, Ji Feng, Xiao Zhuang, Ru Suichu, Tian Chuanjun, Yan Wu
Translators: Wang Mingjie, Carole Murray, Li Chunjia
Translation consultant: Yang Xianyi
Artist: Fu Mali

Chronology of Chinese Dynasties

Xia	*c.* 22nd century–17th century BC
Shang	*c.* 17th century–11th century BC
Zhou	*c.* 11th century–771 BC
Qin	221–206 BC
Western Han	206 BC–AD 25
Eastern Han	25–220
Three Kingdoms	220–280
Jin	265–420
Southern and Northern Dynasties	420–589
Sui	581–618
Tang	618–907
Five Dynasties	907–960
Song	960–1279
Liao	907–1125
Jin	1115–1234
Yuan	1206–1368
Ming	1368–1644
Qing	1644–1911

Introduction

China is an ancient civilization with a long history. The Chinese people have created a brilliant culture, and made great contributions to world science and technology. It was in China that the compass, gunpowder and printing were invented. Achievements in astronomy, medicine, metallurgy, and the production of textiles and porcelain date back several thousand years and are recorded in numerous early histories.

Trade and cultural exchanges between China and other countries began as early as two thousand years ago. In the Western Han dynasty the Silk Road was established, linking China with the countries of Central Asia and Europe. China's silks and embroidered brocades were greatly admired abroad and at the same time various textiles and fruits were introduced to China along this route. The spread of Buddhism, Islam and Catholicism helped promote an exchange of knowledge in science and other subjects. The monk Xuanzang sought Buddhist scriptures in India; the monk Jianzhen travelled to Japan; Admiral Zheng He made seven visits to Asian and African countries; Buddhism was spread by Kasyapa-matanga and Dharmaranga from Central Asia; Marco Polo from Venice and Anigo from Nepal worked as officials for the Yuan dynasty.

The one hundred sites selected for this book range from a cave of the Pleistocene Era to monuments built in the last several centuries. They reflect various aspects of Chinese culture as well as early cultural exchanges with other countries.

Ancient graves are treasure troves of Chinese antiquities. A rich variety of human fossils, innumerable stone tools and fossils of extinct animals and plants over half a million years old were discovered at Zhoukoudian, the site of Peking Man. Objects unearthed at Banpo Village in Xi'an illustrate the life of a primitive village of five to six thousand years ago. Relics discovered at Anyang in Henan province have already been widely published. Since great attention was paid to the burial of the dead during these early periods, a large number of artefacts have been found in ancient graves, particularly in imperial mausolea, the scale of which is quite magnificent. Examples of mausolea covered in this book are the Qin Shihuang Mausoleum and its pottery figures of warriors and horses, the Mao Mausoleum of a Han emperor, the Qian Mausoleum of Emperor Gaozong and Empress Wu Zetian, the Xiao Mausoleum of the Ming Emperor Hongwu and the Thirteen Ming Mausolea, the Northern Mausoleum of Abahai and the Eastern Qing Mausolea.

Many of China's ancient monuments rank among the world's great architectural achievements: in or near Beijing the Forbidden City, the Altar of Heaven, Beihai, the Summer Palace, the Great Wall, and the Ming Mausolea; in Chengde the summer mountain resort with its eight outer temples; in Shenyang the Imperial Palace and the Northern Mausoleum; in Hebei province the Eastern and Western Qing Mausolea; and in Nanjing the tombs of the Six Dynasties period and the Ming dynasty Xiao Mausoleum.

The Anji Bridge in Zhaoxian county in Hebei province, built in the Sui dynasty, is the earliest known open spandrel bridge, and the Anping Bridge, 5 kilometres long, in Quanzhou in Fujian province is the longest bridge dating from the Middle Ages. Several thousand pagodas, some as high as 100 metres, tower over towns and villages and become part of mountain scenery. Buddhist and Daoist temples, mosques and cathedrals are all distinctive examples of Chinese architecture.

The Chinese garden is unique in the art of garden design: 'Though made by human hands, it is as natural as if made by Heaven.' Chinese culture is reflected in the art of the garden. Although often to be found within the precincts of imperial palaces, temples, and high officials' mansions, there are also many famous private gardens in China such as the Zhouzheng Garden, the Liu Garden and the Fisherman's Garden in Suzhou, the Narrow West Lake in Yangzhou, and the Yu Garden in Shanghai, all of which are of historical and artistic value.

Cave temples are some of the richest storehouses of ancient Chinese murals and sculpture. The wall paintings and sculpture in the Mogao Caves at Dunhuang in Gansu province, created by artists from the fourth to the fourteenth century, are splendid and of high artistic value. The stone carvings of Yungang in Shanxi province and of Longmen in Henan province, both created over several centuries ago, number as many as ten thousand. Other examples are the Giant Buddha of Leshan and the realistic stone sculptures of Dazu. All of these attract large numbers of artists and tourists.

Among the sites in this book, many bear witness to the cultural exchanges between China and other countries. In the White Horse Temple in Luoyang, the first Buddhist temple in China, for instance, can be seen the tombs of two Indian monks, Kasyapa-matanga and Dharmaranga. At the Large Wild Goose Temple and the Xingjiao Temple in Xi'an Xuanzang translated the Buddhist scriptures he had brought back from India. The Qingjing Mosque in Quanzhou was built by Arabs, and the White Dagoba in Beijing was designed and built by the Nepalese artisan, Anigo, in the Yuan dynasty. Astronomical instruments at Beijing's Ancient Observatory were designed by Ferdinand Verbiest and others. Paintings, sculpture and architecture in many parts of China attest to the cultural exchanges between China and other countries.

Owing to the limitations of this book, we are able to include only one hundred sites of historical interest. However, it is to be hoped that those chosen will provide a general outline of the richness of Chinese civilization.

The City of Beijing
北京市

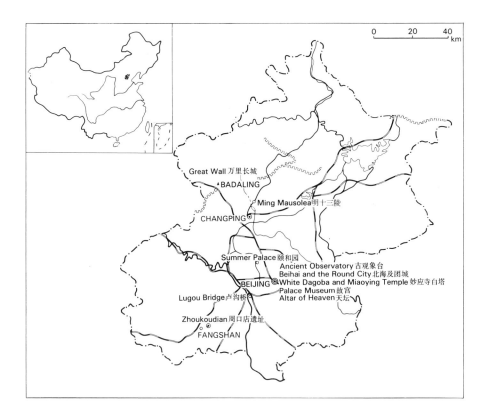

0 20 40
km

Great Wall 万里长城
BADALING
Ming Mausolea 明十三陵
CHANGPING
Summer Palace 颐和园
Ancient Observatory 古观象台
Beihai and the Round City 北海及团城
BEIJING White Dagoba and Miaoying Temple 妙应寺白塔
Lugou Bridge 卢沟桥 Palace Museum 故宫
Altar of Heaven 天坛
Zhoukoudian 周口店遗址
FANGSHAN

Zhoukoudian

ZHOUKOUDIAN, THE HOME OF PEKING MAN
周口店

History
In the early 1920s men working at a limestone quarry near Beijing came across fossilized animal bones in a cave in Dragon Bone Hill (Longgushan), and formal excavations, which began in 1927, led to the discovery of a large quantity of similar bones. Of particular importance were unusual jaw bones and teeth which were believed to be those of either humans or apes. Having analysed them, anthropologists concluded that they were the bones of a hominid, which they named Peking Man. On 2 December 1929 Pei Wenzhong, the noted Chinese paleoanthropologist, discovered the cranium of an early hominid, after which large-scale excavations continued for

more than a decade, uncovering 5 fairly complete skulls, 9 skull fragments, 6 fragments of facial bones, 15 mandibles, 152 teeth and a number of fragmented limb bones, altogether the remains of more than 40 individuals. Scientific analysis revealed that Peking Man lived during the middle period of the Pleistocene Era.

Description

The skull of Peking Man is characterized by a low, flat crown, a receding forehead and heavy brow bones interlocking to form a ridge protruding over the eyes. The bone is 9.7 centimetres thick at the broadest part of the cranium. The average cranial capacity is 1,075 cubic centimetres, comparable to that of an ape. The size, shape, proportion and musculature of the limbs (particularly the thighs) are almost identical to those of modern man, indicating that human limbs developed first through manual labour and that the brain and facial features developed later. Thus Peking Man is characterized by a body similar to that of modern man and by an ape-like brain. About 1.56 metres tall, Peking Man had a communal culture and lived by hunting.

About 100,000 stone tools were found in the cave. These included pebbles which had served as hammers, single- and double-edged choppers, scrapers and points. These were made of hard minerals and rocks such as rock crystal, flint, sandstone, quartz, and quartzite. Also found at the site were the fossilized limb bones of large animals as well as antlers, which had been worked into sharp tools. Roughly fashioned, these stone and bone tools bear the stamp of the early Paleolithic Era.

Layers of soft ash, red, purple, white, yellow and black in colour, were found in the upper, middle and lower strata of the cave. The thickest layer, as deep as 6 metres, provided evidence of the prolonged use of fire. Numerous charred stones and animal bones were found in the ash layers, especially in the black layer. A piece of charred Chinese redbud wood was obtained from the black layer, indicating Peking Man's ability to use and control fire.

Most of the animal fossils accompanying the remains of Peking Man were those of mammals, including sabre-toothed tigers, Sanmen horses and Zhonggu deer. Thirty per cent of these animals are now extinct, a fact which indicates that the climate in the Zhoukoudian area was once warmer and more humid than it is today.

The discovery of the remains of Peking Man provided scientific information of immense value for the study of the origin and evolution of man.

Location

The village of Zhoukoudian is in Fangshan county in the south-western outskirts of Beijing, 50 kilometres from the city centre. There is a bus service from central Beijing to Zhoukoudian.

THE LUGOU BRIDGE
芦沟桥

History

The Lugou Bridge, more commonly known in the West as the Marco Polo Bridge, is named after the river that it spanned, which was renamed the Yongding river in 1698.

The bridge stands at what has always been an important communication point. As long ago as the Warring States period it was a key ferry point for the Beijing area and well before the Jin dynasty there existed a wooden bridge and a pontoon bridge. The Lugou Bridge, which took three years to build, was completed in 1192 after Beijing was made the Jin capital. It was originally known as the Guangli Bridge.

Description

With a length of 266.5 metres, the Lugou Bridge is the longest early stone bridge in north China. Excluding the supports at each end, there are ten stone arches some 16 to 21 metres apart, the distance between them decreasing towards the centre of the bridge. The cross-section of each pier is boat-shaped. The sides of the piers facing the oncoming flow of the river are pointed in order to alleviate the force of the water. An iron triangle, 26 centimetres on each side, is installed at each of these points, its sharp angle facing the oncoming flow of water; these are known as 'dragon cutting swords'. To fortify these points, each is topped with six layers of stone about 1.8 metres thick. The other side of the pillar is shaped like the stern of a boat in order to bear the pressure of the arch. The river bed and both banks consist of thick gravel and sand.

The bridge surface, originally of stone slabs, is now asphalt. There are 280 balusters topped with 485 stone lions, each in a different posture. Many of the adult lions have tiny cubs, and the smallest is only several centimetres high. It is difficult to make an accurate count of the lions, hence the popular saying, 'As numerous as the lions on the Lugou Bridge', in other words, countless. At each side of the east end of the bridge are two male stone lions, while at the

The Lugou Bridge

west end there are two stone elephants. The function of these four animals is to prevent the balustrades from leaning outwards. Most of the stone lions were added after the Ming dynasty.

At each end of the bridge there are four *huabiao* (ornamental stone columns), each 4.7 metres high. At the east end stands a stone tablet with an inscription by Emperor Qianlong (1736–95) saying 'Morning Moon at the Lugou Bridge'. On the west stands a tablet inscribed with a poem by Qianlong which was written when he inspected the river. Each of these tablets is housed in a pavilion.

It was at the Lugou Bridge in 1937 that the Japanese instigated the 'July 7 Incident', marking the beginning of the eight-year Sino-Japanese War.

Location
The Lugou Bridge spans the Yongding River in Fengtai, 15 kilometres southwest of Beijing, from which it is accessible by bus 339.

The west side of the Round City

BEIHAI AND THE ROUND CITY
北海及团城

History

Beihai (the North Lake) was an imperial garden during the Jin, Yuan, Ming and Qing dynasties, and is the oldest and best preserved imperial garden in China.

Beihai first became part of an imperial garden a thousand years ago during the Liao and Jin dynasties. Its hills and lakes were chosen as a pleasure ground by the Liao rulers, who called it Yaoyu (the Jade Islet). Legend has it that the Liao empress dowager had her dressing-tables set on the top of the islet.

After overthrowing the Liao dynasty, the Jin rulers set out to transform Beihai into a paradise for the emperor and his empress, concubines, relatives and ministers. A lake was dug, an artificial hill built and magnificent buildings erected. According to the *History of the Jin Dynasty*, Daninggong (the Palace of Great Tranquillity) was built in 1179 as an outside palace north of the imperial palace.

It was later renamed Shouninggong (the Palace of Longevity and Tranquillity) and then Shouangong (the Palace of Longevity and Peace). In 1191 it was renamed Wanninggong (the Palace of Immense Tranquillity). In Qionglinyuan (the Jade Wood Garden) stood Heng-cuidian (the Horizontal Jadeite Hall). In the west garden of Ning-degong (the Palace of Tranquillity and Virtue) was Yanguangtai (the Terrace of Jade Light). There was also Qionghuadao (the Jade Flowery Island) and Yaoguanglou (the Tower of Jade Light). Construction was carried out on a large scale. Timber was brought from Tanyuan in Zhending prefecture and rocks for the lake came from Genyue in Bianliang. The group of palaces and pavilions, the Gold Sea and the Jade Flowery Island together formed an imperial garden.

After the Yuan overthrew the Jin, Beihai became an imperial garden for Yuan rulers. The lake was expanded southwards to the area now known as Zhonghai (the Central Lake) and named the Lake of Great Waters. To the east of the Lake of Great Waters was the great inner palace where the Forbidden City is located. To the west were two other palaces, Xingshenggong (the Palace of Rising Sages) and Longfugong (the Palace of Great Happiness). The Jade Flowery Island was renamed Wansuishan (the Hill of Long Life).

The Lake of Great Waters, made during the Yuan dynasty, remained the imperial garden during the Ming, and was renamed Xiyuan (the West Garden). Another lake, Nanhai (the South Lake), was dug to connect with the Central Lake and the North Lake. Changes took place in the original features of the lakeshore. The Terrace in Waters was extended to the east shore and became a peninsula, Tuancheng (the Round City). In the Round City, Yitian-dian (the Hall of Service to Heaven) was renamed Chengguangdian (the Hall to Receive Light). All the destroyed buildings on Jade Flowery Island were rebuilt and many new buildings were constructed around the Lake of Great Waters to form several scenic spots, each with its own distinctive features.

After the Qing dynasty had established its capital in Beijing in 1651, a white Tibetan-style Buddhist dagoba was built on the ruins of Guanghandian (the Hall of Vast Cold). On the south of the island, a temple, now known as Yongansi (the Temple of Eternal Peace) was built. More construction was carried out over a thirty-year period during the reign of Emperor Qianlong (1736–95).

The Round City, located to the west of the south gate of the Beihai Park and to the east of the Beihai Bridge, is skirted by the North Lake, the Central Lake, Jingshan Park and the Imperial Palace. More

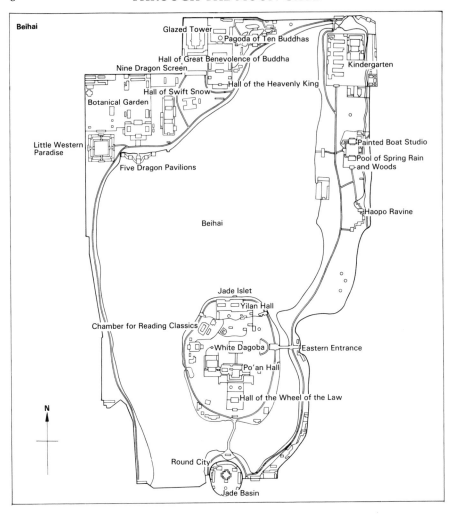

Beihai

Glazed Tower
Pagoda of Ten Buddhas
Hall of Great Benevolence of Buddha
Nine Dragon Screen
Kindergarten
Hall of the Heavenly King
Hall of Swift Snow
Botanical Garden
Little Western
Paradise
Painted Boat Studio
Pool of Spring Rain
and Woods
Five Dragon Pavilions
Haopo Ravine
Beihai
Jade Islet
Yilan Hall
Chamber for Reading Classics
White Dagoba
Eastern Entrance
Po'an Hall
Hall of the Wheel of the Law
N
Round City
Jade Basin

than eight hundred years ago, when the Round City and Beihai were used by the Liao and Jin rulers as an imperial garden, they were considered one of the three 'immortals' hills'. During the late Ming, the lake area southeast of the islet was filled in, levelled and turned into a terrace enclosed by a brick wall. Beihai Lake now covers an area of 4,553 square metres and has a perimeter of 276 metres. The main building on the terrace is the Hall to Receive Light.

Description
After 1949 Beihai became a public park and underwent large-scale reconstruction and renovation. The lake was dredged and the bridge

repaired. Beihai Park covers a total area of 68,000 square metres. The White Dagoba is in the centre of the park. The Temple of Eternal Peace in the south of Jade Flowery Island and the Hall to Receive Light in the Round City are linked by a bridge. Climbing the hill from the Temple of Eternal Peace at its southern foot, the visitor passes through several Buddhist halls before reaching the summit, from which there is a panoramic view of the surroundings. To the south the golden-tiled roofs of palaces and halls glisten in the sun; to the north the blue waters of the lake are dotted with pleasure boats. The northern slope takes the visitor through a beautiful complex of rockeries and caves and then down to the semi-circular gallery which skirts the northern shore of the island. On the east of the island is a stele inscribed 'Spring over Jade Island'. On the north shore of the lake are the Five Dragon Pavilions which extend into the water. To the west are Guanyindian (the Hall of the Goddess of Mercy) and Wanfolou (the Ten Thousand Buddha Tower). To the north is Chanfusi (the Temple of Explaining Happiness), and to the east are Tianwangdian (the Hall of the Heavenly King) and Jingxinzhai (the Studio of the Calm Mind). Beihai also boasts a rich store of artefacts such as the Jade Basin and the Jade Buddha in the Round City, the stelae bearing inscriptions by famous Chinese calligraphers in Yuegulou (the Chamber for Reading the Classics), Jiulongbi (the Nine Dragon Screen), the Yuan dynasty Tieyingbi (the Iron Shadow Screen) and the sixteen-sided stone pillar in the Ten Thousand Buddha Tower.

See Plate 1

Location
Beihai is situated to the west of the Imperial Palace and Jingshan in the western district of Beijing. Buses 5 and 101 and trolley-buses 103 and 109 pass the southern entrance to the park, while buses 13, 27, 42 and trolley-bus 111 pass the northern entrance to the park.

THE WHITE DAGOBA AND THE MIAOYING TEMPLE
妙应寺 白塔

History
The White Dagoba in Miaoyingsi (the Mysterious Manifestation Temple) was constructed between the years 1271 and 1279. Designed and built by Anigo, a Nepalese artisan, during a mission to China,

it is one of the largest Yuan dynasty Lamaist dagobas in China. Its name derives from the fact that the entire body of the dagoba is white; hence the temple in which it is located, the Miaoying Temple, is also popularly known as the White Dagoba Temple.

Description

The White Dagoba Temple consists of the following structures laid out on a central axis: the Hall of the Heavenly Kings, the Purity of Heart Hall, the Hall of the Seven Buddhas and the courtyard where the dagoba stands. This courtyard, which is located at the northern extremity of the complex, is 2 metres above ground level, and is completely surrounded by a red wall. The Hall of the Six Transcendental Powers stands immediately to the south of the dagoba, and there are four corner towers surrounding the white structure. The dagoba, which is 50.9 metres high, consists of three parts: the base, the body and the crown. The Sumeru base has three levels and its ground-plan resembles a Maltese cross. The massive rounded body of the dagoba creates a striking contrast with the angular base. The base is echoed by another similar base which supports the conical upper part of the body of the dagoba. This upper part is divided into thirteen layers known as Heavens, and is capped by an elaborate crown, the main component of which is a gilded bronze pinnacle weighing 4.6 tonnes. The pinnacle is secured to the body of the dagoba by eight steel chains.

In 1961 the State Council listed the Miaoying Temple among the important cultural relics to be protected by the state, and in 1964 it underwent a major rehabilitation. The Tangshan earthquake of 1976 damaged the body of the dagoba, and when repairs were carried out in 1978 a cache of precious relics dating from 1758, the year in which Emperor Qianlong had the structure repaired, was discovered in the crown of the dagoba. Among the cache were bronze images of the Buddhas of the Three Ages, a pure gold Buddha, a yellow sandalwood image of Guanyin, the complete Buddhist canon (Tripitaka) in 724 cases, a copy of the Heart Sutra in the hand of Emperor Qianlong, and a Tibetan version of the Mantra of the Honoured and Victorious One, as well as a brocade Five Buddha Cap and a brocade monk's robe.

The Hall of the Seven Buddhas contains a display of three over life-sized Yuan dynasty *nan* wood images of the Buddhas of the Three Ages which were repaired in 1980. The side walls of the hall are lined with lifelike bronze images of the eighteen Protectors of the Truth (Lokapalas), cast in the mid-Ming dynasty.

The White Dagoba of the Miaoying Temple

The Hall of the Six Transcendental Powers is a typical Buddhist structure. In the centre of the hall are images of the Buddhas of the Three Ages, and on the walls are displayed eight late Qing dynasty Lamaist scrolls.

Location
The White Dagoba and the Miaoying Temple are located in Fuchengmennei Street in Beijing. The temple can be reached by buses 42, 103 and 202.

The Palace Museum

THE PALACE MUSEUM
故宫

History
The Palace Museum was the imperial palace of the emperors of the
Ming and Qing dynasties, and was known as the Purple Forbidden
City. It is the largest architectural complex in China.

The palace was built during the reign of the Ming dynasty Emperor
Yongle (1403–24) and was completed between 1406 and 1420.
Later emperors expanded and improved Yongle's palace, but its basic
design has remained the same for over five hundred years. A total
of twenty-four emperors made the palace their home and seat of
government, and it was not until 1911, with the overthrow of the
Qing dynasty, that it ceased to perform these functions. The Purple
Forbidden City was opened to the public as a museum in 1925.

Description
The Palace Museum occupies an area of 724,000 square metres and
its 8,700 rooms and chambers occupy 160,000 square metres. It is

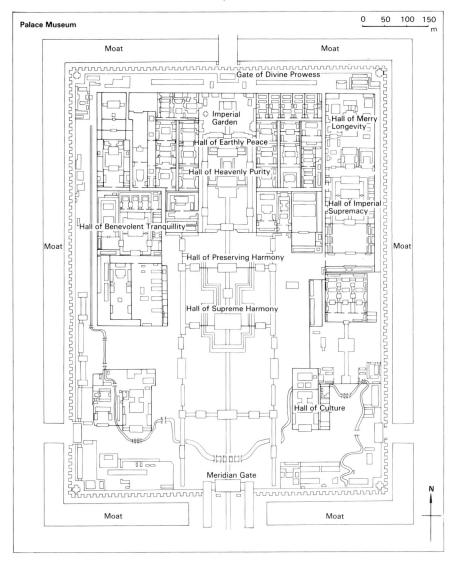

Palace Museum

0   50   100   150
m

Moat

Moat

Gate of Divine Prowess

Imperial
Garden

Hall of Merry
Longevity

Hall of Earthly Peace

Hall of Heavenly Purity

Hall of Imperial
Supremacy

Hall of Benevolent Tranquillity

Moat

Moat

Hall of Preserving Harmony

Hall of Supreme Harmony

Hall of Culture

Meridian Gate

N

Moat

Moat

enclosed by a rectangular wall with a total length of 3.4 kilometres, and there is a gate on each of the four sides. The wall itself is surrounded by a moat.

The main gate of the Palace Museum is Wumen (the Meridian Gate), which is U-shaped and opens towards the south. The Meridian Gate tower is composed of a large nine-bay structure with multiple eaves which is connected to the four square pavilions situated on the flanks of the gate by a number of roofed corridors. The five separate buildings on the stone base give the gate its alternative name of the

Five Phoenix Towers. To the south of the Meridian Gate is the wall surrounding the palace, further to the south of which stands Tiananmen (the Gate of Heavenly Peace). The northern gate of the palace is Shenwumen (the Gate of Divine Prowess), beyond which stands Jingshan, formerly known as Coal Hill. To the east is Donghuamen (the Eastern Flowery Gate) and to the west Xihuamen (the Western Flowery Gate). Each of the four corners of the palace wall is provided with an elaborate watchtower. The central axis of the palace lies on the central axis of the city of Beijing. From south to north, this axis runs through the Martial Gate, the Three Great Halls (the Hall of Supreme Harmony, the Hall of Complete Harmony and the Hall of Preserving Harmony), the Three Rear Palaces (the Hall of Heavenly Purity, the Hall of Vigorous Fertility and the Hall of Earthly Peace), the Hall of Imperial Peace in the Imperial Garden, and finally the Gate of Divine Prowess.

The buildings in the Palace Museum are distributed according to the ancient ritualistic principle of placing 'official halls in the front (south) and residential quarters in the rear (north)'. The two sections are separated by Qianqingmen (the Gate of Heavenly Purity).

The axial Three Great Halls and Three Rear Palaces are the major buildings in the palace; the building complexes to either side of these six structures play a subsidiary role in the overall design of the palace.

The largest building in the palace is the Hall of Supreme Harmony, which stands on a white marble base. The hall is 28 metres high, 64 metres wide, 37 metres deep and has a total floor area of 2,380 square metres. The roof of the hall, with its overhanging multiple eaves, is covered with yellow glazed roof tiles, and on each end of the ridge there stand large dragons of the same material. The eave extensions are provided with ten decorative figures of immortals and mythical beasts whose functions reflect their positions. The 'jack of all trades' — the figure of a winged man — occupies the highest position and is found only on the Hall of Supreme Harmony. In the centre of the hall is a platform, upon which stands a throne decorated with gilded entwined dragons. To each side of the throne are three giant columns decorated with golden dragons, and directly above it is an exquisitely carved interior cupola filled with a coiled dragon from whose mouth hangs a mirrored sphere on a chain. This was the throne upon which the emperor sat while holding court. Here grandiose ceremonies would be held at the lunar New Year, the winter solstice and the emperor's birthday, as well as on such occasions as an emperor's ascension to the throne, the promulgation of imperial edicts, the announcement of successful candidates in the imperial examinations and the dispatching of ministers on missions abroad.

To the north of the Hall of Supreme Harmony is the Hall of Complete Harmony, a square pavilion-like building which also contains a throne. Here the emperor would have a brief rest before proceeding to the Hall of Supreme Harmony, though sometimes he would hold intimate audiences with more trusted officials or rehearse certain rituals with those in charge of ceremonial affairs.

The Hall of Preserving Harmony was where Qing dynasty emperors held fêtes for missions from tributary states, and from the Yongzheng period (1723–35) it was the site of the palace examinations.

The two building complexes to the east and west of the Three Great Halls are the Hall of Culture and the Hall of Martial Heroism. Here the emperors would discuss state affairs with their ministers or exchange views on literary subjects with scholars assigned to the palace.

The Gate of Heavenly Purity is the main entrance to the Inner Palace residential quarters. During the Qing dynasty emperors, seated on a throne placed before the gate, occasionally held audiences here with leading officials. The Son of Heaven lived with his family on the other side of this gate. The Hall of Heavenly Purity was the emperor's quarters, while the empress lived in the Hall of Earthly Peace. Between the two stands a small square building called the Hall of Vigorous Fertility. To the east and west of these three halls are the six Eastern and Western Palaces, which, from the Yongzheng reign, were the emperor's private offices and living quarters.

Beyond the Hall of Earthly Peace is the Imperial Garden, which is a finely landscaped retreat filled with old pines and scholar trees, curiously shaped stones, jade benches, flowerbeds, miniature landscapes and paths paved with coloured pebbles in amusing designs.

The Hall of Tranquil Longevity, with its own garden, is located in the southwest section of the Inner Palace; it was built by the Qianlong emperor in 1772. To the southeast are the Halls of Benevolent Tranquillity, Peaceful Longevity and Healthy Longevity. These were all the residences of the favoured consorts and concubines of the emperor, and for this reason the Buddhist temples situated in this section are particularly exquisite.

See Plates 2, 3 and 4

Location
The Palace Museum is situated in the centre of Beijing, on the north side of Tiananmen Square.

THE MING MAUSOLEA
明十三陵

History
The thirteen Ming imperial mausolea were built at the foot of the southern side of the Tianshou Hill in Changping county near Beijing during the period from 1409 to 1644. The mausolea are scattered over a natural basin approximately 40 square kilometres in area, and the site is screened by hills to the north, east and west.

Description
The first monument encountered within the area is a splendid marble archway, which marks the beginning of the 7-kilometre

Nan wood pillars in the Ling'an Hall of Changling

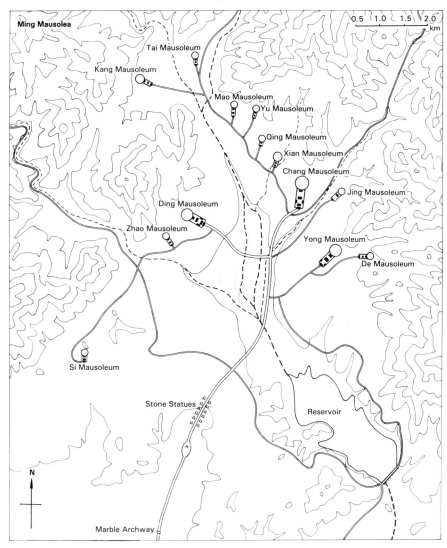

approach to the mausolea. About 1 kilometre to the left of this is the imposing Great Red Gate, beside which is the Stele Pavilion containing a stele inscribed on all four sides. At the four corners of this pavilion stand four marble *huabiao*, ornamental columns which were traditionally placed in front of palaces or tombs. Beyond the pavilion is an avenue lined with 18 pairs of stone statues including 24 animals — lions, camels, elephants, unicorns, horses and mythical animals — and 12 generals and ministers. Each is carved from a single rock. At the end of this approach stands a triple-

Dingling, the mausoleum of Emperor Wanli and his two empresses

arched portico called the Dragon and Phoenix Gate through which
would have passed the imperial bier.

The best-known of the mausolea are Changling, famous for its
magnificent buildings, and the underground Dingling.

Changling lies at the foot of the principal peak of the Tianshou
Hill. It is the earliest and largest of the thirteen mausolea, and it
is here that Emperor Yongle (1403–24) and his empress are buried.
This mausoleum was completely restored in 1955. The Ling'an Hall
in the second compound is celebrated for its sixty rare *nan* wood
pillars. All of the beams, posts, purlins, rafters and brackets are also
made of *nan* wood. Though built some five hundred years ago, the
structure appears as solid as if it were new, and it is the only large
nan wood structure still in existence in China.

The 'underground palace' of Dingling was excavated in 1958.
Buried in it are the Emperor Wanli (1573–1620) and his two empresses, Xiaoduan and Xiaoqing. Wanli ascended the throne when
he was only ten years old, his reign lasted for forty-eight years and

1 Beihai, Beijing (*see p. 6*)

2 The Palace Museum, Beijing (*see p. 12*)

3 The Palace Museum, Beijing *(see p. 12)*

4 The interior of Chuxiugong, the Palace Museum, Beijing *(see p. 12)*

5 The Hall of Prayer for Good Harvests, the Altar of Heaven, Beijing *(see p. 19)*

6 The Great Wall at Badaling, near Beijing (*see p. 24*)

7 The Summer Palace, Beijing (*see p. 26*)

8 The Dule Temple, Tianjin (*see p. 33*)

9 The Eastern Qing Mausolea, Hebei province (*see p. 46*)

he was notorious for his debauchery and cruelty. To construct the mausoleum, between twenty and thirty thousand men worked for six years, and the project cost millions of taels of silver, an amount equal to two years' national revenue. The underground palace, 27 metres beneath the ground, is constructed in the form of a vault and consists of three main chambers flanked by two smaller chambers. The rear chamber is the largest; in the centre of it are three coffins with outer cases, which are those of Wanli and the two empresses. Beside these coffins were jades and red lacquer chests full of funerary objects. When the mausoleum was excavated over 3,000 artefacts were found. Dingling is open to the public and some of the artefacts are displayed in two galleries at the entrance to the mausoleum.

Location
The Ming Mausolea lie to the northwest of Beijing, and may be reached by bus 345 from Deshengmen.

THE ALTAR OF HEAVEN
天坛

History
The Altar of Heaven (Tiantan), which was first built in 1420, was where Ming and Qing emperors came to worship heaven and to pray for good harvests. It was originally called the Altar of Heaven and Earth, but the harvest rites were later transferred to four new sites on the outskirts of Beijing. In 1530 the Altar of Earth was built in what was then a northern suburb of Beijing and the Altar of Heaven and Earth became known as the Altar of Heaven.

Description
The building complex and surroundings are enclosed by a wall which is semicircular to the north and square to the south, symbolizing the ancient belief that heaven was round and earth square. The main structures are two groups of buildings set on a north-south axis, and connected by a paved way. To the north stands the Hall of Prayer for Good Harvests, and to the south the Round Altar and the Imperial Vault of Heaven.

The Hall of Prayer for Good Harvests is where imperial ceremonies were held to worship heaven and earth. In 1889 the hall was struck by lightning and burned down. Rebuilding began the following year

The Altar of Heaven

and was completed in 1896. The circular hall has triple eaves and
a cone-shaped deep blue tiled roof crowned with a gilded knob. It
rests on a circular stone terrace on three levels, each edged with
a balustrade of carved white marble. Three huge stone slabs carved
with a dragon-and-cloud motif are inset between steps on both the
southern and northern sides. Inside the hall are twenty-eight massive
wooden pillars of which the four central ones represent the
four seasons. These are surrounded by two concentric rings of
twelve columns which symbolize and twelve months of the year
and the twelve divisions of day and night in accordance with the
traditional Chinese method of reckoning time. In the centre of the
floor is a round marble slab with natural veining in a dragon-and-
phoenix pattern, under a caisson ceiling painted with dragons.

The main hall is flanked by side halls behind which stands the
Heavenly Emperor Hall. The auxiliary structures are the Gate to
the Hall of Prayer for Good Harvests, the Divine Warehouse, the

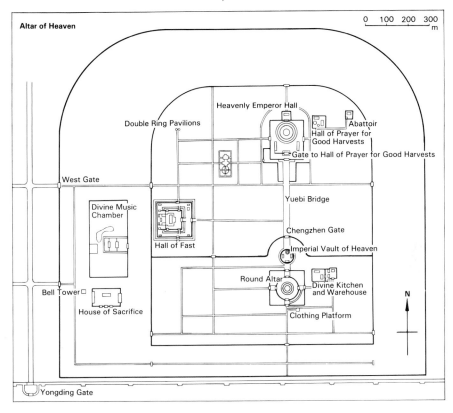

Altar of Heaven

0 100 200 300 m

Heavenly Emperor Hall

Double Ring Pavilions

Abattoir

Hall of Prayer for Good Harvests

Gate to Hall of Prayer for Good Harvests

West Gate

Yuebi Bridge

Divine Music Chamber

Chengzhen Gate

Hall of Fast

Imperial Vault of Heaven

Bell Tower

Round Altar

Divine Kitchen and Warehouse

N

House of Sacrifice

Clothing Platform

Yongding Gate

Divine Kitchen, the abattoir, a walkway specially built for sacrificial animals, and a seventy-two-bay corridor. To the south of the corridor lie several stones known as the Seven Stars Stones which were set here during the reign of the Qing Emperor Jiaqing (1796–1820). They are carved with small cloud motifs.

The Round Altar, built in 1530, lies in the southern section of the complex. In imperial times emperors came here on the Winter Solstice to worship heaven. It is a three-tiered white stone terrace surrounded on each tier by a marble balustrade. When first built, the terrace and the balustrade were faced with blue glazed tiles. However, when the terrace was enlarged in 1749, the balustrade tiles were replaced by marble and the terrace was paved with stone slabs. Since the number nine was symbolic of heaven and the emperor, the slabs on the terrace surface, the balusters and the steps are arranged in multiples of nine. In the centre of the top tier is a round stone encircled by nine fan-shaped slabs. The altar is enclosed by a round inner and a square outer wall, and there is a small archway on each of the four sides. Nearby are the Imperial Vault of Heaven and three lamp-watching terraces.

The Imperial Vault of Heaven, which lies to the north of the Round Altar, stands on a stone foundation with a marble balustrade, and housed a tablet inscribed with the names of various deities. Built in 1530, it originally had a two-tiered cone-shaped roof of green glazed tiles. It was renovated in 1753 and the roof was resurfaced with blue glazed tiles and crowned with a gilded knob.

The Imperial Vault of Heaven is flanked by two side halls which house wooden memorial tablets. It is surrounded by a wall of polished bricks, known as the Echo Wall, because if a person stands near the wall and whispers, his or her voice can be heard distinctly at any other point along the wall.

There is also an imperial residential chamber and a music chamber where training in ceremonial music took place.

See Plate 5

Location
The Altar of Heaven is located in the southern suburbs of Beijing. It is accessible by buses 20, 35 and 116 and trolley-buses 105 and 106.

THE ANCIENT OBSERVATORY
古观象台

History
The Ancient Observatory in Beijing, which symbolizes China's astronomical tradition, has been a centre for observation and research over the centuries. During the Yuan dynasty an imperial college of astronomy and an astronomical observatory were established near the site of the present observatory, which was built in 1442. The first observatory in Beijing was built in the Jin dynasty, and in 1127 astronomical instruments were shipped to Beijing from Kaifeng and installed in it. In 1279 new astronomical instruments were made by Wang Xun, Guo Shoujing and other astronomers, and a new observatory was constructed, the remains of which are inside Jianguomen. During the early years of the Ming dynasty astronomical instruments were shipped to Nanjing and installed at an observatory on Jiming Hill. In 1442 reproductions of an armillary sphere, an abridged armilla and a celestial globe were made from

the original instruments, and various buildings, including Ziweidian (the Celestial Abstruseness Hall) and Louhufang (the Clepsydra Room), were erected on the site of the present observatory to house these instruments.

Western natural sciences were introduced to China after the reign of Emperor Wanli (1573–1620) and Chinese astronomers such as Xu Guangqi and Li Tianjing made a number of astronomical instruments. In 1669 Ferdinand Verbiest designed and supervised the making of six new instruments including a zodiac theodolite, an equatorial theodolite, an altazimuth and a quadrant. Later, more instruments were added to the observatory. In 1900, during the Boxer Uprising, French and German troops looted the observatory. The French forces took the equatorial theodolite, the altazimuth and various other instruments to the French embassy in Beijing, but these were returned to the Chinese government in 1902. Instruments taken by German troops were displayed in Potsdam and Berlin and returned to China after the First World War in accordance with the Treaty of Versailles. They were re-installed at the ancient observatory in 1921. In 1931 Chinese authorities transported the

The Ancient Observatory

armillary sphere, abridged armilla and five other precious Ming instruments to the Purple Hills Observatory in Nanjing. All of the astronomical instruments now remaining at the Beijing observatory were made either in 1674 or in 1744.

Description

The recently repaired ancient observatory in Beijing is a high brick terrace on which are displayed several large astronomical instruments. At the foot of the terrace are a number of buildings including the Celestial Abstruseness Hall and Guiyingtang (the Sundial Hall). The formerly solid structure has been hollowed out to make a spacious three-storey exhibition hall, the external appearance of which is exactly as it was in the Ming and Qing dynasties. The duty chamber at the top of the terrace, which was converted into a two-storey house in the 1920s, has been rebuilt according to historical records. Exhibits and models of ancient astronomical instruments are displayed in the first two storeys of the inner hall and in the Celestial Abstruseness Hall. New replicas of the Ming dynasty abridged armilla and armillary sphere have been placed in the compound. The display provides a general outline of the development of Chinese astronomy.

Location

The Ancient Observatory is in the eastern part of Beijing, just southwest of the highway flyover at Jianguomen. Buses 1, 4, 9, 43, 44 and 48 pass by the observatory and there is an underground station opposite the entrance.

THE GREAT WALL AT BADALING
八达岭长城

History

Badaling is an important section of the Great Wall, which is altogether 6,700 kilometres long. Construction of the wall began in the Warring States period, and it is now one of the major monuments of early Chinese civilization. High walls were first built by the states of Yan, Zhao and Qin to resist the nomadic peoples to the north. When the first Qin emperor unified the country, he ordered these walls to be repaired and linked together, thus laying the foundations of the Great Wall. It was reinforced or renovated by succeeding rulers from the Han to the Ming dynasty. During the Han it was expanded

The Great Wall at Badaling

1,000 kilometres westwards to Dunhuang and Jiuquan and many
fortifications were built on its northern side. During the Ming
dynasty several important towns were established near the wall and
some of the earthen sections were replaced by bricks and stones.
By then the Great Wall stretched across north China from the Jiayu
Pass in the west to the Shanhai Pass in the east. Also built along
the wall were beacon towers. If the enemy appeared during the day,

smoke signals would be given to alert others; if at night, beacons would be lit.

Description

The section of the Great Wall at Badaling, where it snakes over the mountainous terrain, dates from the Ming dynasty. Varying in height and width, this section is on average 6 to 7 metres in height and the width at the base is about 6.5 metres and at the top 5.8 metres, broad enough for five horses or ten soldiers to walk abreast. The lower part of the wall is composed of rectangular stone slabs while the upper part has crenellated walls and a pathway. It is faced with regular bricks and the inside is filled with earth and rubble. The top is paved with large slabs. On the north is a crenellated wall with embrasures through which soldiers could keep watch and fire on attackers. Towers were built at bends or at strategic points. These are of two types: two-storey forts and lower terraces, the latter built on level ground and of the same height as the wall.

Badaling is not only of historical importance but also serves as a communications link even today. The road from Beijing to Zhangjiakou passes through Badaling as does the Beijing-Baotou railway line. A bronze statue of the famous engineer Zhan Tianyou stands at Badaling's Qinglongqiao railway station, to commemorate the man in charge of the design and construction of the railway over the difficult terrain from Nankou to Qinglongqiao from 1905 to 1909.

There are also a number of scenic spots and places of historical interest in the area around the Great Wall.

See Plate 6

Location

Badaling is in the south of Yanqing county near Beijing. It is accessible by car, coach or train.

THE SUMMER PALACE
颐和园

History

Beijing's Western Hills, where the Summer Palace (Yiheyuan) is located, were chosen as early as eight hundred years ago by the emperors of the Jin dynasty to serve as their summer resort. It was there, upon Jinshan (the Gold Mountain), later renamed Wengshan, that they built the Gold Mountain Summer Palace.

The Summer Palace

With the establishment of the Qing dynasty in 1644, the Manchu emperors made the Forbidden City in Beijing the seat of state power, and it was during the reigns of Kangxi (1662–1722) and Yongzheng (1723–35) that they carried out the large-scale construction of parks and gardens to the west of the city. They built, in turn, the Garden of Repose and Brightness, the Garden of Repose and Ease, the Garden of Joyful Spring and the Garden of Perfect Brightness. During the Qianlong period (1736–95), not only were these four gardens enlarged and further embellished, but a fifth major garden, the Garden of Pure Ripples, was begun in 1749. To commemorate his mother's sixtieth birthday, Emperor Qianlong in 1751 carried out major improvements to the temple in the garden known as the

Temple of Perfect Repose and renamed it the Temple of Gratitude and Longevity. At the same time he renamed Wengshan as Wanshoushan (Longevity Hill). Emperor Qianlong was also responsible for changing the name of Wengshan Lake to Kunming Lake. In so doing he emulated the Han dynasty Emperor Wu, whose navy carried out military exercises on Kunming Lake in the capital city of Chang'an. Construction and expansion continued for fifteen years, until 1764, during which time the Garden of Pure Ripples had been transformed into a large-scale imperial garden that combined the regal splendour of a palace with the refinement of a southern Chinese garden. At this time the northwestern suburbs of Beijing were home to the famous Three Hills and Five Gardens: the Garden of Peace and Brightness on Jade Spring Hill, the Garden of Repose and Ease on Fragrant Hill, the Garden of Pure Ripples on Longevity Hill, as well as the Garden of Joyful Spring and the Garden of Perfect Brightness.

Following the golden age of the Kangxi and Qianlong reigns, the Qing dynasty began its gradual decline. In 1860 the Garden of Pure Ripples was destroyed by allied English and French troops. In 1886, when power was in the hands of the notorious Empress Dowager Cixi, the official in charge of naval affairs, Prince Chun, appropriated funds originally allocated to the navy and began a major expansion programme in the Garden of Pure Ripples. Ostensibly, he was to build a 'naval academy' on the banks of Kunming Lake, where the navy could perform military displays, but his real motive was to ingratiate himself with the all-powerful empress dowager. The enlarged Garden of Pure Ripples was renamed Yiheyuan, an abbreviated form of a phrase meaning 'to nurture and harmonize'.

In 1900 the Eight Allied Armies sacked Beijing, and the Summer Palace (the English name given to Yiheyuan) suffered extensive damage. Two years later, in 1903, it was rebuilt.

During the reign of Emperor Guangxu (1875–1908), the Summer Palace served both as the residence and as the court of the empress dowager and the emperor.

Description

The Summer Palace today is the largest and best preserved traditional garden in China. It consists of two major areas, Longevity Hill and Kunming Lake. The entire Summer Palace occupies an area of almost 3 square kilometres, three-quarters of which are lakes. The buildings in the garden can be divided by their functions into residential, official and recreational. The official buildings stretch

The Long Corridor

from the Eastern Palace Gate to the eastern foot of Longevity Hill, the most important being the Hall of Humanity and Longevity. In these splendid and imposing buildings the empress dowager and the emperor would manage court affairs and hold audiences.

The emperor and his family lived in a group of buildings which included the Hall of Happiness and Longevity, the Hall of Jade

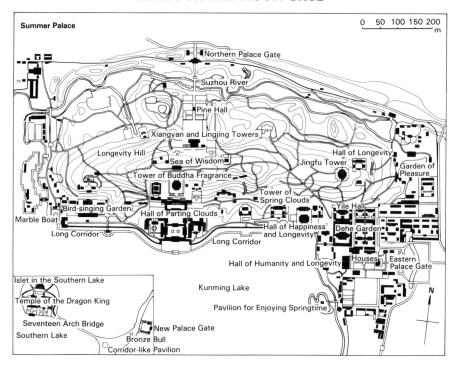

Waves and the Hall of Pleasing Eve. But the principal area of interest in the park is the scenic area made up of Longevity Hill and Kunming Lake. The formidable buildings standing along a south-north axis on the south side of Longevity Hill, such as the Hall of Parting Clouds, the Hall of Luminous Virtue, the Tower of Buddha Fragrance, and the Sea of Wisdom, were the site of major ceremonies, both religious and secular, carried out by the imperial household during the Qing dynasty. The Hall of Parting Clouds is the architectural centrepiece, as well as the most exquisite building in the entire garden. The octagonal Tower of Buddha Fragrance, with its three storeys and four sets of eaves, is 38 metres high and starts some 60 metres up from the base of the hill. The Sea of Wisdom, which stands at the top of Longevity Hill, is made of bricks and is the most important structure dating from the Qianlong period to have survived the destruction of the Garden of Pure Ripples.

Kunming Lake, located to the south of the Longevity Hill, was originally a natural lake fed by a spring in the northwestern outskirts of Beijing. In the Qianlong period it was enlarged to its present area of over 2 square kilometres. Several islands dot the lake, and the Western Dyke, modelled after the Su (Dongpo) Dyke on the West

Lake in Hangzhou, spans the lake, interrupted by six stone bridges, each one different in design. The finest of these is undoubtedly the Jade Ribbon Bridge.

Across the lake from the Western Dyke is the Eastern Dyke. Other famed sites include the Pavilion for Enjoying Springtime, the Temple of the Dragon King, the Bronze Bull and the Seventeen Arch Bridge. On the north shore of Kunming Lake stands the splendidly painted Long Corridor, 726 metres in length, which links up the various clusters of buildings to the south of Longevity Hill. At the end of the corridor is the famous Marble Boat. The entire garden is a triumph of design and layout. Most exquisite of all is the view of the Summer Palace with the pagoda atop Jade Spring Hill and the undulating pattern of the Western Hills in the background.

See Plate 7

Location

The Summer Palace is situated in Haidian district to the northwest of central Beijing. Bus 332 runs from the Beijing Zoo to the Summer Palace. The ride takes approximately 30 minutes.

The City of Tianjin
天津市

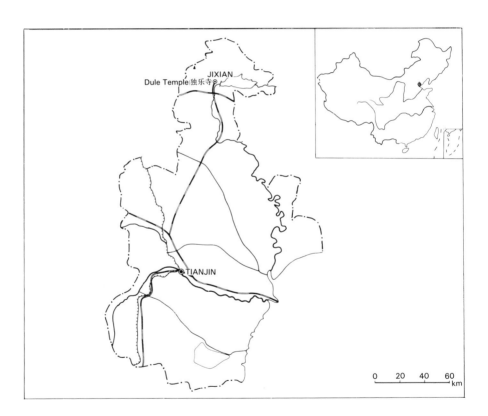

The Guanyin Tower of the Dule Temple

THE DULE TEMPLE
独乐寺

History

Dulesi (the Temple of Singular Happiness), also known as the Great Buddha Temple, is generally considered to have been built in AD 636. In AD 984 it was rebuilt by a prince of the Liao dynasty; it was subsequently repaired and repainted in the reign of the Ming Emperor Wanli (1573–1620), and in the reigns of the Qing Emperors Shunzhi (1644–61), Qianlong (1736–95) and Guangxu (1875–1908). The principal structures of the temple, the Guanyin Tower and the main gate in front of the tower, are preserved as they were following the rebuilding of the temple in the Liao dynasty. In 1753 a reflecting wall was constructed in front of the temple, four wooden columns were added to support the roof of the Guanyin Tower, and an imperial summer residence was built on the eastern side.

Description

The temple is composed of eastern, western and central sections, the eastern and western sections having served initially as monks'

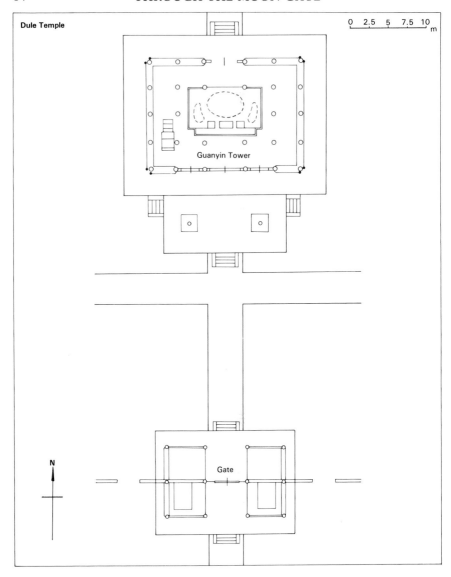

Dule Temple

Guanyin Tower

Gate

0 2.5 5 7.5 10 m

N

quarters and then as the imperial summer residence. The central section is the temple proper, and is made up of the main gate and the Guanyin Tower, both of which are situated on a north-south axis. The main gate stands on a low platform and is three bays wide. The central bay is the entranceway itself, with clay images of the traditional door gods, Generals Heng and Ha, standing to either

10 The Puning Temple, near Chengde, Hebei province (*see p. 52*)

11 The Four Gate Pagoda, near Ji'nan, Shandong province *(see p. 58)*

12 The Hall of Great Achievement at the Temple and Mansion of Confucius, Qufu, Shandong province *(see p. 59)*

13 The Fisherman's Garden, Suzhou, Jiangsu province (*see p. 76*)

14 The Narrow West Lake, Yangzhou, Jiangsu province (*see p.79*)

15 The Six Harmonies Pagoda, Hangzhou, Zhejiang province *(see p. 90)*

16 The Taibai Memorial Hall, Caishiji, Anhui province (*see p. 99*)

17 The Kaiyuan Monastery, Quanzhou, Fujian province *(see p. 104)*

18 The Guangxiao Temple, Guangzhou, Guangdong province (see p. 113)

19 The Chen Family Memorial Hall, Guangzhou, Guangdong province
(see p. 115)

20 The Du River Dyke of the Min river, Sichuan province (*see p. 131*)

21 The great statue of Maitreya at Leshan, Sichuan province (*see p. 135*)

Clay statue of the Eleven-headed Guanyin

side. The eastern gate is the earliest extant roofed temple gate in China. It has five ridges, four sloping sides and eaves which rise up in sweeping curves. The animal figures on the ends of the main roof ridge, with their fish-like tails pointed inwards, are some of the earliest examples of such decorative figures in China.

Passing through the main entrance, the visitor enters a courtyard

in which stands the Guanyin Tower. The tower is an imposing
structure 23 metres high, five bays wide and four bays deep. It has
three storeys, but as the second storey is concealed, the effect is of
two storeys only. Between the two extended eaves is a balustrade
and balcony which runs around the tower. The tower itself has a
single-eaved gabled roof. The rafters, brackets and joists number in
the thousands, and are arranged with great precision. There are
twenty-four different types of brackets alone, each with its own
particular function. The excellence of the design is apparent from
the fact that the temple has withstood several earthquakes over the
centuries, to become the oldest extant multi-storey wooden tower
in China.

Inside the tower is a Liao dynasty standing Guanyin which leans
slightly forward. The plump face, relaxed shoulders and stately
posture preserve the style of a Tang dynasty work. Because the
ten small heads attached to the top of the bodhisattva's head
share the features of Guanyin, the sculpture is called the Eleven-
headed Guanyin. Sixteen metres in height, it is one of the tallest
clay sculptures in China. The painted bodhisattva images on the
western side of the tower are rare works of the Liao dynasty. The
interior walls of the lower storey of the tower are completely covered
with paintings. The main subjects are the sixteen arhats and three
six- and four-armed *rajas*. These figures are interspersed with
landscapes and scenes of daily life.

See Plate 8

Location

The Dule Temple is located in Xiguan Street in the Western Gate
district of Jixian, the city of Tianjin. Buses and trains run from Beijing
and Tianjin to Jixian.

Hebei Province
河北省

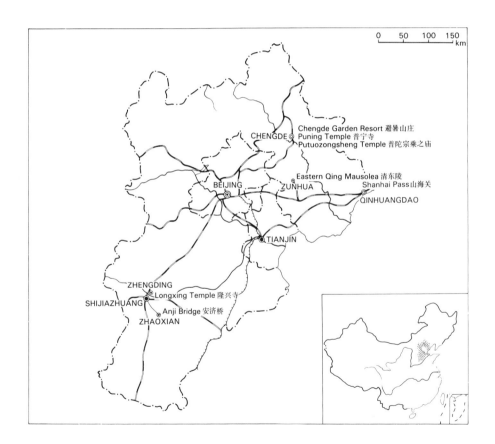

CHENGDE ⊚   Chengde Garden Resort 避暑山庄
Puning Temple 普宁寺
Putuozongsheng Temple 普陀宗乘之庙

Eastern Qing Mausolea 清东陵
ZUNHUA   Shanhai Pass 山海关
QINHUANGDAO

BEIJING

TIANJIN

ZHENGDING
Longxing Temple 隆兴寺
SHIJIAZHUANG
Anji Bridge 安济桥
ZHAOXIAN

0   50   100   150
km

The Anji Bridge

THE ANJI BRIDGE
安济桥

History
The Anji Bridge is also known as the Zhaozhou Bridge and, since it is constructed entirely of stone, more popularly as the Zhaozhou Great Stone Bridge. It was designed and built between AD 590 and 616 by a stonemason named Li Chun and is the oldest surviving arched bridge in China.

In AD 793, about two hundred years after the bridge was built, cracks caused by flooding began to appear. Regular repairs were carried out during the Song, Ming and Qing dynasties. In 1949 only twenty of its twenty-five original arches were in reasonable condition. To protect the bridge, which is of great architectural importance, the government carried out a detailed survey and thoroughly renovated it between 1955 and 1958, restoring it to its former appearance.

Description
The Anji Bridge is 10 metres wide and its arches have a span of 37.4 metres and a height of 7.2 metres. It is 50.8 metres long and is set low with a fairly gentle gradient for the convenience of pedestrians and vehicles.

The size of the arches and width of the apertures ease the flow of water as well as the passage of boats. The bridge was built according to the *changjiangong* (open-shouldered-arch) technique, a major innovation at the time. In this technique two small stone arches are built on the shoulders of larger stone arches, giving the bridge a graceful appearance. The technique is economical in its use of materials, and as a result the overall weight of the bridge is reduced. The arches alleviate the impact of flooding, as well as increasing the stability of the bridge.

The Anji Bridge is comprised of twenty-eight arches in all. The most significant advantage of the open-shouldered-arch technique of bridge building is that each arch may be made individually before being reinforced crosswise to complete the structure. This enables repairs to be carried out to individual arches if one is damaged, instead of the whole bridge having to be closed. Each end of the bridge rests on natural rough sand banks, on which flat stone slabs were laid as a foundation; these have proved capable of sustaining the weight of the bridge.

Apart from being a remarkable technical achievement, the Anji Bridge is noteworthy for its elegant profile and its carved decoration. On its railings are delicate carvings of dragons, animals such as flying horses, animal heads and floral motifs, and on the columns between the railings are vivid carvings of dragons and bamboo. Combining strength and delicacy, the bridge has been likened by poets to a crescent moon, a rainbow and a dragon.

According to an ancient legend, the donkey hoofprints and the wheelmarks on the bridge were left by Zhang Guolao, one of the Eight Immortals, and by Prince Chai.

Location
Spanning the Xiaoshui river, the Anji Bridge is 2.5 kilometres south of Zhaoxian, Hebei province. It is accessible by bus from Handan.

THE LONGXING TEMPLE
隆兴寺

History
Longxingsi (the Flourishing Dragon Temple) was first built in AD 586, in the early Sui dynasty. At that time it was called Longcangsi (the Concealed Dragon Temple). In the early Song dynasty its name was changed to Longxingsi and during the reign of the

The Longxing Temple

Emperor Kangxi (1622–1722) it assumed its present name. Because the temple contained a large bronze statue of the Buddha, it was also popularly known as the Giant Buddha Temple.

Legend has it that the original giant Buddha image once stood in the Pavilion of Great Compassion in the Temple of Great Compassion in the western outskirts of Zhengding (in present-day Hebei province). In the year AD 944, the Khitan invaded from the north and burned the Pavilion of Great Compassion to the ground, as a consequence of which the upper half of the statue was melted into scrap. In AD 955 the emperor ordered that all bronze Buddha images be melted down and made into coins, and so the lower half of the Buddha was also destroyed. When the first emperor of the Song made an official inspection tour of Zhengding in AD 968 and learned the story of the destruction of the giant bronze statue, he gave orders for the statue in the Longxing Temple to be recast and a pavilion, to be named the Pavilion of Great Compassion, built to house it.

The Longxing Temple preserves the basic Song dynasty layout. Of particular interest are the Revolving Scripture Library, the Cishi Pavilion and the Mani (Luminous Pearl) Hall, which are among the few extant Song dynasty buildings in China.

The Guanyin of a Thousand Arms and a Thousand Eyes

Description

The Longxing Temple occupies an area of 50,000 square metres. All of its buildings stand on a south-north axis as follows: the Hall of the Heavenly Kings, the Hall of the Six Masters of Great Enlightenment, the Mani Hall, the Ordination Platform, the Cishi

Clay figure of seated Guanyin

Pavilion, the Revolving Scripture Library, the Pavilion of Great Compassion, the Amitabha Hall and the Vairocana Hall. In addition, there are two pavilions containing stelae with inscriptions by the Kangxi and Qianlong emperors.

The Pavilion of Great Compassion, also known as the Pavilion of Buddha Fragrance or the Pavilion of Heavenly Peace, is the

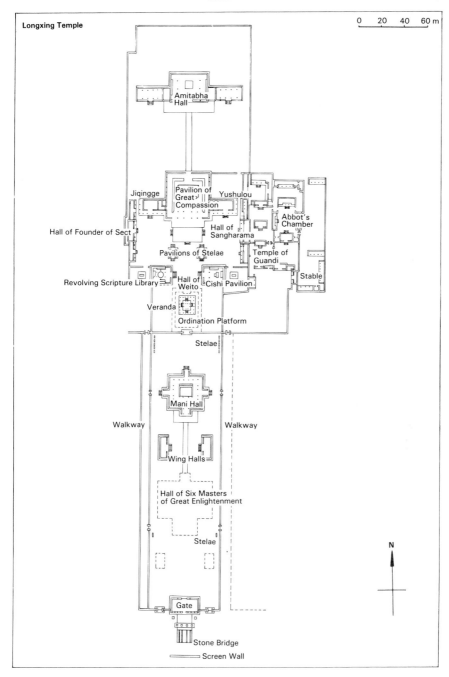

Longxing Temple

0 20 40 60 m

Amitabha Hall

Jiqingge

Pavilion of Great Compassion

Yushulou

Abbot's Chamber

Hall of Founder of Sect

Hall of Sangharama

Temple of Guandi

Pavilions of Stelae

Revolving Scripture Library

Hall of Weito

Cishi Pavilion

Stable

Veranda

Ordination Platform

Stelae

Mani Hall

Walkway

Walkway

Wing Halls

Hall of Six Masters of Great Enlightenment

Stelae

N

Gate

Stone Bridge

Screen Wall

principal building in the Longxing Temple. It contains a 22-metre-high bronze bodhisattva, cast in AD 971, and popularly called the

Guanyin (Avalokitesvara) of a Thousand Arms and a Thousand Eyes, although it has only forty-two arms. It is one of the largest bronze statues of a bodhisattva in China, and it is said to have been cast seven times in all. Another popular name for the statue is the Giant Bodhisattva of Zhengding. It is one of the 'Four Precious Relics of Northern China', the other three being the Anji Bridge, the lions of Cangzhou, and the pagoda in Yingzhou.

The Mani Hall, popularly known as the Great Pavilion of the Five Flowers, was built in the year 1052. Designed in the shape of a cross, the pavilion contains an altar on which stand clay images of Sakyamuni, Ananda, Kasyapa and two other bodhisattvas. Of these, the image of Sakyamuni and his two favourite disciples are Song dynasty relics. Seated in the sculpted Mount Sumeru which hangs at the rear of the pavilion is a Ming dynasty clay figure of Guanyin, with its rather sensuous full chest exposed. One foot is placed on a lotus and the other is raised; the two hands are placed on the knees, and the face reveals a state of bliss. The entire effect is one of great sobriety and refinement, with the naturalness of the form surpassing the conventional rigidness of most religious sculpture.

The stele preserved in the Concealed Dragon Temple dates from the time of the construction of the temple. The inscriptions on it are a valuable source for the study of the evolution of Chinese calligraphy from the Han official script (lishu) to the Tang regular script (kaishu). In addition, there are more than thirty other inscribed stelae dating from the Sui, Song, Jin, Yuan, Ming and Qing dynasties.

Location
The Longxing Temple is located in the northeastern suburbs of Zhengding, Hebei province, 14 kilometres to the south of Shijiazhuang. Shijiazhuang is on the Beijing-Guangzhou railway line, and a bus runs from Shijiazhuang to the temple.

THE SHANHAI PASS
山海关

History
The Shanhai Pass (Shanhaiguan) has always been a place of great strategic importance. In 1381, when the place was known as Shanhaiwei, troops headed by General Xu Da were billeted there. The pass was built the following year, and it marks the starting point of the eastern end of the Great Wall.

The Shanhai Pass

Description

There are four entrances to the Shanhai Pass: Zhendong in the east, Ying'en in the west, Wangyang in the south and Weiyuan in the north. Ramparts were built outside both the eastern and western entrances. The largest and best preserved of the entrances is the eastern gate which serves as a landmark. It is 13 metres high, 20 metres wide, 11 metres deep and is built on a rectangular terrace 12 metres high. There are sixty-eight windows on the north, east and south sides. On the upper part of the gate hangs a horizontal plaque with the characters meaning 'The First Pass Under Heaven'. The characters were written in 1472 by a Ming scholar named Xiao Xian, and the original is now on display in the lower part of the structure. All land east of the gate is known as Guanwai (Beyond the Pass).

Four kilometres south of the pass the Great Wall meets the sea at a place called Old Dragon Head, which was built by Qi Jiguang, commander of the troops stationed there. The northern part of the wall is linked with the section of the Great Wall which extends eastwards to the Yalu river.

Location

The Shanhai Pass is to the northeast of Qinhuangdao, Hebei province. It is accessible by train from Beijing.

THE EASTERN QING MAUSOLEA
清东陵

History

The Eastern Qing Mausolea are located to the east of Beijing, hence the name. The complex comprises fifteen tombs, in which are buried five emperors, namely Shunzhi, Kangxi, Qianlong, Xianfeng and Tongzhi, as well as fourteen empresses and 136 concubines.

The earliest and most important mausoleum in the complex is Xiaoling, built in 1663; the other tombs are located to both sides of it.

Description

Near the high main peak of the Changrui mountain, with low hills to the north and the Yandun and Tiantai mountains to the south, lies a level area of 50 square kilometres; this is the site of the Eastern Qing Mausolea. Skirted by rivers, the setting is one of great natural beauty.

The tombs of Cixi and Ci'an

Yuling, the mausoleum of Qianlong

A Sacred Way, 5 kilometres long, leads from a stone archway straight to Xiaoling. Lining this road are eighteen pairs of statues, including three pairs of human figures and two pairs each of stone horses, unicorns, elephants, camels, *suanni* (fierce mythical animals) and lions. Each of these is carved with its base from a single rock. Between these statues and the structures known as Fangcheng and Minglou are the Dragon and Phoenix Gate, the Stone Bridge on the Sacred Way, and the Stele Pavilion. The mausolea are similar in design, but the length of the Sacred Way leading to each, and the number and size of the stone statues lining it vary according to the rank of the tomb's occupant.

The most extravagant of the tombs is that of the Empress Dowager Cixi. The marble balustrade surrounding the Longen Hall is carved with dragon-and-phoenix and cloud scroll motifs, and the stone in front of the hall has a splendid carving of a dragon and phoenix dancing around a pearl amidst multi-coloured clouds. The stone pillars are encircled by dragons in high relief, and the horizontal plaques inside the hall are painted with gold and polychrome.

To the west of Xiaoling is the mausoleum of Emperor Qianlong, two of his empresses and three of his concubines. This mausoleum,

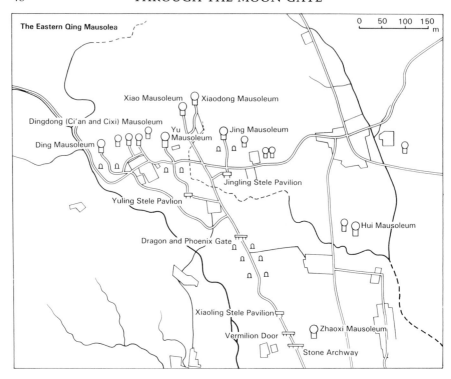

known as Yuling, is an underground palace of unique architectural distinction. It is a vaulted structure with three chambers and four double doors all made of stone. The decorative eaves, tiles and brackets of the first door are all made of marble, and on each side of the door are sculptures of the four Heavenly Kings. One chamber is flanked by eight niches in which imperial records and seals are laid, and its ceiling is carved with five illustrations in bas relief. On the ceiling of another chamber are twenty-four bas-relief images of the Buddha. The fourth stone door leads to the central chamber of the palace, the four walls of which are covered with Buddhist scriptures in Sanskrit and Tibetan. On a Sumeru base lie the coffins of Qianlong, his two empresses and three concubines. The sumptuousness of this underground complex illustrates the prosperity of Qianlong's reign.

See Plate 9

Location

The Eastern Qing Mausolea are in Zunhua county, Hebei province, 125 kilometres east of Beijing. They are accessible by coach.

The Jinshan Pavilion in the Chengde Garden Resort

THE CHENGDE GARDEN RESORT
避暑山庄

History
The garden resort at Chengde is the largest surviving imperial garden complex in China.

Construction began in 1703 and was completed in 1790. The building and development of the resort were closely linked with the political situation in north China at the time, for it was frequently used as a temporary residence by Qing emperors while hunting or making military inspection tours. In order to strengthen northern defences and maintain contact with Mongolian rulers and high officials, the Qing Emperors Kangxi and Qianlong made such tours an almost annual practice. Before 1701 the Qing court had been too preoccupied in fighting northern tribes to build a summer resort, but in 1703, when the border areas were secure and the domestic situation was stable, Emperor Kangxi began construction. Emperors from Kangxi to Xianfeng established temporary courts and received foreign envoys and ethnic minority leaders in Chengde, with the result that it became a second political centre.

Description

The Chengde resort covers an area of 5.6 square kilometres and is surrounded by a wall 10 kilometres long. Within this precinct are about 110 original buildings, which can be divided into two categories, palaces and garden complexes. The former include the

The Yanyu Pavilion

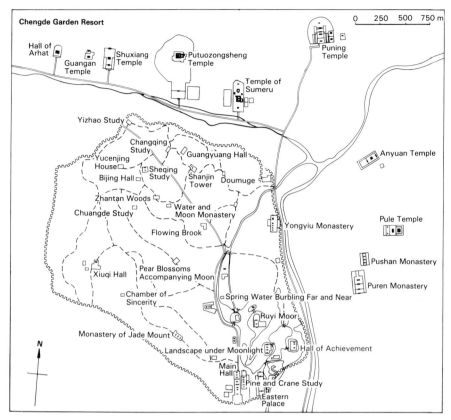

Chengde Garden Resort

Hall of Arhat
Guangan Temple
Shuxiang Temple
Putuozongsheng Temple
Puning Temple
Temple of Sumeru
Yizhao Study
Changqing Study
Yucenjing House
Guangyuang Hall
Sheqing Study
Bijing Hall
Shanjin Tower
Doumuge
Anyuan Temple
Zhantan Woods
Chuangde Study
Water and Moon Monastery
Flowing Brook
Yongyiu Monastery
Pule Temple
Pushan Monastery
Xiuqi Hall
Pear Blossoms Accompanying Moon
Puren Monastery
Chamber of Sincerity
Spring Water Burbling Far and Near
Monastery of Jade Mount
Ruyi Moor
Landscape under Moonlight
Hall of Achievement
Main Hall
Pine and Crane Study
Eastern Palace
N
0   250   500   750 m

main hall, the Pine and Crane Study, the Eastern Palace and many others, and it was in these that the Qing emperors stayed during the hot season and performed their official duties. The gardens are set out on a flat plain and around a lake which lies to the north of the palaces. Scattered throughout this area are small islands, pavilions and towers which were designed to allude to different scenic spots in south China. Further to the north is a lush forested area, characteristic of the northern grasslands, and mountains which make up four-fifths of the total area of the resort.

The Emperors Kangxi and Qianlong gave names to seventy-two places in Chengde. Of the thirty-six given by Qianlong, the first is Lezhengmen, the main entrance to the resort. These names were written on plaques in Chinese, Mongolian, Tibetan, Manchu and Uygur. The main palace complex consists of nine courtyards with the Nanmu Hall at the centre, a symbol of imperial power and the place where important ceremonies were usually held. The imperial quarters are behind this palace. The resort contains many buildings of architectural distinction, the design and construction of which have been dictated to a certain extent by the natural terrain, whether by a hillside or by water. Although the dimensions and proportions are less grandiose than those of the imperial buildings in Beijing, the overall effect is at once elegant and imposing. All the palaces are built of grey bricks and tiles, and are interspersed with rockeries, pines and cypresses.

Location
The resort is located in Chengde, Hebei province, and is accessible by train.

THE PUNING TEMPLE
普宁寺

History
Puningsi (the Temple of Universal Peace) was built in 1755 in the reign of Emperor Qianlong to commemorate the quelling of the armed uprising in Zhungar (in present-day Xinjiang province) and to appease whose who reverted their loyalty to the emperor.

Description
The Puning Temple occupies an area of 23,000 square metres. The front section of the temple complex is in typical Han Chinese style, while the rear section is a copy of the Sanmoye Temple in Tibet; the temple therefore displays a mixture of Han Chinese and Tibetan architectural styles. The principal buildings in the front section are laid out along a central axis, with auxiliary buildings to either side.

General view of the Puning Temple

Colossal clay statue of Guanyin

These buildings include the entrance gate, the Stele Pagoda, the Hall of the Heavenly Kings and the Mahavira Hall. The Stele Pagoda contains three stone stelae inscribed in Chinese, Manchu, Mongolian and Tibetan scripts. Behind the Mahavira Hall begins the Tibetan-style section of the temple, with the Mahayana Pagoda occupying the prime position. The pagoda is 36.8 metres high, is wide at its base and narrows towards the top. The lowest level is seven bays wide and five bays deep, and from the front, six sets of eaves can be counted.

Inside the pagoda is a colossal clay image of Guanyin, 22.2 metres tall. In addition to its normal hands and eyes, it has twenty hands extending from either side with an eye in each, a total of forty hands and forty eyes, symbolizing the bodhisattva's penetrating awareness of all tragedy and happiness, the ability to relieve all suffering, and the limitless powers of the Buddhist faith. The bodhisattva holds a wheel, conch, umbrella, roof, flower, bottle and fish, all Buddhist ritual objects symbolic of good fortune, as well as several types of daggers, swords and halberds for the suppression of evil spirits. The seated Buddha on the statue's crown is the Buddha of Limitless Light (Amitabha), said to be the bodhisattva's teacher. Its position on the crown is an expression of respect. The statue of Guanyin is made of elm, fir, pine, linden and cypress, as well as iron, the gross weight being 120 tonnes. The imposing, well-proportioned statue is the largest extant wooden statue in China. Beside it stand images of the Buddha's servants, Sudhana and the Dragon Maiden.

To each side of the pagoda are halls representing the sun and the moon, and on each of the four sides of the pagoda are terraces in the form of a ladder, a square, a crescent and an oval, which symbolize the Four Major Continents and the Eight Minor Continents described in the Buddhist scriptures. There are also four Lamaist dagobas, red, green, black and white, which represent the Buddha's four kinds of wisdom. To the east and west of the pagoda are the Miaoyan Chambers and the Scripture Explication Hall, where the Living Buddhas expounded the scriptures, and where the Qing princes participated in Buddhist rituals and listened to the monks reciting the scriptures.

See Plate 10

Location
The Puning Temple is located to the northeast of the Chengde Garden Resort, Hebei province.

General view of the Putuozongsheng Temple

THE PUTUOZONGSHENG TEMPLE
普陀宗乘之庙

History

The Putuozongsheng Temple is the largest of the eight 'outer temples' of Chengde. Because it was modelled after the Potala Palace in Tibet, it is called Putuozongsheng, which is the Chinese transliteration of the Tibetan 'Potala'. The temple was built between the years 1767 and 1771 in the reign of Emperor Qianlong to commemorate the emperor's sixtieth birthday and to accommodate visiting ethnic minority leaders. Its construction coincided with the submission to the Qing of the leader of the Torgut tribe of the Western Mongols, who had freed his people from the enslavement of Tsarist Russia and made the long journey from the Volga river basin to have an audience, along with other ethnic minority chieftains, with the emperor. On this occasion Qianlong wrote three inscriptions, the 'Record of the Putuozongsheng Temple', the 'Record of the Torgut Mongols Pledging Allegiance', and the 'Record of

Imperial Commiseration with the Torgut Mongols', which were carved in Manchu, Chinese, Mongol and Tibetan scripts on stone stelae which now stand in the Pavilion of Stelae.

Description

Designed to blend harmoniously with the mountainous landscape, the Putuozongsheng Temple rises gradually from south to north. The buildings within the temple complex are not arranged according to a rigid pattern and they vary in style. The temple complex may be divided into three sections: front, central and rear. The front section includes the main entrance, the Pavilion of Stelae and the Five Pagoda Gate, which has on top of it five Lamaist pagodas representing five Lamaist sects. This gate is an expression of the religious tolerance shown by the Qing rulers towards the various Lamaist sects.

The central section starts at a glazed tiled archway and rises towards the Great Red Terrace. It is made up for the most part of the Tibetan-style White Terrace, which contains monks' quarters and halls for Buddhist worship. The rear section contains the principal and tallest building in the entire temple complex, the Great Red Terrace, which is 25 metres high and is built on the White Platform. With the Hall of the Merciful Boat of Universal Salvation which stands on the northwest corner of the Great Red Terrace, the entire structure reaches the imposing height of 60 metres. The southern face of the outer wall is designed to resemble the Potala Palace in Lhasa; although it has several rows of windows, it is actually a false facade. With the four-storey structure beneath it, the Great Red Terrace is a building of truly monumental proportions. The square Temple of the Unity of the Myriad Truths in the centre of the Great Red Terrace, with its multi-eaved roof which rises to a point and its gilded roof tiles, is the principal hall in the entire Putuozongsheng. In addition, the Hall of Loka Shengjing (Fairy Scene of the Loka) and the Quanhengsanjie Pavilion are located in the eastern part of the Terrace, and the Pavilion of the Merciful Boat of Universal Salvation to the north. Both pagodas have roofs with gilded bronze tiles made in fish-scale style. The grounds are planted with pines, scholar trees and birch trees, giving the temple the air of a garden.

Location

The Putuozongsheng Temple is located to the north of the Chengde Garden Resort, Hebei province. It is accessible by bus from Chengde.

Shandong Province
山东省

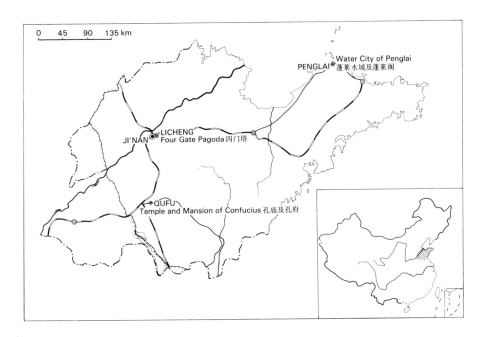

0   45   90   135 km

Water City of Penglai
PENGLAI 蓬莱水城及蓬莱阁

LICHENG
JI'NAN Four Gate Pagoda 四门塔

QUFU
Temple and Mansion of Confucius 孔庙及孔府

The Four Gate Pagoda

THE FOUR GATE PAGODA
四门塔

History

The Four Gate Pagoda (Simenta) was built in AD 611, and has arched openings on each of its four sides. It assumed its present name in the Song dynasty.

In AD 351 a monk by the name of Lang came to preach Buddhism in the area around Mount Tai, and a temple named the Langgong Temple was built at the foot of Green Dragon mountain. The name of this temple was changed to the Shentong Temple in AD 584.

The complex was neglected, however, and gradually fell into ruin. All that survive today are some pagodas, a number of rock carvings and stone tablets. The best known of these remains is the Sui dynasty Four Gate Pagoda.

Description

The Four Gate Pagoda is a square one-storey structure made of huge blocks of stone. Its overhanging eaves are supported by five corbelled layers of bricks and its roof is composed of twenty-three layers of corbiesteps. The cylindrical pinnacle rests on a square base and is decorated with palm leaf carvings and a Buddhist Wheel of the Law.

Inside the pagoda are sixteen triangular stone beams, and at the centre is a square stone pier. There were originally three stone statues on each side of the pier, but now there is only one on each side; these were brought here at a later date. Each statue is carved from a single block of marble. Both have high topknots and lively expressions; they sit in a cross-legged position, with both hands folded in front of their abdomens and others with hands on their knees or raised in a preaching gesture. The drapery of their garments hangs in graceful flowing curves. Set into the northern altar is a stone tablet referring to a man named Yang Xianshu. This inscription is not the original but was carved from a rubbing of the original.

Behind the pagoda towers an ancient cypress tree which, because it forks into nine main branches at the top, is known as the Nine-top Cypress. The nearby chain of hills is covered with lush cypress groves. Clear brooks in deep ravines and graceful bamboo forests are reminiscent of the beautiful scenery of southern China.

See Plate 11

Location

The Four Gate Pagoda lies at the foot of Green Dragon mountain in Licheng county, Shandong province, on the road linking Ji'nan and Tai'an.

THE TEMPLE AND MANSION OF CONFUCIUS
孔庙及孔府

History

Confucius or Kong Qiu (551–479 BC) was a philosopher, statesman, educator and founder of the Confucian school of thought who lived during the late Spring and Autumn period of the Eastern Zhou. The Temple of Confucius is the place where he has been worshipped for many generations.

In 478 BC, the year after Confucius' death, Duke Ai of Lu transformed the three rooms of Confucius' residence into a temple, which was to become the site of annual sacrifices in his honour. Emperor Wu of the Han dynasty 'discredited all other schools of thought and elevated the school of Confucius to the status of a religion'. To the Chinese people Confucius became a sage. Subsequent emperors of China maintained and enlarged the temple, so that today it is one of the largest extant examples of traditional architecture in China.

The Mansion of Confucius, located to the east of the Temple of Confucius, was formerly known as the Mansion of the Descendants of Confucius through the Ages; it served as the offices and residence of generations of descendants. It was the first emperor of the Han dynasty who conferred the responsibility for carrying out sacrifices to Confucius on the ninth generation of the master's descendants; Emperor Renzong of the Song conferred the title of Duke Yansheng upon Kong Zongyuan, Confucius' forty-sixth-generation descendant; and this tradition was observed by Emperor Huizong of the Song. In 1377 the Ming Emperor Hongwu had a residence built to the east of the Queli Residence. It is this fourteenth-century residence which, following repeated repair and enlargement in the Ming and Qing dynasties, is the residence which stands today.

Description

The Temple of Confucius comprises nine courtyards, the whole surrounded by a high wall. The following structures, dating from the Jin, Yuan, Ming and Qing dynasties, are laid out on the central axis from south to north: the Lingxin Gate, the Shengshi Gate, the Hongdao Gate, the Dazhong Gate, the Tongwen Gate, the Pavilion of the Constellation of Scholars, the Stelae Pavilion of Thirteen Emperors, the Gate of Great Achievement, the Apricot Terrace, the Hall of Great Achievement, the Hall of Repose and the Hall of the Sage's Accomplishments.

The Shengshi Gate, the second entrance to the temple, was built in the Ming dynasty. In the courtyard beyond the gate stand two Han dynasty columnar stone figures. The Pavilion of the Constellation of Scholars, situated at the centre of the temple complex, was begun in the Song dynasty and enlarged to three storeys in the Ming. It is one of the finest examples of wooden pagoda

Entrance to the Mansion of Confucius

architecture in China, and formerly held a collection of inscriptions donated to the temple by a number of China's emperors in the course of history.

The Gate of Achievement, the seventh entrance to the temple, is an example of Ming dynasty architecture. To the north of this gate the temple divides into three parallel series of courtyards and buildings. Immediately inside the gate, and located directly on the central axis of the temple, is a square open-air pavilion with carved beams and painted rafters, and set upon a base of dark stone. In front of the pavilion is the Apricot Terrace where Confucius used to give lectures; on it are four apricot trees and a stone incense burner.

The Hall of Great Achievement is the main structure within the Temple of Confucius. In the Tang dynasty it was known as the Hall of Prince Wenxuan, and it assumed its present name in the Song. The present hall was rebuilt in the Qing dynasty. It has multiple eaves and a nine-section roof covered in yellow glazed tiles. The ten columns which support the roof are decorated with high-relief

An avenue in the garden

carvings of paired dragons sporting with pearls; beneath the dragons
are wave patterns and above them are cloud patterns. These fine
stone carvings date from the Ming dynasty.

The wide terrace in front of the hall was where 'eight groups of
dancers performed in the hall' during sacrificial rituals held in
Confucius' honour. In the hall is a plaque bearing the inscription,
'The Most Holy Sage, the First Teacher', and an altar containing

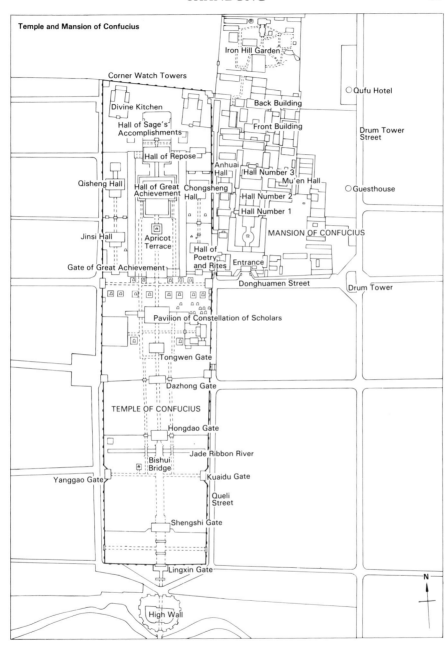

Temple and Mansion of Confucius

Iron Hill Garden

Corner Watch Towers

Divine Kitchen

Hall of Sage's
Accomplishments

Hall of Repose

Qisheng Hall

Hall of Great
Achievement

Chongsheng
Hall

Anhuai
Hall

Mu'en Hall

Hall Number 3

Hall Number 2

Hall Number 1

Jinsi Hall

Apricot
Terrace

Hall of
Poetry
and Rites

Entrance

MANSION OF CONFUCIUS

Gate of Great Achievement

Donghuamen Street

Back Building

Front Building

○ Qufu Hotel

Drum Tower
Street

○ Guesthouse

Drum Tower

Pavilion of Constellation of Scholars

Tongwen Gate

Dazhong Gate

TEMPLE OF CONFUCIUS

Hongdao Gate

Jade Ribbon River

Bishui
Bridge

Yanggao Gate

Kuaidu Gate

Queli
Street

Shengshi Gate

Lingxin Gate

N

High Wall

an image of Confucius, flanked by those of the four disciples and twelve philosophers, his disciples and followers of the Confucian school of thought.

Behind the Hall of Great Achievement is the Hall of Repose, where sacrifices to the memory of Confucius' wife were carried out; to the north of the Hall of Repose is the Hall of the Sage's Accomplishments which dates from the Ming dynasty. This hall contains a series of 120 stone carvings known as 'The Sage's Accomplishments', which depict the life of Confucius. These carvings are some of the earliest examples of this genre of carving in China. Also in this hall are stone reliefs entitled 'Confucius Engaged in Teaching' based on a painting reputedly by the famous fourth-century painter Gu Kaizhi, and 'Confucius as Minister of Justice in the State of Lu' by the Tang painter Wu Daozi, as well as the 'Stele in Praise of Confucius' rendered in seal script by the Song calligrapher Mi Fei.

The residence of Confucius, on the eastern axis of the Temple of Confucius, is also known as the Queli Residence. Legend has it that this was the home of Confucius, though all that remains is the well. Inside the courtyard is the Hall of Poetry and Rites, built to commemorate his teaching of poetry and rites to his son Kong Li.

The Mansion of Confucius is laid out on three parallel axes and contains nine courtyards in all. The major buildings stand on the central axis. In the front section are the official buildings, consisting of three halls and six offices. The residential buildings are located in the rear. On the western axis are buildings for studying poetry, practising rites, reading, and entertaining guests, and on the eastern axis are the clan temple and various workshops. At the northern end of these axes stands the garden of the Mansion of Confucius. As the stones which make up the garden contain a high percentage of iron ore, it is known as the Iron Mountain Garden.

The Mansion of Confucius contains historical archives dating from 1534 to 1948, which are a rich source of information on Chinese philosophy, culture, and politics, including valuable data on peasant uprisings. Of the many historical artefacts in the collection, the most famous are ten bronze vessels from the Shang and Zhou dynasties, paintings by Zhao Mengfu and Zheng Banqiao, calligraphy by Dong Qichang and Wen Zhengming, seals by He Zhen and Wen Peng, rare woodblock editions from the Song, Yuan and Ming dynasties, fine jades, wood carvings, ceramics and bronzes. There is also an interesting collection of garments, weapons, official plaques and household goods from the Yuan, Ming and Qing dynasties, including a rare seven-tiered Yuan dynasty crown.

See Plate 12

Location

The Temple and Mansion of Confucius are located in Qufu, Shandong province. Travelling by train from Beijing or Shanghai, visitors should alight at Yanzhou and take a bus from there to Qufu.

THE WATER CITY OF PENGLAI
蓬莱水城及蓬莱阁

History

Penglai is also known as Beiwo. It was originally called Daoyu Fort, and in 1042 troops were stationed here to guard against Khitan invaders. In 1376 the Japanese began to cause trouble in the region, and so in order to strengthen its defences the village and the surrounding area were upgraded into a prefecture. The town expanded during the Ming and Qing dynasties when warships were moored and naval forces were billeted here. It became an important

The Water City of Penglai

military port and was a base from which ships patrolled the coast. Qi Jiguang, a Ming dynasty general, trained his navy and fought the Japanese here.

Penglai, Fangzhang and Yingzhou are known as the three 'fairy isles'. Legend had it that they were the dwelling places of deities and that an elixir of immortality was to be found on them. According to historical records, both the first Qin and the first Han emperor visited these isles in search of the elixir. An alchemist by the name of Xu Fu was entrusted by Qin Shihuang to set sail from here in search of the immortals. The pavilion on Penglai, built in the reign of Jiayou (1056–63), was enlarged in 1589 and further renovated in 1819.

Description

Penglai lies at the base of the eastern slope of Danya mountain in northern Penglai county, with the mountain as its backdrop. From the site the Changshan archipelago can be seen in the distance. The rectangular town walls of earth, stone and bricks were built on foundations of rammed earth. In 1596 brick and stone were used to reinforce the wall, which is on average 7 metres high and 8 metres thick, with a perimeter of 2,200 metres. The town has two entrances, the Zhenyang Gate to the south, which links the town with a road, and the Water Gate, which leads to the sea. A narrow lake known as the Lesser Sea was dug from south to north, dividing the town into two. Sea water was channelled into it and it was used as a naval training base. Docks, a breakwater and a dyke were built near the Water Gate in order to decrease the force of the sea, with the result that, no matter how stormy the ocean, the water in the Lesser Sea was always calm. Boats were able to come and go at any time without waiting for the tide. Both inside and outside the town there were navy barracks, a blockhouse, a lighthouse, sluice gates and a moat, forming a complete marine defence system. As the location, planning and building of the town are unique, it has an important place in the history of Chinese port construction.

The Penglai Pavilion stands on the top of Danya mountain. It has a double-eaved roof and eight curved corners, and is surrounded by a balustrade. A broad horizontal plaque has 'The Penglai Pavilion' written on it in gilt characters by a Qing dynasty calligrapher named Tie Bao. To the south of the pavilion are the Sanqing Hall, the Patriarch Lü Hall, the Queen Mother Palace, the Dragon King Palace and the Sramanera Temple. Together they form a complex of classical buildings known as Penglaige. Visitors to the pavilion at the time when summer is turning into autumn may be fortunate enough to see a mirage to the north. Su Shi (Su Dongpo), the great Song dynasty poet, wrote a poem on the mirage he witnessed:

> Tier upon tier are the eastern clouds
> Where flocks of fairies come and go.
> A myriad images in their changing shapes,
> How can the Shell Tower hide the Pearl Palace?

In the Su Shi Memorial Hall, which lies to the east of the Penglai Pavilion, the following couplet has been carved on stone: 'All mirages are but illusions. Only loyal ministers and filial sons are immortals.' To the southeast stands the Pavilion for Watching the Waves, from which can be seen not only a vast expanse of ocean but also sunrise and moonrise. Penglaige has been frequented by literati for centuries. Approximately two hundred tablets with inscriptions about the place by some of these visitors are to be found here.

Location
Penglai is situated at the foot of Danya mountain in northern Penglai county, Shandong province. Visitors may take a train to Yantai and complete the journey by bus.

Jiangsu Province
江苏省

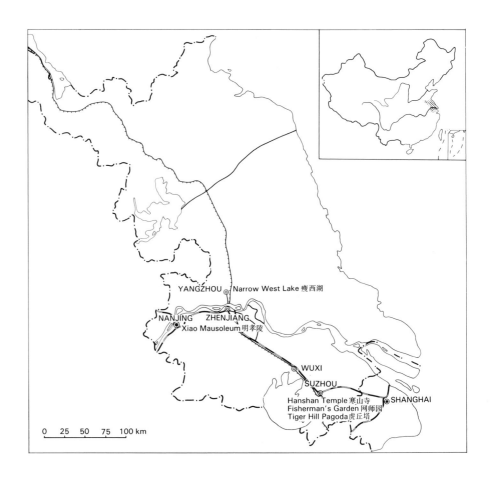

The canal by the Hanshan Temple

THE HANSHAN TEMPLE
寒山寺

History

The Cold Mountain Temple (Hanshansi) was formerly called
the Sariputra Temple and was built during the reign of Tianjian
(AD 502–19). It is said that in the Tang dynasty an eminent monk
by the name of Hanshan served as its abbot and that the temple
was subsequently renamed in his honour. The temple buildings
have been destroyed by fire on several occasions, and in 1860 war
again left the temple in ruins. The existing structures were all
built during the late Qing dynasty. The Tang poet Zhang Ji once
visited the temple and wrote the following poem, 'Night Mooring
by Maple Bridge', which has brought fame to the temple both in
China and abroad:

> As the moon goes down, a crow caws through the frost,
> Under the shadows of maple trees a fisherman moves with his torch,
> And I hear, from beyond Suzhou, from the temple on Cold Mountain,
> Ringing for me, here in my boat, the midnight bell.

The Bell Tower of the Hanshan Temple

Description

In the centre of the temple is the Mahavira Hall. Set into the walls behind and on each side of the main altar are thirty-six poems by Hanshan and numerous poems by Wei Yingwu and other poets. There are also striking stone images of Hanshan, Shide and Fenggan, and inscriptions by celebrated artists such as Luo Pin and Deng Wenzhuo of the Qing dynasty. In the two side chambers of the hall are five hundred small wooden figurines of arhats and statues of Hanshan and Shide. Behind the hall is the Sutra Repository on the circular wall of which is inscribed the *Diamond Sutra* carved by Zhang Chuliao in the Song dynasty. The corridor to the left of this building leads to the Bell Tower. The bell mentioned in Zhang Ji's poem disappeared long ago, and another huge bell cast in the reign of Jiajing (1522–66) is said to have been taken to Japan. When the Hanshan Temple was rebuilt in 1905, a small bronze bell, which had been paid for by Japanese donations, was given to the temple and it hangs to the right of the central hall. In the stele corridor are scores of tablets with inscriptions or poems in praise of the temple by renowned figures such as Wei Yingwu, Yue Fei, Lu You, Tang Yin, Wang Shizhen and Kang Youwei. Zhang Ji's poem was carved on a tablet in the calligraphy of the famous Ming artist Wen Zhengming but this was unfortunately damaged. It was recarved by Yu Yue in the reign of Emperor Guangxu (1875–1908). A postscript was also carved on the rear. To the south of this corridor stands the structure called the First Building of Fengjiang, which was moved here in 1954.

Location
The Hanshan Temple is situated in Fengjiaozhen outside Changmen in Suzhou, Jiangsu province. It is accessible by bus from the centre of Suzhou.

THE TIGER HILL PAGODA
虎丘塔

History
The Tiger Hill Pagoda stands on Tiger Hill, once described as the 'most beautiful place in the state of Wu'. It has a history of some 2,400 years. During the late Spring and Autumn period the Wu King Fu Chai buried his father here. Legend has it that three days after the burial a white tiger mounted the tomb and so the place came to be called Tiger Hill. Another story tells that the hill was so named because the tomb is shaped like a tiger.

Work on the Tiger Hill Pagoda began in AD 959 and was completed in AD 961. Between then and 1860 the pagoda caught fire seven times, and the top and overhanging eaves were destroyed.

The Tiger Hill Pagoda

Its iron pinnacle was also destroyed and now only the brick base for the pinnacle remains.

Description
The seven-storey octagonal pagoda is 47.5 metres high, built of brick, and designed in pavilion style.

The pagoda consists of an outer wall, winding corridor and main body, and is similar in design to the Leifeng Pagoda in Hangzhou. It is characteristic of the brick pagodas constructed along the Yangtze river in the tenth century. The passage linking the outer wall and the winding corridor has four openings. Inside the pagoda are small chambers, square in shape except for those on the second and seventh floors which are octagonal. The brick caisson ceilings on each storey, supported by *dougong* brackets, are rectangular, square or octagonal. The inner walls are painted with delicate colourful peonies.

The pagoda, which tapers towards the top, has a complex structure, and is inclined to the northwest. The corners of the octagon protrude as half columns. In the centre of each facade is an entrance flanked by windows with vertical lattices. The bracket system at the top and bottom of each storey supports the protruding eaves. The brickwork is designed to imitate wood and is painted pale grey, red and black. The horizontal plaques, doors, *dougong* brackets and caisson ceilings are painted with intricate geometric designs.

Subsidence caused the Tiger Hill Pagoda to incline. After several years of repair and reinforcement its foundations have now firmly settled, and the leaning pagoda has become one of the landmarks of Suzhou.

Location
The Tiger Hill Pagoda, 3.5 kilometres from the centre of Suzhou, is located on Tiger Hill outside Changmen. It is accessible by car.

THE XIAO MAUSOLEUM
明孝陵

History
The Xiao Mausoleum (Xiaoling), built between 1381 and 1383, is the mausoleum of Zhu Yuanzhang, the founding emperor of the Ming dynasty. The emperor himself decided on the setting and design. Basing his design on Han and Tang imperial burial mounds, he introduced a number of innovations, and in so doing established a style which was followed for six hundred years. The former square burial mounds became round, and the convention of lining the Spirit Way (the approach to the mausoleum) with stone sculptures was introduced.

The Treasure City

Description

The Xiao Mausoleum has twice been seriously damaged, first when Nanjing fell to the Manchus and again during the suppression of the Taiping Rebellion. The majority of the existing structures were rebuilt during the late Qing dynasty. Many of these have been repaired or renovated since 1949.

Of the more than ten Ming imperial mausolea, the Xiao Mausoleum is the only one in Nanjing. It can be divided into two areas, the Spirit Way and the mausoleum itself. The approach to the mausoleum begins at the Dismount Arch, continues through the Great Golden Gate, the Square City and the Spirit Way, and ends at the Lingxing Archway. Inside the Square City stands a stone tablet dated 1413 and carved with a eulogy of Zhu Yuanzhang composed by his fourth son, the Emperor Yongle (1403–24). One of the largest stone tablets in China, it is 8.9 metres high and is inscribed with some 2,700 characters. To the northwest of the Square City is the Spirit Way, flanked by twelve massive pairs of stone animals — lions, camels, elephants, unicorns, horses and mythical

The Spirit Way

beasts. The passage then turns north to two *huabiao* followed by two pairs of stone statues of officials wearing ceremonial hats and holding *hu* (a tablet held before the chest by officials when received by the emperor). There are also two pairs of generals in full armour and holding weapons. At the end of the Spirit Way, which extends for 1 kilometre, stands the Lingxing Archway, behind which are five parallel bridges leading to the entrance to the mausoleum.

The main parts of the Xiao Mausoleum are the entrance, the Tablet Pavilion, the Sacrificial Hall, the Square City and the Treasure City. The entrance formerly had three large and two small square doors, but now there is only a gate built during the reign of the Qing Emperor Tongzhi (1862–73). On its lintel is a stone tablet with the characters 'Ming Xiaoling'. At the foot of the central gate stands a stele pavilion inside which is a tablet with an inscription by the Qing Emperor Kangxi (1662–1722). The Sacrificial Hall, situated behind this pavilion, is the principal structure of the mausoleum. It is nine bays wide, five bays deep and flanked by side chambers. The imperial kitchen, the slaughterhouse and many other buildings were destroyed long ago. All that survives today are the Sumeru bases, the plinths of fifty-six huge columns and a hall built during the reign of the Qing Emperor Tongzhi. In front of the Treasure City stands the Square City, the roof of which has collapsed. Behind this are the graves of Zhu Yuanzhang and his wife, surrounded by a brick wall.

Location
The Xiao Mausoleum lies on a southern slope of the Purple and Gold Hills on the eastern outskirts of Nanjing. It is accessible by bus from the centre of the city.

THE FISHERMAN'S GARDEN
网师园

History
The Fisherman's Garden (Wangshiyuan) was originally the site of a library known as the Ten Thousand Volume Chamber which

A pavilion in the Fisherman's Garden

The Dianchun Hall

belonged to Shi Zhengzhi, a Southern Song official. It subsequently fell into ruin and was later rebuilt by Song Zongyuan, an official in the reign of Emperor Qianlong (1736–95). Song retired to live in seclusion in the garden, renaming it the Wangshiyuan after a nearby street called Wangshi Lane.

Description
Covering an area of 5,000 square metres, the garden can be divided into three sections: the residential dwellings to the east, the main garden in the centre and the inner garden to the west.

Typical of medium-scale houses of feudal officials, the dwelling area consists of an entrance, front hall, main hall and rear chamber. The rooms are compact, and decorated in a refined and attractive manner. A small door on the west side of the front hall leads to the garden.

To the south of the main garden are several chambers where the owner would have entertained guests. To the north is a library named the Five Peaks. Jixuzhai served as a study. The square pond in the centre of the garden is surrounded by gazebos, pavilions and a corridor. The Duck Shooting Corridor, the Zhuoying Pavilion and a small stone bridge extend across the water.

In the inner garden stands the Dianchun Hall which was once a study, and where peonies used to grow and blossom in late spring.

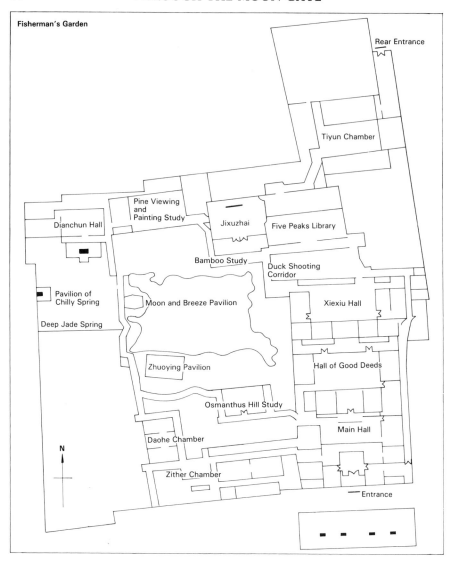

In the southwest corner is a spring. A replica of this part of the garden was created in the Metropolitan Museum of Art in New York in 1980.

See Plate 13

Location

The Fisherman's Garden is located in Shiquan Street, Fengmen, Suzhou. It is accessible by bus from the town.

The Narrow West lake

THE NARROW WEST LAKE
瘦西湖

History

The Narrow West lake (Shouxihu), so called because it is narrower than the West lake in Hangzhou, is at the confluence of two streams flowing from the Tiny Wave valley and the Dabie mountains in the western outskirts of the city of Yangzhou. It has been a famous scenic spot since the Six Dynasties period. In the mid-eighteenth century the Small Golden Hill, the Five Pavilion Bridge and the White Dagoba were added to the site.

Description

The meandering Narrow West lake is 4.3 kilometres long, and the surrounding scenic area covers more than 300,000 square metres. The main places of interest are the Great Rainbow Bridge, the Long Dyke, the Xu Garden, the Small Golden Hill, the Angler's Terrace, the Five Pavilion Bridge and the White Dagoba.

The Great Rainbow Bridge, shaped like a rainbow, marks the beginning of the lake. The original late Ming dynasty bridge was

The Five Pavilion Bridge

made of wood, but this was replaced by a stone bridge in the Qing dynasty. Scholars often came here to drink and write poetry.

The Long Dyke, shaded by rows of willow trees, is on the western bank. In the pavilion on the middle of the dyke is the inscription 'Spring willows over the dyke'; this is one of the twenty-four scenic spots of Yangzhou. At the northern end of the dyke lies the Xu Garden (Xuyuan) in which the Listening to Orioles Pavilion is situated. In front of this pavilion stand two iron cauldrons which are said to have been used to regulate the streams during the Northern and Southern dynasties.

The Small Golden Hill, originally known as Evergreen Ridge, is named after the Golden Hill on the Yangtze river at Zhenjiang which it resembles. It is said that there were buildings and gardens here as early as the Six Dynasties period although the existing buildings and rockeries all date from the Qing dynasty. On top of the hill stands the Wind Pavilion, and at the foot of the western slope of the hill are the Green Shade Chamber, the Jade Buddha Cave and the Lesser South Sea.

The Angler's Terrace is located on the western slope of the hillside, and has water on three sides. The terrace has four openings, one square and three round; all are laid with bricks. Across an expanse of water stand the Five Pavilion Bridge and the White Dagoba, both of which can be seen from the openings of the Angler's Terrace.

Built on a lotus-shaped causeway, the Five Pavilion Bridge is also known as the Lotus Bridge. It has five pavilions on it and was built by a salt merchant in order to welcome the Qing Emperor Qianlong when he was on an inspection tour of the south.

South of this bridge is the Lianxing Temple, which was built by a rich Yangzhou merchant to greet Emperor Qianlong. In 1784 a three-storey white dagoba was erected on the fifty-three-step square base of the temple. There is an altar on the second storey and a round pinnacle on the top storey. In appearance and style it is similar to the White Dagoba in the Beihai Park in Beijing.

See Plate 14

Location

The Narrow West lake is on the western outskirts of Yangzhou, Jiangsu province. It is accessible by car from the centre of the city.

The City of Shanghai
上海市

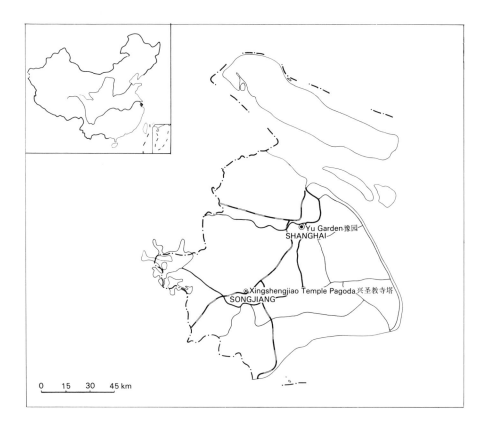

Yu Garden 豫园
SHANGHAI

Xingshengjiao Temple Pagoda 兴圣教寺塔
SONGJIANG

0   15   30   45 km

The Xingshengjiao Temple Pagoda

THE XINGSHENGJIAO TEMPLE PAGODA
兴圣教寺塔

History

The Xingshengjiao Temple Pagoda in Songjiang, one of the oldest buildings in Shanghai, was erected in the reign of the Northern Song Emperor Shenzong (1068–94).

Songjiang was originally part of the state of Wu during the Spring and Autumn period. The king of Wu used to hunt in the area, and maintained a residence there called Huating. During the reign of Wudi of the Liang dynasty (AD 502–47) Buddhism flourished in the

Yangtze valley. According to one contemporaneous record, 'There are more than five hundred temples in the capital and its surrounding area, all of which are grand and splendid.' During the Sui dynasty Songjiang grew into a small town where troops were stationed. In AD 751, it became a county and then gradually developed into a densely populated city. By the Tang and Five Dynasties periods, Buddhist temples were to be found throughout the region south of the Wusong river. The Xingshengjiao Temple, erected in AD 949 on the foundations of a residence belonging to the son of Zhang Ai, a minister of the Latter Han Kingdom of the Five Dynasties period, was one of the four great temples in Huating county. The pagoda was built about one hundred years after the temple. During the late Yuan dynasty the temple itself was destroyed, but the pagoda remains.

Description

The Xingshengjiao Temple Pagoda is a nine-storey wood and brick structure. All of its overhanging eaves, still intact, are supported by *dougong* brackets constructed primarily of *nan* wood. Of 177 brackets, over half date from the Song dynasty, rare amongst surviving early pagodas. Two fine Song paintings of seated Buddhas can be seen on the wall between the brackets on the western side of the third storey. On the ground floor is a vault with a brick ceiling, and inside is a stone case on top of which lie forty-two Song dynasty coins and a bronze seated Buddha. The case contains a bronze reclining Buddha. On each side of the stone case are silver boxes in which are fossilized animal bones, symbolizing the teeth of the Buddha. The pinnacle of the pagoda, which greatly enhances the structure, consists of an inverted basin shape, a Buddhist Wheel of the Law, a gourd and chains, all made of iron. These iron objects are attached to a wooden pole planted on the floor of the eighth storey in order to lower the structure's centre of gravity and enable it to withstand the wind.

Despite repeated restoration throughout its history, the Xingshengjiao Temple Pagoda was in a dilapidated state on the eve of Liberation in 1949. Years were spent surveying and collecting suitable materials so that by 1975 the pagoda could be restored to its original grandeur.

Location

The Xingshengjiao Temple Pagoda is located in Songjiang county in the southwestern suburbs of Shanghai. It can be reached by car.

The Exquisite Jade boulder in the Yu Garden

THE YU GARDEN
豫园

History
Work on the Yu Garden (Yuyuan) commenced in 1559 and was completed in 1577. One of the greatest gardens of its age, it was created by a certain Pan Yunduan for his father, a retired Minister of Punishment in the Ming government. The garden later changed hands several times. It underwent large-scale restoration in 1982.

Description
The Yu Garden occupies an area of 50,000 square metres. At the centre is a huge rockery made of unique yellow stones from Wukang in Zhejiang province. Created by Zhang Nanyang, a celebrated Ming rockery designer, the rockery is composed of stones of different sizes imitating mountain scenery such as cliffs, ravines and caves.

To the east of the rockery stands the Cuixiu Chamber. In the winding corridor leading from the chamber is a stone tablet with the inscription, 'A serene view of mountains and streams', by the famous Ming scholar Zhu Zhishan. Not far from the rockery, and jutting out over the pool, is a two-storey structure called the Yang-shan Pavilion. Behind it lies a winding corridor where visitors may rest or view the rockery. Here the pool branches into two streams, one flowing northwest into the rockery, the other eastwards, skirting the Hall of a Myriad Flowers and reaching the Appointment of Spring Hall. In 1853 the latter served as the headquarters of the Small Sword Society which rose in rebellion against foreign domination, and then, with the Taipings, jointly ruled Shanghai for over seventeen months. Today the hall is a museum displaying weapons, coins and proclamations issued by the rebels.

There are more than twenty pavilions, towers and other buildings, linked by winding corridors. The decorative walls, with their variously shaped windows and latticework, provide a number of different views of the garden.

In front of the Yuhua Chamber stands an immense boulder called the Exquisite Jade. Transported from Lake Tai, it has been carved naturally by flowing water. It is said that water poured into an opening at the top will spurt from all its many holes, while incense smoke burned underneath will rise and curl from every hole. The Exquisite Jade boulder was handed down from the Tang or Sui dynasty and was acquired by the Song Emperor Huizong. It was, however, lost en route to Kaifeng, the Northern Song capital, where the emperor stored precious stones and rare flowers; later the boulder came into the possession of the Pan family. When it was transported to the garden, the boat carrying it capsized and the stone fell into the Huangpu river. The Pan family was forced to send divers to locate it and haul it to the bank. A section of the city wall had to be felled in order for it to be brought into Shanghai.

Location
The Yu Garden is located in the Nanshi district of Shanghai and is accessible by bus.

Zhejiang Province
浙江省

HANGZHOU◎Six Harmonies Pagoda 六和塔
West Lake 西湖

NINGBO◎Baoguo Temple 保国寺
Tianyige Library 天一阁

0 25 50 75 100
km

General view of the temple

THE BAOGUO TEMPLE
保国寺

History
The Defend the Country Temple (Baoguosi), once known as the
Lingshan Temple, is said to have been first built during the Eastern
Han dynasty and later destroyed. When rebuilt in AD 880 it was
named the Baoguo Temple. The existing buildings, which are
the earliest wooden structures in the Yangtze valley, were erected
in 1013. They were renovated from time to time and large-scale
repairs were carried out in the reign of the Qing Emperor Kangxi
(1662–1722). The central hall dates from the Song dynasty.

Description
The main buildings in the Baoguo Temple, the Heavenly King Hall,
the Mahavira Hall, the Avalokitesvara Chamber and the Sutra
Chamber lie on a north-south axis. To the east and west are monks'
quarters, meditation rooms and a Bell and Drum Tower. The central
hall is an outstanding example of traditional wooden architecture,

A large hall

The caisson ceiling of the Mahavira Hall

without a single nail in the entire structure. The weight of the roof is supported by *dougong* brackets. The hall is deep and wide, the beams are crescent-shaped and the *dougong* brackets thick and strong. The ceiling has three engraved sunken panels characteristic of Song dynasty wooden structures.

Location
The Baoguo Temple is situated at the foot of Ma'an mountain, north of Hongkuang in Ningbo, Zhejiang province. It is about 15 kilometres from the town and is accessible by bus.

THE SIX HARMONIES PAGODA
六和塔

History
The Six Harmonies Pagoda (Liuheta) was built in AD 971 by Qian Chu, ruler of the Wuyue Kingdom, in order to control the destructive tidal waves of the Qiantang river. The original pagoda had nine storeys and was approximately 60 metres high. With a lantern installed at the pinnacle, it also served as a lighthouse.

The pagoda was originally built of brick and wood, but in 1153 it was renovated mainly in brick. The pinnacle and the top storey were rebuilt in the Ming dynasty. In 1899 the thirteen-eaved wooden exterior was renovated. The pagoda has since been reduced to seven storeys, yet it still retains much of its original splendour and is an important example of traditional Chinese wood and brick architecture.

Description
The Six Harmonies Pagoda, also known as the Six Points Pagoda (the four points of the compass plus heaven and earth), occupies an area of 870 square metres. The octagonal base is made from long slabs of rock, and the seven-storey octagonal pagoda, 59.9 metres high, is built of rectangular bricks. Of the thirteen upturned wooden eaves, only seven are built over windows, an arrangement which allows visitors to see great distances. Over one hundred large iron bells hang from the corners of the eaves, which are so dense as to make the body of the pagoda barely visible. Inside the pagoda, each storey consists of two levels and each has a small chamber surrounded by a corridor. A staircase leads to the top. The bricks

The Six Harmonies Pagoda

of the Sumeru base are elaborately carved with realistic human, animal and floral motifs. These include celestial beings, dancing figures, leaping lions, unicorns, blooming peonies, roses, camellias and a variety of decorative patterns.

See Plate 15

Location

The Six Harmonies Pagoda stands on the Yuelun hill on the northern bank of the Qiantang river in Hangzhou, Zhejiang province. It is accessible by bus from central Hangzhou.

THE TIANYIGE LIBRARY
天一阁

History

Tianyige was first built in 1561 and was the library of Fan Qin, an assistant Minister of War in the mid-sixteenth century. It is the earliest surviving private library in China.

Fan obtained his books by purchases of individual titles, by large-scale acquisition of books from other libraries, among them Wanjuanlou (the Library of Ten Thousand Volumes) in Ningbo, and by copying rare items in the possession of other collectors. By these means he built up his library to a total of 70,000 volumes. Some of the books in his collection were block-printed by Fan himself.

The books are extremely well preserved due to the measures taken to ensure proper ventilation, the correct degree of humidity, and protection from bookworms. In the main structure, the Precious Books Building, a piece of limestone was laid beneath each bookcase, and *yuncao* grass was used to keep away bookworms. In 1665 Fan Qin's grandson Fan Guangwen built a splendid garden by making use of the mounds of earth and grotesque rock forms around the buildings and by planting numerous trees and bamboos. This added greatly to the charm of the library's grounds and even attracted the attention of the emperor.

In 1773 the Qing court decided to compile *Si ku quan shu* (the *Complete Library in Four Branches of Literature*, namely, Classics, History, Philosophy and *Belles-lettres*). For this project a nation-wide search for manuscripts which were dispersed throughout the country was launched. Fan Mouzhu, Fan Qin's eighth-generation descendant, responded to the appeal by presenting 683 books to the court, for which he was highly praised. In recognition of his generosity the emperor later bestowed on him a set of the encyclopaedia *Gu jin tu shu jicheng* (the *Synthesis of Books and Illustrations of Ancient and Modern Times*), which comprises 10,000 volumes, as well as presenting other rare books to the Tianyige Library.

The Tianyige Library

The Precious Books Building

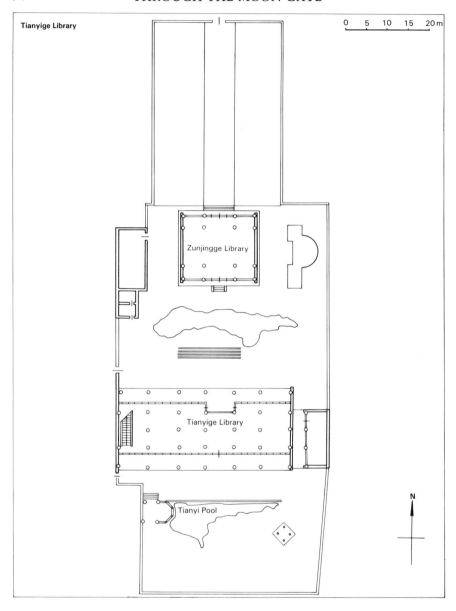

In order to provide better storage for *Si ku quan shu* the emperor decided to build several more libraries throughout the country. He asked a local official in Zhejiang province to prepare drawings of the buildings and bookcases in the Tianyige Library to be used as specifications for the new libraries. These new libraries were the Wenyuange Library in the Forbidden City in Beijing, the Wenlange Library in Hangzhou, the Wenjinge Library in Chengde, the Wensuge Library in Shenyang, the Wenhuige Library in Yangzhou, the Wenyuange Library in the Old Summer Palace in Beijing and the Wenzongge on Jinshan in Zhejiang. Thus the reputation of the Tianyige Library was firmly established.

However, as the Fan family declined, the library and its courtyard were neglected and became dilapidated. It was not until 1933 that money was collected to repair the library and move the Zunjingge Library from the Temple of Confucius in Ningbo to the rear courtyard of Tianyige. A number of Song and Yuan stelae in the area were moved here also, and became known collectively as the Mingzhou Forest of Stelae. Many of the original books have been lost. In 1949 only 1,591 titles, totalling 13,038 volumes, remained; these included the 10,000 volumes added in the Qing dynasty.

Description

The library's main structures are Tianyige (the library building), the Tianyi Pool, Zunjingge and the Mingzhou Forest of Stelae, as well as several pavilions and rockeries. The library building is a two-storey wooden building of six rooms. In front of it is a pond, which suggests that fire precautions were taken into account when the library was built.

Since 1949 an administrative office has been set up to oversee the renovation work and gardening. A further 3,000 volumes, which were originally part of the collection, were recovered and books donated by local people were added. Today the library houses about 300,000 volumes including 80,000 rare books. Special camphor boxes have been made for valuable editions. From the *Selected Local Histories of the Ming Dynasty Housed in the Tianyige Library* 170 titles have been photo-offset and published.

Location

The Tianyige Library is situated by the Moon lake in the south-western suburbs of Ningbo, Zhejiang province. There is a bus service from the centre of town.

THE WEST LAKE
西湖

History

The West lake (Xihu) was formed gradually from a shallow sea and in the Han dynasty was called the Wulin lake. Legend has it that

Three Pools Mirroring the Moon

there once emerged from the lake a golden ox which was believed
to herald the appearance of a brilliant emperor; the lake was therefore
given yet another name, the Mingsheng (Brilliant Emperor) lake. In
the Tang dynasty the county seat of Qiantang was moved to a place
called Qiantangmen and since the lake was to the west of the town
it was then given the name of the West lake.

Of the many projects to control the West lake throughout history,
the most famous are those organized by Bai Juyi in the Tang dynasty
and Su Dongpo in the Song dynasty, both celebrated poets in their
time. In AD 822 Bai Juyi was appointed governor of Hangzhou.
Under his aegis a long dyke was built outside Qiantangmen and stone
sluices were installed to control the water. Su Dongpo held two
official appointments in Hangzhou: as *tongpan* (assistant governor)
from 1071 to 1074; and as prefect from 1089 to 1091. He ordered
the lake to be weeded and dredged, and a dyke to be built from
south to north with the mud taken from the lake. Six stone bridges
were built along this. To commemorate the projects the dyke was
called the Su Dyke and the long causeway from west to east the
Bai Causeway.

Description
The West lake is surrounded on three sides by mountains and on
the fourth by the town of Hangzhou. The lake is fringed with dense

forests and a variety of flowers. It covers an area of 5.6 square kilometres, has a circumference of 15 kilometres and an average depth of 1.5 metres. It is divided by the Su Dyke and Bai Causeway into five parts: the Outer lake, the Inner lake, Yue lake, Xili lake and the small Southern lake. The enchanting Solitary Hill stands by the side of the lake. On small islands in the lake are the Three Pools Mirroring the Moon, the Mid-lake Pavilion and Ruan Yuan's Mound. Within the surrounding 49 square kilometres there are over forty scenic spots including the Ten Famous Scenes, and more than thirty spots of historical interest such as monasteries, ancient pagodas, mountains, caves and cliff carvings. Since 1949 a botanical garden and a zoo have been built, and the parks known as Viewing Fish at Flower Harbour, Listening to Orioles Singing in the Willows, Autumn Moon on Calm Lake, the Jade Spring and the Solitary Hill have been enlarged. The ancient Temple of the Soul's Retreat, the Six Harmonies Pagoda and Yue Fei's Tomb and Temple have also been renovated, all of which has added greatly to the charm of the West lake. On Solitary Hill is a provincial museum and library. Wenlange, now part of the museum, is one of the seven buildings where a copy of the *Complete Library in Four Branches of Literature* is kept. The Xilin Epigraphy Society has preserved many early stone carvings which are of considerable historical importance.

Location

The West lake is situated to the west of Hangzhou, Zhejiang province. Buses and boats go to a wide variety of scenic spots, and the lake itself is within walking distance of Hangzhou.

Anhui Province
安徽省

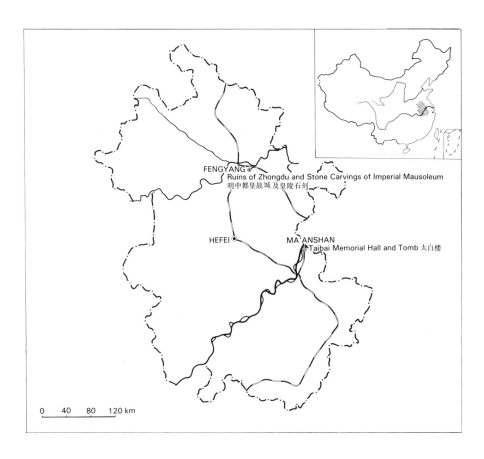

FENGYANG⊙
Ruins of Zhongdu and Stone Carvings of Imperial Mausoleum
明中都皇故城及皇陵石刻

HEFEI⊙   MA'ANSHAN
⊙Taibai Memorial Hall and Tomb 太白楼

0   40   80   120 km

THE TAIBAI MEMORIAL HALL AND TOMB
太白樓及李白衣冠冢

History

The Taibai Memorial Hall was built in commemoration of the great Tang romantic poet Li Bai (AD 701–62), also known as Li Taibai; hence the name of the building. Li Bai was born in the town of Sujab near Lake Balkash in Central Asia, and at the age of 5 moved with his father to Zhangming (present-day Jiangyou) in Mianzhou, Sichuan province. Later he moved to Dangtu in Anhui province, very close to Caishiji where he often went sightseeing and wrote poems. The memorial hall was built in the reign of Yuanhe (AD 806–20), but was destroyed and rebuilt several times in the Song, Yuan, Ming and Qing dynasties. The existing structure was built in the reign of the Qing Emperor Guangxu (1875–1908).

Both the Taibai Memorial Hall and a memorial containing Li Bai's robes and cap, otherwise known as his tomb, are at Caishiji. Legend has it that Li Bai had become drunk and, in an attempt to catch the moon whose reflection he saw in the river, had drowned. Fishermen went to his rescue but found only his clothes and hat. These were buried first in the Shenxiao Temple at Caishi village and were later moved to the present tomb. The Tang poet Bai Juyi wrote in his poem 'Li Bai's Tomb': 'By the Caishi river lies Li Bai's tomb. The grassy fields surrounding it stretch to infinity and merge with the clouds.' This poem is taken as proof that the tomb of Li Bai is at Caishiji.

Description

The Taibai Memorial Hall is comprised of a group of buildings set on a mountain side, the most important of which are three halls with side wings and verandas. A flight of stone steps leads from the entrance gate to the main hall, a three-storey structure with yellow and green glazed tile roof, upturned eave corners, carved rafters and painted beams. The top storey commands a view of the complex. On the lintel hangs a horizontal plaque inscribed in gold: 'The Memorial Hall of Li Bai of the Tang Dynasty'. Set into the walls beneath the eaves are two inscribed stone tablets, one of which gives a record of the renovation of the hall, while the other provides a brief biography of the poet. On the ground floor of the hall is a huge screen with a painting of Li Bai at Caishiji, and on the walls hang paintings of Li Bai journeying to various places. On the first floor are two boxwood sculptures of the poet. Also displayed on this floor are rubbings of his calligraphy and various editions of his works. There are poems, couplets in praise of Li Bai and paintings from later periods.

The base of Li Bai's tomb is made of azurite. The grass-covered loess mound is about 2 metres high and the marble tablet in front of the mound is inscribed: 'The great Tang poet Li Bai's robes and cap'.

On a precipice at Caishiji beside the Chang river stands the Moon Catching Pavilion, from which Li Bai is said to have jumped into the river to catch the moon.

See Plate 16

Location

The Taibai Memorial Hall and tomb are situated at Caishiji, 7 kilometres southwest of Ma'anshan in Anhui province. They are accessible by train or car from Hefei and Nanjing.

THE RUINS OF ZHONGDU AND THE STONE CARVINGS OF THE IMPERIAL MAUSOLEUM
明中都皇城遗址及皇陵石刻

History

Zhongdu was the first of the three Ming capitals, the other two being Nanjing and Beijing. In 1369 Zhu Yuanzhang, the founder of the Ming dynasty, decided that he would establish his capital in Fengyang which he renamed Zhongdu, after the place where his rebellion began. All the palaces and walls were built according to the traditional design of a capital. When after six years of work it was almost completed, the emperor decided that Nanjing was a more favourable location for a capital. He issued an order to halt construction, claiming that it was too extravagant, and then established his capital at Nanjing.

The Ming imperial mausoleum at Zhongdu is where Zhu Yuanzhang's parents were buried. They had died while he was still poor, and a neighbour had given him a small plot of land for a burial place. When he became emperor he wanted to build them a mausoleum but as he was afraid to dig up the graves he enlarged the original tomb to a mausoleum. The project was begun in 1369 and completed in 1380.

Stone sculptures lining the Spirit Way

Description

Zhongdu had three walls, an outer one 25 kilometres long, a middle one 6.5 kilometres long and an inner one 3 kilometres long. The inner part of the city is known as the Imperial City, after its equivalent in Beijing, and this is where the imperial palaces were situated. Its wall is 15 metres high, higher than that of the Forbidden City in Beijing. All the palaces in the Imperial City are on a grand scale with elaborate carving and decoration. *The Gazetteer of Zhongdu* states: 'The scale of the complex is the greatest under heaven.' The builders not only inherited the architectural tradition of the Song and Yuan but also developed a characteristic Ming style of city planning and architecture. For this reason the site is of great importance.

All of the magnificent buildings have long since collapsed, but the composition of the structures can still be discerned from the ruins. A wall 1 kilometre long from the former Xihua Gate to the Wu Gate still stands, and several foundations of buildings, balustrades and stone carvings survive. These are among the best preserved ruins of ancient palaces.

The imperial mausoleum, 5 kilometres to the southwest of

Zhongdu, was surrounded by three walls: an imperial wall, a brick wall and an earthen wall. The imperial wall was 6 metres high and 2 kilometres long, and within it were the Main Hall, the Golden Gate, side chambers, tablet pavilions, an imperial bridge, *huabiao* columns and thirty-six pairs of stone statues of men and animals. The brick wall was 6 metres high and 3.2 kilometres long, and within it were the Garment Chamber, the Kitchen, the Official Chamber, the Lingxing Gate, the Red Bridge, the Divine Kitchen, the Divine Storehouse, a pond and a Drum Chamber. The earthen wall was 14 kilometres long, and within it were the Sacred Way, the Official Chamber, dormitories, the sluice gate, the Imperial Bridge and the Dismount Tablet.

This mausoleum is one of the largest of its kind to have been built during the Ming and Qing dynasties. Unfortunately it was completely destroyed by war at the fall of the Ming dynasty, although the stone sculptures which once stood on the Sacred Way have survived. There are more of these sculptures than at any other imperial mausoleum. Although carved during the Yuan, they exhibit a distinct Song influence and are particularly precious since large stone sculptures from this period are extremely rare.

Location

The ruins of the Ming capital of Zhongdu lie to the south of Phoenix mountain, which is northwest of Fengyang, Anhui province. The imperial mausoleum is located 8 kilometres southwest of the county seat.

Fujian Province
福建省

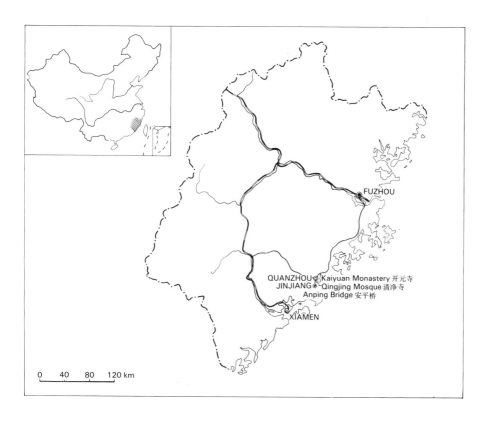

FUZHOU

QUANZHOU Kaiyuan Monastery 开元寺
JINJIANG Qingjing Mosque 清净寺
Anping Bridge 安平桥

XIAMEN

0   40   80   120 km

The Kaiyuan Monastery

THE KAIYUAN MONASTERY
开元寺

History

The Kaiyuan Monastery (Kaiyuansi), originally known as the Lotus Monastery, was built in AD 686 and the current name was adopted in AD 738. In 1285 the complex was destroyed by fire and it was rebuilt in the late fourteenth century. It is the largest and best preserved Buddhist monastery in Fujian province.

A pair of pagodas, the largest stone pagodas in China, stand in front of the monastery. The Zhenguo Pagoda to the east was originally built in wood in AD 865 and then rebuilt in brick. From 1238 to 1250 it was again rebuilt, as a five-storey octagonal granite structure. To the west is the Renshou Pagoda, which was first built in AD 916 and later rebuilt in brick, before being converted to a stone pagoda in 1228.

Description

The Kaiyuan Monastery comprises the Heavenly King Hall, the Homage Court, the Mahavira Hall, the Ganlu Ordination Hall and

The Eastern Pagoda

the Sutra Repository, all built on a north-south axis, as well as several auxiliary structures.

The Mahavira Hall, the principal structure, covers more than 1,000 square metres. It is 20 metres in height, nine bays wide and six deep, and has double sloping eaves. It is said that while it was being built a purple cloud hovered above it and thus it is also known as Purple Cloud Hall. Since it has almost one hundred columns it is sometimes called the One Hundred Column Hall.

The Ganlu Ordination Hall has a double-eaved roof with eight curving corners. It is one of the three largest ordination halls in use since the late Ming dynasty, the others being the Jietai Temple near Beijing and the Zhaoqing Temple in Hangzhou.

The two granite pagodas in front of the monastery are built in the style of wooden pavilions. The Eastern Pagoda has thirty-nine bas-relief carvings depicting the life of Sakyamuni, while the Western Pagoda is decorated with bird and flower motifs. The buildings are similar in design. Each floor has four doors and four altars, the location of which varies in order to achieve a balanced distribution of weight. Both pagodas have balconies and pinnacles. Internal staircases lead to the top, and inside both buildings are solid

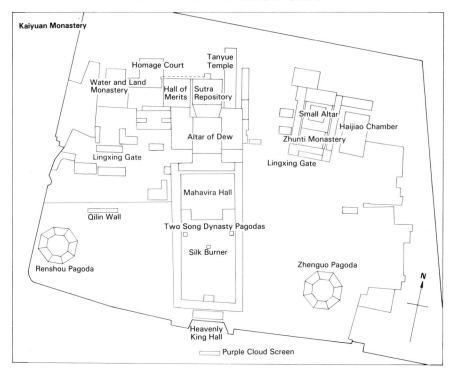

octagonal stone columns which have survived for several hundred years. The plinths of the pagodas are exquisitely carved Sumeru bases. On the doors and altars are altogether eighty realistic bas-relief images in typical Song dynasty style.

See Plate 17

Location
The Kaiyuan Monastery is in Xijie Street in Quanzhou, Fujian province. It is accessible by car or bus from Fuzhou or Xiamen.

THE QINGJING MOSQUE
清净寺

History
The Qingjing Mosque (Qingjingsi) in Quanzhou was first built in 1009 by Muslims who had come to Quanzhou from Western Asia.

The Qingjing Mosque

It was originally known as the Mosque of Sacred Friends, and is the earliest extant Islamic structure in China.

In 1310 the mosque was renovated in a Syrian architectural style by a man named Ahmed from Jerusalem. According to historical records the mosque was repaired in 1350 and 1609, and inside it is a stone tablet inscribed with an instruction issued in 1407 by the Ming Emperor Yongle to protect the mosque and Muslims.

Description

The principal surviving structures in the mosque are the gates, the Fengtian Altar and the Mingshan Chamber. The three successive arched gateways in front of the main building are made of green and white slabs of granite. On the roof of the main gate is the Terrace for Observing the Moon, which is surrounded on three sides by a crenellated wall. It was on this terrace that the commencing date of Ramadan was determined and announced. There used to be a tower for observing the moon and a pointed pagoda on the roof, but both collapsed early in the Qing dynasty. Two stone tablets

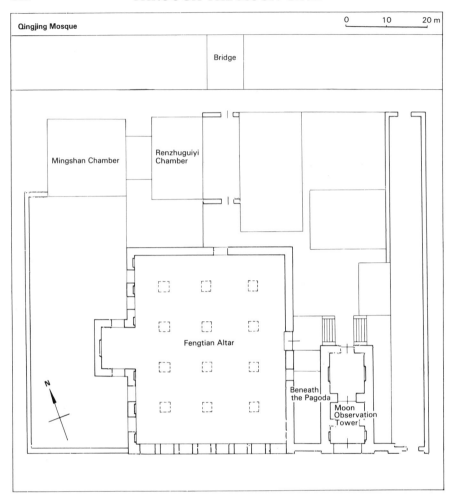

with inscriptions in Arabic are inset in the northern wall of the gate. These inscriptions record the origin of the mosque and the dates of subsequent renovations.

Only the four stone walls of the Fengtian Altar remain, the roof having long since collapsed. It was here that congregations gathered and religious services were performed. In the middle of the western wall was a dais from which an imam led prayers. On this dais is an arched shrine with seven lines in ancient Arabic carved on it. The shrine is flanked by two rectangular doors.

To the north of the Fengtian Altar is the Mingshan Chamber, which has been damaged and rebuilt several times, the present structure being of fairly recent date. The wall of this chamber is also inset with Song and Yuan tablets inscribed in Arabic. Quotations from the Koran are visible in several places, such as on the lintel of the archway, on the southern exterior of the Fengtian Altar and in various niches. Other surviving structures include the Zhusheng Pavilion.

Location
The Qingjing Mosque is in Tumen Street in Quanzhou, Fujian province. It is accessible by car from Fuzhou or Xiamen.

THE ANPING BRIDGE
安平桥

History
The Anping Bridge, also known as Five *Li* (Wuli) Bridge (a *li* is a Chinese mile), is a stone bridge with supports, and is modelled after the Luoyang Bridge. With a length of over 2,000 metres it was, in medieval times, the longest stone bridge in the world.

The bridge was begun in 1138 when Anhai was an important coastal town and a key communication point for Jinjiang and Nan'an

The Anping Bridge

The Central Pavilion

counties. Built in response to economic development, the Anping Bridge played a significant role in linking Quanzhou with the outside world. It took thirteen years to complete, and was finished in 1151 under the supervision of Governor Zhao Lingjin.

Description

The Anping Bridge is made of granite and sandstone. According to Zhao Lingjin's *A Record of the Anping Bridge in the Town of Shijing* 'It is 811 *zhang* [2,676 metres] long, 1.6 *zhang* [5.3 metres] wide' and it was said: 'There is none longer anywhere in the world.'

The bridge surface comprises six or seven huge flagstones. There are still 331 piers: where the water is calm these are rectangular in shape; where the water is deep on one side of the bridge they are boat-shaped, with one pointed and one flat end, the pointed end being placed on the deeper side; where the water is deep on both sides of the bridge they are pointed at both ends. *The Gazetteer of Anping* states: 'The bridge has five pavilions from east to west'. These were the Water Pavilion, the Central Pavilion, the Palace Pavilion, the Rain Pavilion and the Luo Pavilion. Today only the Central and Water Pavilions remain. These were built during the

Qing dynasty and have been repaired several times. The bridge has railings on each side and is decorated with carved stone generals and lions. There are thirteen stone tablets inscribed with records of repairs. Formerly there were several towers at each end of the bridge, but all except a white brick tower built during the Song dynasty have been destroyed. This tower is a five-storey, cylindrical structure with six eave corners.

In the course of time, owing to large deposits of sand and mud, the river spanned by the Anping Bridge has silted up and become farmland.

Location

The Anping Bridge is located in the bay between Jinjiang and Nan'an counties, 30 kilometres south of Quanzhou, Fujian province. It is accessible by bus from Quanzhou.

Guangdong Province
广东省

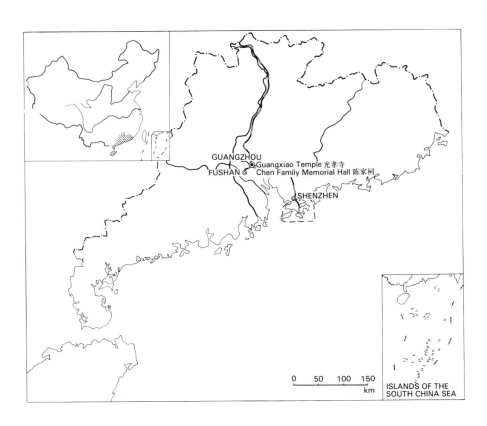

GUANGZHOU
Guangxiao Temple 光孝寺
FUSHAN   Chen Family Memorial Hall 陈家祠
SHENZHEN

0   50   100   150
km

ISLANDS OF THE
SOUTH CHINA SEA

The Mahavira Hall

THE GUANGXIAO TEMPLE
光孝寺

History
There is a saying in Guangzhou: 'The Guangxiao Temple existed before the Town of Rams.' Although this is not quite true, the Guangxiao Temple is certainly the earliest and most famous Buddhist temple in Guangzhou. In AD 397 an Indian monk named Dharmayasa went to Guangzhou to preach Buddhism and built the main hall of the temple, in which, up until the Tang dynasty, a succession of Indian monks preached and promoted Buddhism. In AD 676 Huineng had his head shaved beneath the bodhi tree in the temple complex. He later founded the Southern branch of Buddhism and became known as the Sixth Patriarch of the Chan (Zen) Sect. In 1137 the name of the temple was changed to Bao'en Guangxiao Temple. The present name was adopted in 1151. The main temple buildings date from different periods: the Mahavira Hall was built in AD 397, the main hall in the Song dynasty, the Yifa (Hair-storing)

The bodhi tree

Pagoda in AD 676, the Eastern Iron Pagoda in AD 963, and the Western Iron Pagoda in AD 967.

Description

The Mahavira Hall, the Sixth Patriarch Hall, the Samgharama Hall, the Reclining Buddha Hall, the Yifa Pagoda and the Eastern and Western Iron Pagodas are of great importance in the study of early Chinese architecture. The Mahavira Hall is a particularly imposing structure. Its beams are supported by shuttle-shaped posts and the weight of the lower eaves is partly taken by *dougong* brackets. On the right is the Samgharama Hall named after a deity who was thought to guard the temple. On the left is the Sixth Patriarch Hall, formerly known as the Ancestor Hall, which was built for the worship of the Sixth Patriarch of the Chan Sect. It is five bays wide and four bays deep with sloping roofs. The Yifa Pagoda contains the hair of the Sixth Patriarch which was collected by Abbot Facai and buried beneath a bodhi tree. The seven-storey pagoda is octagonal, and each storey has eight niches inlaid with exquisite statues of the Buddha.

To the east and west of the central hall are two iron pagodas cast in the Five Dynasties period. The seven-storey Eastern Iron Pagoda is 7.7 metres high, with over nine hundred niches each containing small statues of the Buddha, all of which were originally gilded. Sometimes known as the Thousand Gilded Buddha Pagoda, although it has long since lost its gilding, it is the largest and most complete pre-Song iron pagoda surviving today. It was made as a replica of the Western Iron Pagoda which had been cast four years previously, but of which only three storeys now remain. Both pagodas illustrate the high level of casting technology in ancient China. The other four pagodas were destroyed when a building collapsed on them during the Sino-Japanese war.

See Plate 18

Location
The Guangxiao Temple is located at the northern end of Hongshu Street, close to Zhongshanliulu in Guangzhou, Guangdong province. It can be reached by bus from the city centre.

THE CHEN FAMILY MEMORIAL HALL
陈家祠

History
The Chen Family Memorial Hall is where members of the Chen family offered sacrifices to their ancestors and held clan activities. It was common in ancient China for large families to place tablets inscribed with the names of celebrated or respected clan members on altars in a memorial hall. On specific occasions and at festivals, memorial ceremonies would be held. Such halls usually had strong regional architectural characteristics. The Chen Family Memorial Hall also served as a school for the clan, and so was sometimes called the Chen Family School.

The Memorial Hall was built over a five-year period from 1890 with donations from the clan. With the decline of the clan the hall was neglected and became dilapidated, until, in 1958, the government allocated a large sum to have it restored on account of its great artistic and architectural value. The hall has since been used as a museum for local folk arts and crafts.

The Chen Family Memorial Hall

Description

The Chen Family Memorial Hall is in traditional courtyard-house style, and is a superb example of late nineteenth-century architecture. The complex, occupying an area of 10,000 square metres, consists of nine halls and six courtyards linked by three corridors. The main buildings are on the central axis and include the entrance gate, a screen wall immediately behind the gate, and a main hall, five bays wide, in front of which is a terrace with steps on each side and to the front, and a spacious high veranda with stone columns. Flanking this hall are corridors which lead to the left and right of the buildings. This type of layout makes the courtyards seem large and creates a feeling of space. Behind the main hall is a rear hall which is also five bays wide.

All the buildings are decorated with finely carved bricks, stone and wood carvings, clay sculptures and ironwork. Particularly noteworthy are the figures on the glazed tile ridges.

See Plate 19

Location
The Chen Family Memorial Hall is in Zhongshanbalu in Guangzhou, Guangdong province. It is accessible by bus.

Guangxi Province
广西省

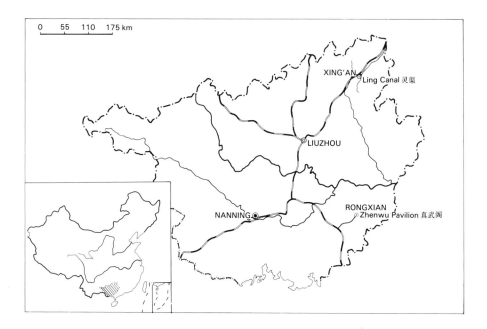

0   55   110   175 km

XING'AN
Ling Canal 灵渠

LIUZHOU

NANNING

RONGXIAN
Zhenwu Pavilion 真武阁

The dividing dykes known as the Large and Small Balances

THE LING CANAL
灵渠

History

The Ling Canal (Lingqu), also known as the Xing'an Canal, is one of the major hydrology projects of ancient China, and one of the oldest canals in the world. In the year 219 BC the first emperor of the Qin dynasty, Qin Shihuang, assigned a general named Shi Lu the task of building a canal that would aid in the unification of southern China and solve problems of grain transport. By 214 BC a canal linked the Xiang and Li rivers, thus connecting the major river systems of the Chang (Yangtze) and Zhu (Pearl) rivers and facilitating the transport of military rations from north to south. The positive results of the building of the Ling Canal were a more thorough unification of the country, increased communication between the south and the central plains, and the development of the culture and economy of the southern regions. History records a total of twenty-three major rehabilitation projects on the canal, the most significant being those of General Ma Yuan in the Han dynasty, of Li Po and Yu Mengwei in the Tang dynasty, and of Yan Zhenzhi in the Ming dynasty. The Ling Canal has also served up to the present day as a means of irrigating the fields along its length. Since 1949 the area under irrigation has increased from approximately 2 to 29 square kilometres.

Description

The Ling Canal links the Haiyang river in the upper reaches of the Xiang river with the Liujiaodong river in the upper reaches of the Li river, in the region of Xing'an, Guangxi province.

The main division takes place at the dyke to the southeast of Xing'an, where the canal divides into its northern and southern sections. The northern section, 4 kilometres in length, connects with the Xiang river; the southern section, 30 kilometres long, connects with the Li river. The whole canal is 34 kilometres long, 5 metres wide and about 2 metres deep, with the flow moving approximately 1 metre in depth.

The major components of the canal are the ploughshare divide, the dividing dykes (known as the Large and Small Balances), the canal bed, the Qin Dyke, the spillways and the locks. The ploughshare divide and the dividing dykes form a V shape, with the ploughshare divide located at the point where the two dykes meet. The function of the ploughshare divide is to direct the rushing water of the Xiang river into the Li river. It accomplishes this by diverting the water of the Haiyang river into the Liang and Xiang rivers through the southern and northern sections of the canal respectively. However, the distribution is not equal: 'Three parts go to the Li river and seven to the Xiang'. A pavilion atop the ploughshare divide houses two stone stelae marked 'The place where the waves were quelled', and 'The dividing of the Li and the Xiang rivers'.

The 2-kilometre Qin Dyke, so named because it dates from the Qin dynasty, is built of stone between the Ling Canal and the former bed of the Xiang river. The dyke stands at the part of the canal which presented the builders with the greatest engineering challenge; it is also the most scenic spot in the area. There are three important sites here: the so-called Flying Rock, the Temple of the Four Sages, and the Tombs of the Three Generals.

The Flying Rock is a large squarish rock some 4 metres high, with a perimeter of 20 metres. Its four sides are covered with inscriptions dating from several dynasties. The Temple of the Four Sages, built in 1355, commemorates the four builders of the canal mentioned

The Ling Canal

above, namely Shi Lu, Ma Yuan, Li Po and Yu Mengwei. The Tombs of the Three Generals are said by some to be those of three generals who died while building the canal during the short-lived Qin dynasty, and by others to be the tombs of three noted stonemasons. Legend has it that during the reign of Qin Shihuang, two generals named Zhang and Liu were put to death for their failure to complete the canal, while a third general named Li, taking a lesson from their errors and subsequent demise, succeeded in completing the difficult project. Reluctant to take credit where his colleagues had failed, Li killed himself once the canal began to function. The tombs are believed to honour the three generals' contributions towards the project.

The two spillways, built of stones arranged in a fish-scale pattern, are Ming dynasty additions. The larger of the two is located on the eastern dyke of the southern section of the canal, and functions as an emergency floodgate. When the water level exceeds the capacity of the dividing dykes, the spillways take over this function, diverting the water into the former bed of the Xiang river, and preventing flooding along the length of the canal.

The locks of the Ling Canal performed a function similar to that of present-day canal locks, permitting the passage of vessels along the entire length of the canal. Most of the thirty-six extant locks are located at places where the water level is comparatively low.

Location

The Ling Canal is located in Xing'an county, 66 kilometres to the north of Guilin, Guangxi province. Trains from Guilin go to the site of the canal.

THE ZHENWU PAVILION
真武阁

History

Legend has it that the Drill Tower which originally occupied this site was built by the Tang dynasty poet Yuan Jie in the period between AD 758 and 779, when Yuan held the post of military governor in Rongwan (present-day Rongxian in Guangxi province). The tower served as an observation post for military exercises, as a venue for court ceremonies, and as a place for enjoying the surrounding scenery. When the tower was destroyed it was replaced by the Wudang Palace, which eventually fell into ruin. The present Zhenwu Pavilion dates from 1573. The three-storey pavilion is the only remaining structure on the site, the covered corridors, walls, bells and incense burners which once surrounded it having disappeared.

Description

The Zhenwu Pavilion is a three-storey pagoda-style building with roofs of extended eaves covered with green ridge tiles, and a golden ridge along the roof-top. The pavilion is constructed of three thousand hardwood beams of various sizes. The structure is based on the lever-arm principle, a form of construction in which the various structural elements support each other as well as limit each other's movements.

The four main interior vertical pillars of the second storey support the massive weight of the upper floorboards, beams and rafters, auxiliary columns, roof tiles and ridge decorations, although the feet of these columns are actually suspended in the air. This extraordinary effect is achieved in the following manner: a total of eighteen square posts, divided into upper and lower levels, are set

The Zhenwu Pavilion

into the eave columns, forming two structurally complex systems of lever-type bracket arms. The external bracket-beams support the wide eaves and the ridge tiles while the internal bracket-beams support the entire suspended structure in the interior of the pavilion, with the eave column serving as the fulcrum. Most interesting of all, the weight of the roof in the third storey is precisely equal to that of the eaves and ridge tiles of the second storey, with the result that the entire weight of the building is divided like a balance scale. This is a rare phenomenon in world architecture. The fact that the Zhenwu Pavilion has withstood earthquakes and storms is testimony to the high level of knowledge in the realms of physics, mathematics and mechanics on the part of Ming dynasty artisans.

Location
The Zhenwu Pavilion is located in the People's Park in Rongxian, Guangxi province, in the Beiling mountains near the Xiu river. From Nanning trains go to Yulin, where buses leave for Rongxian.

Yunnan Province
云南省

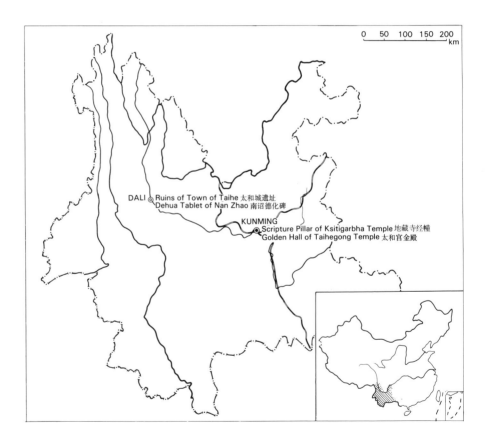

0 50 100 150 200 km

DALI ◎ Ruins of Town of Taihe 太和城遗址
Dehua Tablet of Nan Zhao 南诏德化碑

KUNMING
Scripture Pillar of Ksitigarbha Temple 地藏寺经幢
Golden Hall of Taihegong Temple 太和宫金殿

THE RUINS OF THE TOWN OF TAIHE AND THE DEHUA TABLET OF NAN ZHAO
太和城遗址及南诏德化碑

History
Taihe was the capital of the Nan Zhao Kingdom from AD 739 to 779. The town was neglected through the Tang, Song and early Yuan dynasties and gradually deteriorated. According to historical records, within the town, on the Buddha Head peak there was another small town called Jingong (Vajra), built with rammed earth in an irregular circle. When Taihe was built in AD 747 the Tang court gave the *Vajracchedika-prajnaparamita Sutra* (commonly known as the *Diamond Sutra*) to the Nan Zhao, hence the name Jingong.

Description
Two of the town walls, made of rammed earth, can still be seen among the ruins of Taihe. The northern wall, about 2 kilometres in length, starts on Buddha Head peak in the east and ends at Erhai lake. The best-preserved section is still 3 metres above ground. The earth foundations of Jingong remain and cover an area of about 3,600 square metres.

A tablet, known as the Dehua Tablet, which was erected by King Geluofeng of the Nan Zhao in AD 766, has been found at the site. On one side are carved 3,800 characters in cursive script, a record of the early Nan Zhao and of the two wars waged between the Nan Zhao and the Tang in the reign of Tianbao (AD 742–56). On the other side is a list of names and titles of senior officials and officers. The tablet is a valuable source for the study of the relationship between the Nan Zhao and the Tang.

Location
The ruins of Taihe are to the west of Taihe village, 7.5 kilometres south of Dali, Yunnan province.

THE SCRIPTURE PILLAR OF THE KSITIGARBHA TEMPLE
地藏寺经幢

History
The Ksitigarbha Temple was built by the Shu (present-day Sichuan) monk Yongzhao Yunwu in the late Song dynasty. The Scripture

The Scripture Pillar of the Ksitigarbha Temple

Dragons on the Sumeru base of the pillar

Pillar dates from the middle period of the Dali Kingdom (937–1253) and was built by Yuan Douguan, an official in the employ of the king.

Description
The octagonal stone Scripture Pillar is 8.3 metres high and is divided into seven registers. The Sumeru base is decorated on all sides with

eight dragons, while the four corners are carved with the images of earth gods. The base of the first register is inscribed with an account in Chinese of the erection of the pillar, as well as with two Buddhist texts, while the *Prajnaparamita Sutra* is transcribed in Sanskrit between the Four Heavenly Kings. The second register is carved with images of the *Dharani Sutra*. Beginning at the third register are carvings of Sakyamuni Buddha, bodhisattvas, the Four Heavenly Kings, various buildings and birds. These fine, realistic carvings are an important source for the study of the art and culture of the ethnic minorities of Yunnan.

Location
The Ksitigarbha Temple is located in the Old Pillar Park in Tuodong Road in Kunming, Yunnan province.

THE GOLDEN HALL OF THE TAIHEGONG TEMPLE
太和宫金殿

History
The Golden Hall of the Taihegong Temple is made of bronze, hence its name. Modelled after the Golden Hall on Wudang mountain in Hunan province, it was first cast in 1602. The hall is surrounded by a wall with towers and gates. In 1637 the Golden Hall was moved to the Jinding Temple on Jizu mountain in Bingchuan. The present-day Golden Hall was constructed in 1671 under Prince Wu Sangui.

Description
Square in shape, the Golden Hall is three bays wide and deep and has a two-tiered sloping roof with four overhanging eaves at the corners. Its beams, posts, brackets, doors, windows, horizontal plaques, tables, sacred drapery, platform, side pavilions, flag post and Seven-star Flag are all made of bronze. It is an important example of early Qing architecture and bronze casting.

Location
The Golden Hall is located in the Taihegong Temple on Mingfeng mountain, 7 kilometres northeast of Kunming, Yunnan province. It is accessible by car from Kunming.

The Golden Hall of the Taihegong Temple

Sichuan Province
四川省

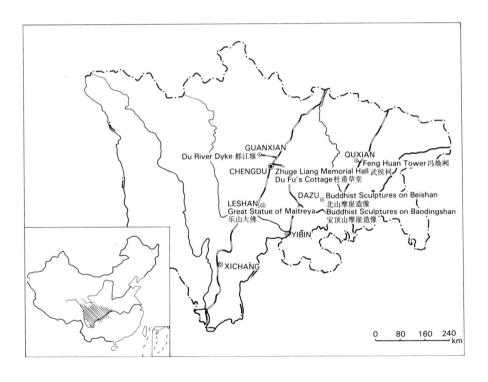

GUANXIAN
Du River Dyke 都江堰

QUXIAN
Feng Huan Tower 冯焕阙

CHENGDU Zhuge Liang Memorial Hall 武侯祠
Du Fu's Cottage 杜甫草堂

DAZU Buddhist Sculptures on Beishan
北山摩崖造像

LESHAN Buddhist Sculptures on Baodingshan
Great Statue of Maitreya 宝顶山摩崖造像
乐山大佛

YIBIN

XICHANG

0   80   160   240
km

The Two Princes Temple near the Du River Dyke

THE DU RIVER DYKE
都江堰

History
The Du River Dyke is a large-scale water conservancy system constructed in 256 BC under the rule of Li Bing, governor of the state of Shu (present-day Sichuan province), and his son. It was repaired and reinforced continuously, and for more than two thousand years has played an important role in water conservancy in the region. After it was built the people of western Sichuan were able to deal effectively with both drought and flooding and ensure good harvests. Sichuan became known thereafter as the Heavenly Kingdom. The system has been repaired since 1949 and now provides irrigation

The Precious Bottle Neck

for an area of more than 5,263 square kilometres, four times as great an area as in 1949.

Description

The Du River Dyke system consists of the Fish Mouth, the Sand-flying Dyke and the Precious Bottle Neck. The Fish Mouth is a breakwater in the middle of the Min river dividing it into an inner and outer river. The former is the primary stream, capable of easing flood water, while the latter meanders across the plains of western Sichuan to be used for irrigation. The Sand-flying Dyke releases both water and sand and regulates the volume of water. The Precious Bottle Neck, dug out of a mountain named Yulei, is the conduit through which the Min river water flows into the inner river. It derives its name from the shape of the river estuary which resembles the neck of a bottle.

There are a number of sites of historical interest near by, such as the Two Princes Temple, the Dragon Subduing Daoist Temple and the Wave Calming Bridge.

Legend has it that Li Bing once subdued a dragon in the area and the Dragon Subduing Daoist Temple was built to commemorate the event. It stands on a cliff on Yulei mountain. There are three halls in the temple and a second-century stone statue of Li Bing discovered in 1973.

The Two Princes Temple at the foot of Yulei mountain was built in AD 497 in memory of Li Bing and his son. The surviving temple buildings date from the Qing dynasty. Li Bing and his son were both designated princes in the Song dynasty, since when the temple has been called the Two Princes Temple. The temple contains statues of Li Bing and his son, and a stone tablet inscribed with Li's words: 'Dredge the river bed when the water is deep and build low dykes when the water is low', as well as other stelae with inscriptions in praise of the pair.

The Wave Calming Bridge, known before the Song dynasty as the Zhupu Bridge and thereafter as the Pingshi Bridge, was originally located at the point where the river divides. It was destroyed during fighting in the final years of the Ming and was rebuilt and given a new name during the Qing. Since the bridge is made of bamboo ropes it is also known as the Bamboo Rope Bridge. It is an ideal spot from which to enjoy the surrounding scenery.

See Plate 20

Location
The Du River Dyke is situated on the upper reaches of the Min river, 57 kilometres west of Guanxian, Sichuan province. It can be reached by car from Chengdu.

THE FENG HUAN TOWER
冯焕阙

History
The Feng Huan Tower in Qu county, Sichuan province, was built in AD 123 at the tomb of Feng Huan, a high Eastern Han official. A good official and loyal to the imperial house, he enjoyed the respect of both the court and the people.

Feng Huan died in AD 122 after his attempt to expose the conspiracy of several court eunuchs had failed; the eunuchs had made use of a fake imperial seal to gain the upper hand. When the truth came to light, the emperor decreed that Feng Huan be

The Feng Huan Tower

posthumously exonerated and the chief instigator put to death. He also gave 100,000 cash to Feng Huan's family and promoted his son to an official rank. Feng Huan's tomb and a tower were built the year after his death.

This type of tower was traditionally a kind of entrance structure, a gate with side buildings erected in front of a hall. After the Tang dynasty it gradually evolved into an archway. Most stone towers of this type date from the Eastern Han.

Description

There were once two parts to the Feng Huan Tower but now only the eastern one remains. It consists of a plinth, body and top, all made of stone. The plinth is a square base, on which stands the body of the tower with an inscription in neat, powerful clerical style. The top consists of a main ridge, purlin ridges, tile ridges, tile ends and brackets, which are large and simple, typical of Han style.

Location

The Feng Huan Tower is located in Zhaojiaping village in the north of Quxian, Sichuan province. Visitors may go by bus to Quxian and then walk to the site.

THE GREAT STATUE OF MAITREYA AT LESHAN
乐山大佛

History

The great statue of Maitreya at Leshan, the largest of its kind in China, was begun in AD 713. It is said that a noted monk by the name of Haitong often saw boats capsize and men drown in the river and so he began to carve a statue of Maitreya, the Buddha of the future, in the belief that it would control the water by its divine power. It was completed ninety years later in AD 803 under Wei Gao, governor of western Sichuan. A seven-storey, thirteen-eaved pavilion was built above the statue but this was destroyed during fighting at the end of the Yuan dynasty. However, the huge statue of Maitreya still towers above the confluence of the Qingyi, Min and Dadu rivers.

Description

The statue of the seated Maitreya, 71 metres high, is carved out of the cliff face. Its head is 14.7 metres high and its shoulders 28 metres wide. Each ear is 7 metres long and can hold two men; and each foot is 8.5 metres wide, large enough to accommodate one hundred seated people. The statue has a graceful, benign and imposing expression and is flanked by statues of armoured warriors.

The great statue of Maitreya

The statue of Maitreya is well proportioned and has a unique technical feature: a drainage system has been installed at its rear to help prevent erosion. No trace of this drainage system can be seen from the front.

To the right of the statue is a winding and dangerous wooden staircase which leads to its base, and from the back of the statue one can climb to the top of Lingyun mountain.

It is said that the Song scholar Su Dongpo once studied here, a story which is commemorated by a pavilion containing a stone statue of him, and stone tablets inscribed with his poetry and carved with images of him. In front of the pavilion is a pond where Su is said to have washed his brushes. A great lover of landscape, he wrote in one of his poems:

> I have no desire to be made a marquis in this life,
> Nor do I hope to make the acquaintance of Han Zhaozong.
> I am happy being a magistrate
> Journeying about like a wine-laden cloud.

See Plate 21

Location

The Great Statue of Maitreya is located on the western cliff face of Lingyun mountain at the confluence of the Qingyi, Min and Dadu rivers. Visitors should take a train from Chengdu, alight at Emei Station and then take a bus to Leshan.

THE BUDDHIST SCULPTURES ON BEISHAN
北山摩崖造像

History

The Buddhist sculptures on Beishan (Northern mountain), one of the principal sites near Dazu, date from the late Tang dynasty to the Northern and Southern Song dynasties. In ancient times Beishan was known as Dragon mountain. In the late Tang dynasty, Wei Junjing, governor of Changzhou and military commander of Changzhou, Puzhou, Yuzhou and Hezhou, established the Yongchang Fort on the mountain, and in AD 892 began the sculpting of Buddhist images in the surrounding cliffs. The work continued for about 250 years, coming to an end around 1150.

Description

The Buddhist sculptures on Beishan are distributed throughout a number of sites in Dazu county: Fowan, Yingpan hill, Guanyin hill, Beita Temple and Fo'er cliff. The sculptures of greatest interest are at Fowan (Buddha bay), where 264 grottoes contain almost 10,000 different images.

The sculptures at Fowan extend for approximately 500 metres on a cliff face in the form of a half-moon. Most of the carvings in the southern section date from the late Tang and the Five Dynasties periods, and most of those in the north date from the Song dynasty; the most outstanding carvings are those in the central section dating from the Song. The most representative sculptures on Beishan are the scenes entitled 'The Vehicle of the Mind and Spirit' and 'The Depiction of the Pure Land'.

The figures in 'The Vehicle of the Mind and Spirit' assume imposing postures, and their fine forms display individual characteristics. The Buddha on the main wall is flanked by eight bodhisattvas: to the left is Manshu (Manjusri), the Bodhisattva of Wisdom, seated upon a fierce lion, and to the right is the sensuous figure of Puxian (Samantabhadra) riding an elephant. Other fine examples of Buddhist art are 'Guanyin Counting her Rosary Beads'

Statue of Guanyin

and 'Guanyin Gazing at the Reflection of the Moon', the latter noted
for its fine rendering of the female figure. In a more vigorous vein
is 'Ksitigarbha [the God of the Earth] Changes his Appearance', a
masterpiece of the Song dynasty.

Location

The Beishan Buddhist sculptures are located 2 kilometres to the northwest of Dazu, Sichuan province. Trains go from Chongqing and Chengdu to Youtingpu, from where buses leave regularly for Dazu.

THE BUDDHIST SCULPTURES ON BAODINGSHAN
宝顶山摩崖造像

History

The Buddhist sculptures on Baoding mountain (Baodingshan) were carved during the period 1179 to 1249, under the direction of the monk Zhao Zhifeng.

Description

The Buddhist sculptures on Baodingshan are perhaps the finest of all those to be found at the thirteen sites in and around Dazu county in Sichuan province, and some of the finest in China.

The Buddha entering Nirvana

Genre scene of maid tending hens

The Great Buddha Bay is a horseshoe-shaped cliff approximately 500 metres long, into the surface of which are carved the sculptures. Of the thirty-one large-scale images, the Thousand-armed Guanyin, the Bodhisattva of Mercy, is the most impressive. Standing less than 3 metres tall, the bodhisattva has a total of 1,030 hands, each holding a Buddhist symbol. These hands are spread out above and to the side of the torso, like the tail of a peacock, and cover some 88 square metres of rock surface. The design and execution of this sculpture are of the highest artistic order. Also of great interest are the nineteen sculptured scenes depicting stories from Buddhist scriptures, each of which displays a sense of continuity attesting to careful planning. The sculptures embrace a broad range of subject matter, and the realism with which they are conceived reveals traces of local characteristics.

In terms of form, a single sculpture group may be made up of as many as twenty or thirty sub-groups, and may depict either a single story or several stories from the Buddhist scriptures. In addition, written texts give these works of art the appearance of an ancient comic strip. Several well-known stories depicted are 'Herding Cattle', 'Parental Benevolence', and 'The Birth of Sakyamuni', all of which are executed with great realism and in novel compositions. Worthy of particular mention is the sculpture of the Buddha entering Nirvana, in which only the upper part of the torso is shown, the lower half remaining hidden in the cliff.

See Plate 22

Location
The Buddhist sculptures on Baodingshan are located 15 kilometres to the north of Dazu, Sichuan province. Trains go from Chongqing and Chengdu to Youtingpu, from where buses leave at regular intervals for Baoding.

THE ZHUGE LIANG MEMORIAL HALL
武侯祠

History
The Zhuge Liang Memorial Hall was built in the fourth century in commemoration of Zhuge Liang, premier of the state of Shu in the Three Kingdoms period. When the famous Tang poet Du Fu visited Chengdu in AD 760, the site of the Memorial Hall was already covered with ancient cypresses. He described it in this way in the poem 'The Temple of the Premier of Shu':

> Where is the temple of the famous Premier?
> In a deep pine grove near the City of Silk,
> With the green grass of spring mantling the steps,
> And birds chirping happily under the leaves.
> The third summons weighted him with affairs of state.
> To two generations he gave his true heart.
> But before he could conquer, he was dead,
> And heroes have wept on their robes ever since.

The Zhuge Liang Memorial Hall

In the Tang dynasty the Zhuge Liang Memorial Hall was beside the temple of Liu Bei, king of Shu. The hall and the temple were combined during the early Ming dynasty, but unfortunately both were destroyed by war. A large portion of the existing Zhuge Liang Memorial Hall was rebuilt in 1672.

Description

Enclosed by a red wall, the Zhuge Liang Memorial Hall occupies a little over 36,000 square metres of densely wooded land. The south-facing hall contains the Entrance Gate, the Second Gate, the Liu Bei Hall, the Passage Hall and the Zhuge Liang Hall. These five structures stand on a north-south axis with the tallest structure at the front.

Between the Entrance Gate and the Second Gate are six stone stelae, each with a pavilion over it. Four of the stelae date from the Qing dynasty, one from the Ming and the largest from the Tang. Erected in AD 804, the Tang stele is inscribed: 'Tablet of the Memorial Hall of Zhuge Liang, Premier of the State of Shu'. This inscription by the Tang statesman Pei Du was carved by Lu Jian

The gold-painted clay figurine of Zhuge Liang

after the calligraphy of Liu Gongchuo of the Tang dynasty. Because of its fine prose, calligraphy and carving it is also known as 'The Tablet of the Three Excellences'.

On passing through the Second Gate, visitors are confronted by the magnificent Liu Bei Hall, inside which stands a gilded clay statue of Liu Bei. To one side of this statue hangs a carving in wood of Zhuge Liang's 'Memorandum Before Setting Out on a Campaign' in the calligraphy of the famous Song general Yue Fei. On the other side is a carving recording Zhuge Liang's visit to Liu Bei at his hermitage at Longzhong. In the side halls are statues of Liu Bei's aides, Guan Yu and Zhang Fei. There are fourteen statues in the side chambers: in the east wing are court officials headed by Pang Tong, and in the west wing are generals led by Zhao Yun.

Behind the Liu Bei Hall lies the Zhuge Liang Hall, inside which is a gold-painted clay seated figurine of Zhuge Liang. Flanking this hall in the front are the Bell Tower and the Drum Tower. Of the dozen horizontal plaques and couplets both inside and outside the hall, the best known is that by the Qing scholar Zhao Fan, which says: 'If you are able to win the hearts of your enemies, all difficulties can be overcome. Since ancient times no great strategist has ever liked war ... Without careful consideration, both strictness and leniency can be an error. Later rulers must think thoroughly when administering Shu.'

The three bronze drums displayed in front of the statue of Zhuge Liang are said to have been cast during his campaign in the south, and are known as the Zhuge Drums.

See Plate 23

Location

The Zhuge Liang Memorial Hall is located in the southern suburbs of Chengdu, Sichuan province, and can be reached by bus.

DU FU'S COTTAGE
杜甫草堂

History

Tucked away in the western suburbs of Chengdu is a thatched cottage, once the home of the great Tang dynasty poet Du Fu.

Du Fu lived during a time of great instability when the Tang empire, after reaching the zenith of its prosperity, began to decline, a trend which was intensified after the An Lushan Rebellion in AD 755. In AD 759 Du Fu left Chang'an and entered Sichuan via Gansu province. The following year he built himself a cottage in Chengdu where he lived for almost four years and wrote over 240 poems, one of which is the famous 'My Thatched Cottage Is Wrecked

The stele pavilion

Entrance to Du Fu's Cottage

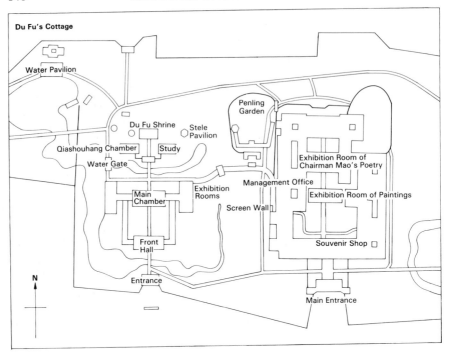

Du Fu's Cottage

Water Pavilion

Du Fu Shrine

Stele Pavilion

Penling Garden

Qiashouhang Chamber

Study

Water Gate

Main Chamber

Exhibition Rooms

Management Office

Exhibition Room of Chairman Mao's Poetry

Exhibition Room of Paintings

Screen Wall

Souvenir Shop

Front Hall

N

Entrance

Main Entrance

by the Autumn Wind'. To commemorate Du Fu, the cottage was rebuilt and a memorial hall in his honour erected in the reign of Emperor Yuanfeng (1078–85) of the Northern Song dynasty. These were later repaired and enlarged in the Yuan, Ming and Qing dynasties. Renovations carried out in 1500 and 1811 laid the foundation for the cottage we see today. It has been repaired several times since 1949 and is now a centre for research on the poet.

Description

The main structures in the courtyard of Du Fu's Cottage include the front hall, the main chamber, the Du Fu Shrine and the exhibition rooms. In the front hall there are two screens made of *nan* wood, one inscribed with a brief biography of Du Fu, the other painted with an illustration of Du Fu's Cottage in traditional Chinese style. Behind this hall stands the main chamber, the centre of the whole complex, in which a statue of the poet is displayed. On the walls between the columns hang rubbings of portraits of the poet copied from stone carvings or woodblocks. In the Du Fu Shrine stand clay and stone statues of Du Fu dating from the Ming and Qing dynasties. Flanking these are statues of the celebrated Song poets

Lu You and Huang Tingjian. Housed in this chamber also are two stone tablets erected in 1793 and 1811, and carved with views of the cottage.

Displayed in the exhibition rooms to the east and west of the cottage are block-printed and handwritten editions of Du Fu's poetry from the Song, Yuan, Ming and Qing dynasties, as well as modern editions and translations in English, French, German, Japanese and other languages. Altogether about 30,000 books relating to Du Fu are on display.

Also exhibited in the rooms before the main chamber are many paintings and examples of calligraphy, all based on themes from Du Fu's poetry.

See Plate 24

Location

Du Fu's Cottage is located beside Huanhua stream in the western suburbs of Chengdu, Sichuan province. It is accessible by car from Chengdu.

Hunan Province
湖南省

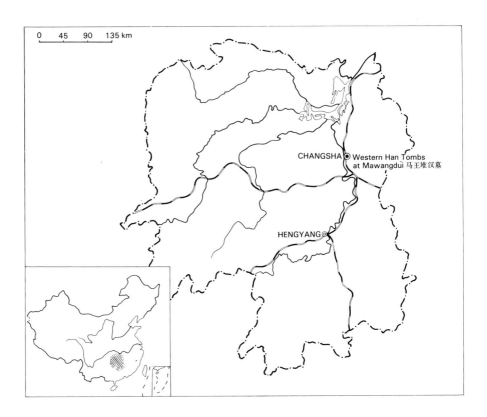

0   45   90   135 km

CHANGSHA ◉ Western Han Tombs
at Mawangdui 马王堆汉墓

HENGYANG ◉

Excavation site at Mawangdui

THE WESTERN HAN TOMBS AT MAWANGDUI
马王堆汉墓

History
The Western Han site at Mawangdui comprises three tombs, that of the Marquis of Dai, prime minister of the kingdom of Changsha, that of his wife Xin Zhui and that of one of their sons whose name is unknown.

It was formerly believed that Mawangdui was the tomb of a prince of Chu named Ma, of the Five Dynasties, which explains the origin of the name (*wang* in Chinese means king, *dui* means mound). Other historical records state that the tombs are those of Lady Cheng, an imperial concubine and mother of Prince Liu Fa of Changsha of the Western Han, and of another concubine named Lady Tang.

In 1951 experts from the Institute of Archaeology of the Academy of Social Sciences surveyed and studied the two earth mounds and concluded that they were definitely Western Han tombs. In 1956 they were listed as cultural sites under provincial protection. In March 1972 archaeologists began excavating Tomb No. 1 and discovered a well-preserved coffin case and a large quantity of lacquer and silk. The colours were still as bright as new, and the skin of the female corpse still retained its elasticity. Tombs Nos 2 and 3 were excavated between November 1973 and January 1974. It was finally determined that the occupant of Tomb No. 1 was Xin Zhui, of Tomb No. 2 the Marquis of Dai, and of Tomb No. 3 their son. The objects excavated from these three tombs provided valuable information on Han dynasty politics, economics, science and culture and aroused great interest both in China and abroad. These precious objects and the female corpse are now housed in a specially built museum, and Tomb No. 3 is open to the public.

Description

The Mawangdui tombs occupy an area of 250,000 square metres. At the centre are two mounds, each 16.5 metres high, joined by a horseshoe-shaped passage. This is all that remains above ground.

Each tomb consists of a covering layer of earth, a passageway, a burial pit and burial chamber. The whole tomb is in quaternary period reddish clay which is as hard as rock. Tomb No. 1 is rectangular and the rammed earth structure is over 50 metres in diameter. It is 20.5 metres from the top of this clay layer to the bottom of the tomb. The upper portion of the pit is 19.5 metres from north to south and 17.8 metres wide from east to west, and from the entrance of the pit to the bottom of the tomb is 16 metres. The burial chamber where the coffin lies is in the lower portion of the pit. The coffin was completely encased by 6,000 kilograms of charcoal and plaster 1 metre thick. The construction of the inner and outer coffins is very complex, and consists mainly of a wooden

Opposite: Silk painting from Tomb No. 1 at Mawangdui

Over 3,000 items have been excavated from the three tombs. Tomb No. 1 yielded more than 1,400 artefacts in all: 184 pieces of lacquer, 51 earthenware vessels, 162 wooden figurines, 48 rectangular bamboo containers, silk fabrics, over 100 garment decorations, over 100 musical instruments and other bamboo or wooden objects, 44 baskets of clay and some funeral paper money, as well as wooden and bamboo slips. About 1,000 artefacts were found in Tomb No. 2 and more than 1,100 in Tomb No. 3. Of these, the most precious are the numerous lacquers, silks, texts and paintings on silk, which are rich in variety and well preserved. Mawangdui is one of the great treasures of early Chinese culture.

Location

The Mawangdui tombs are at Wulipai in the eastern suburbs of Changsha, about 4 kilometres from the centre of the city. The museum, which houses excavated artefacts, is in the compound of the provincial museum in the northeast of the city. Visitors can reach the site by bus.

Hubei Province
湖北省

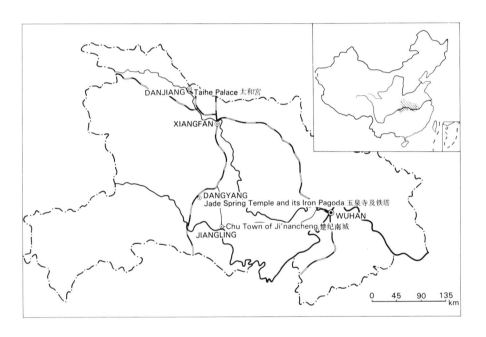

DANJIANG ⊙ Taihe Palace 太和宫

XIANGFAN ⊙

DANGYANG ⊙
Jade Spring Temple and its Iron Pagoda 玉泉寺及铁塔
⊙ WUHAN
⊙ Chu Town of Ji'nancheng 楚纪南城
JIANGLING

0   45   90   135
km

THE CHU TOWN OF JI'NANCHENG
楚纪南城

History
Ji'nancheng was the capital of the state of Chu in the Spring and Autumn and the Warring States periods, when it was known as Yingdu. Since it ·was situated south of the Ji mountain, later generations called it Ji'nancheng (literally, the town south of Ji). Unfortunately all that remains today is a vast expanse of ruins.

According to historical records, King Wen of Chu founded his capital here in 689 BC and it was renovated and enlarged several times. Up to the time when it finally fell to Qin troops led by Bai Qi in 278 BC and King Qingxiang moved to Chen (present-day Huaiyang, Henan province), Yingdu was the capital during twenty Chu reigns over a period of 411 years. The political, economic and cultural centre of Chu, Yingdu was the largest town in south China and one of the largest state capitals in the country. After the Chu king moved his capital east in 278 BC, Yingdu was neglected and fell into ruin. By the Qin and Han dynasties it was nothing more than open country and graveyards. In 1956 the Hubei provincial government decided that the ruins of the town should be classified as a 'historical monument under provincial protection', and in 1961 it was listed as a 'historical monument under state protection'. Surveying and large-scale excavation from 1975 to 1979 have revealed the vast scale of this famous town.

Description
Ji'nancheng was fundamentally rectangular in shape, with a perimeter of 15,506 metres. The town measured 4,450 metres from east to west and 3,588 metres from north to south, making a total area of about 16 square kilometres. Most of the town walls are still fairly well preserved and vary in height from 3.9 to 7.6 metres.

There are various ruins in the surrounding area, most of which belong to the Spring and Autumn or the Warring States period. Many contemporaneous building foundations, as well as cylindrical earthenware tiles, have been discovered outside the southern wall of the town. Within a radius of 30 to 40 kilometres are many groups of Chu period tombs, which can be divided into two types: those with and those without burial mounds. Twenty-five groups of about 2,000 graves without mounds have been found so far, and about 800 large graves with mounds have also been discovered. There are about 40 graves over 40 metres in diameter and mounds over 6 metres high. The largest so far discovered is that of Fan Sheng, a Chu nobleman, which has a mound 9.5 metres in height. Fifteen steps lead to the burial pit which holds a coffin with three separate cases. However, this is classified as a medium-sized tomb. The diameter of large mounds is sometimes as much as 100 metres or more. Thousands of artefacts have been found in the few Chu tombs that have been excavated. Among these are the famous sword of King Gou Jian of the state of Yue, the sword of King Zhou Guo of Yue, the dagger-axe of King Sun Yu of Chu, and a bronze wine cup with phoenix design. A large number of Chu bamboo slips which bear contemporaneous records have also been excavated, and recently a piece of a Warring States period brocade was found. These are all valuable and important artefacts of the period.

Location
Ji'nancheng lies about 5 kilometres north of Jiangling, in Hubei province. From Wuhan, visitors may travel by air, coach or boat to Shashi, and then by bus to Jiangling.

THE JADE SPRING TEMPLE
AND ITS IRON PAGODA
玉泉寺及铁塔

History
The Jade Spring Temple is an ancient Buddhist temple, said to have been originally a simple thatched structure built by a monk named Pujing in the Jian'an period (AD 196–220) at the end of the Eastern Han. In the Southern Dynasties the structure was rebuilt as a temple, and in the Sui dynasty was enlarged under the aegis of a monk named Zhizhe. It then became known as one of the 'four finest temples under heaven', the other three being the Xixia in Nanjing, the Lingyan in Shandong province and the Tiantai in Zhejiang province. The Jade Spring Temple was renovated and added to in the Tang, Song, Yuan, Ming and Qing dynasties. It formerly had 9 buildings, 18 halls and 3,700 monks' cells, and covered an area of 12.5 square kilometres.

On a cliff to the east of the temple stands the Iron Pagoda cast in the Northern Song dynasty in 1061. An inscription records the name of the pagoda, its weight, the date on which it was cast, and names of artisans involved.

The Iron Pagoda

Description
The Jade Spring Temple stands at the foot of the Fuzhou (Inverted Boat) mountains, which are renowned for the more than four

Detail of the base of the Iron Pagoda

hundred rare species of flora and fauna to be found there on the banks of winding brooks. In a poem the Tang poet Zhang Jiuling described the setting thus: 'Rare birds chirp amidst pine trees, clear springs gurgle beneath bamboos.'

The main structures at the temple include the Heavenly King Hall, the Mahavira Hall, the Vairocana Hall, the Eastern Chamber, the Western Chamber, the Banzhou Chamber and the Scripture Repository. The Mahavira Hall, a magnificent structure with double eaves and upturned eave corners, is 21 metres in height. It is seven bays wide, and has seventy-two enormous columns. Its beams and brackets are all made from massive logs and it has an extremely colourful ceiling. In front of this hall is a huge Sui dynasty iron cauldron, and a Yuan iron axe and bell. The side wall of the hall has a stone carving of a bodhisattva in bas relief, said to be based on a drawing by the famous Tang artist Wu Daozi. Inside the temple's grounds grow many ancient cypresses, ginkgos, osmanthus trees and double lotuses.

Originally known as the Sarira-stupa, the Iron Pagoda is made entirely of iron. Its foundation is laid with bricks and the structure is an imitation of an octagonal wooden pavilion. The thirteen-storey pagoda, 17.9 metres high, weighs 48.5 tonnes and is the best preserved ancient iron pagoda in China. The double-tiered Sumeru base is cast on all sides with scenes of the 'Eight Immortals Crossing the Sea', 'Two Dragons Playing with a Pearl' and other marine motifs.

At each corner of the plinth is a statue of an armoured guardian standing on mythical mountains and supporting the pagoda with his shoulders or hands. The eaves of each storey, held by four *dougong* brackets, protrude gracefully. On each storey a face with a door alternates with a face carved with Buddhist figures or floral motifs.

Location

The Jade Spring Temple is located at the foot of the east side of the Jade Spring mountains 15 kilometres west of Dangyang, Hubei province. It is accessible by train or bus from Wuhan.

THE TAIHE PALACE
太和宫

History

The Taihe Palace is one of the major buildings on Sky Pillar peak, the principal peak of the Wudang mountains in Hubei province.

The Wudang mountains were where Daoist ascetics had lived in seclusion, and in the Tang dynasty rulers began to build altars there. Daoism flourished during the Song and Yuan dynasties and the new Quanzhen Sect was particularly favoured by Yuan rulers. Together with other Daoist sects, the Quanzhen Sect built temples on a large scale on the Wudang mountains. In 1307 a bronze hall was erected on Sky Pillar peak, the earliest of its kind still in existence. Halfway up Sky Pillar peak, where the Taihe Palace once stood, new buildings were erected and old ones were repaired and restored. During the period of political turmoil towards the end of the Yuan, most of these temples and palaces were ruined, and on Sky Pillar peak itself only the bronze hall remains.

During the early Ming dynasty, Emperor Yongle (1403–24) sent 30,000 men, supervised by his high officials, and spent a large sum on building temples and palaces in honour of the Daoist deity Zhen Wu. During the reign of Yongle, 33 complexes, including 8 palaces, 2 other Daoist temples and 30 bridges, were built; one of the palaces was Taihe. The scale of this construction was unparalleled in

Chinese history. The emperor gave the Wudang mountains the title Da Yue Taihe mountains, from which the Da Yu Taihe Palace derives its name. Emperor Yongle thought that the Yuan bronze hall at the top of Sky Pillar peak was not large enough, and that its architectural style was inappropriate for the deity Zhen Wu, so he had the hall moved to the Little Lotus peak in the compound of the Taihe Palace, and had another bronze hall made for Sky Pillar peak. For five hundred years the Taihe Palace has been an important centre for Daoist priests and pilgrims.

After 1949 the Taihe Palace and the Golden Hall on Sky Pillar peak were designated cultural sites under state protection, with an administrative office to look after them.

Description
The Main Hall of the Taihe Palace is situated near the Southern Heavenly Gate of the town on Sky Pillar peak. Its name is written on the lintel. In front of the palace is the Hall of Worship of which only the pillars remain. To the left stands the Bell Tower, inside which hangs a bronze bell cast in the fourteenth year of the reign

The Golden Hall

Clay statue in the Golden Hall

of Yongle. This is one of the two largest Ming bells on the Wudang mountains. To the right stands the Drum Tower. Between the Hall of Worship and the Main Hall is the Little Lotus peak on which stands a brick and stone building called the Zhuanzhan Hall. On the cliff face to the east of this is carved in forceful strokes: 'A single pillar can support the sky.' The Zhuanzhan Hall houses the bronze hall that was cast in 1307 and moved from Sky Pillar peak by imperial order. Basically square in shape, the hall is a plain structure with two sloping roofs joined by a ridge. It is slightly smaller in scale than the Ming Golden Hall on Golden peak. In front of the Bell Tower is the Ten Thousand Buddha Chamber which houses icons in bronze, iron and clay. Flanking the entrance to the Main Hall are many stone stelae dating from the Ming and Qing dynasties. In front of the Hall of Worship, down a flight of steps to the right, is the Huangjing Chamber, which was restored during the Qing dynasty.

Beneath the eaves are Daoist figures, finely carved in high relief. To the west is a two-storey building, and to the north are the priests' living quarters, which, together with the Huangjing Chamber, form another courtyard. There are also the remains of other buildings near by. All of these monumental buildings were made of stone and lined the single pathway to the peak.

Location

Visitors may take a coach from Wuhan and change at Laoyingzhen in Junxian county, Hubei province. Alternatively visitors may take a train from Wuhan or Luoyang, get off at Danjiang, Junxian county, and then take a coach to Laoyingzhen. After passing the Zi Xiao Palace, visitors should get off at Crow Ridge and climb about 5 kilometres along the path to the road leading to the Taihe Palace.

Henan Province
河南省

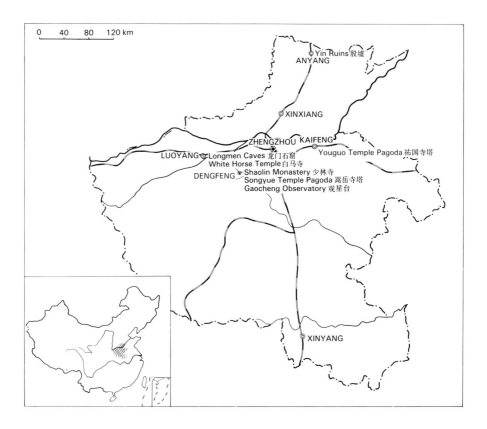

THE YIN RUINS
殷墟

History

Early in the fourteenth century BC the Shang Emperor Pan Geng moved his capital, known as Beimeng, to the site of the present-day Yin ruins. The capital was destroyed after 273 years of rule by twelve emperors spanning eight generations. The Shang dynasty was replaced by the Zhou who referred to their predecessors as Yin, and for this reason the remains of the Shang capital were subsequently known as the Yin ruins.

Description

The Yin ruins cover an area of approximately 24 square kilometres, and the remains of fifty-six imperial buildings have been discovered. The majority of the foundations are built on either a north-south or an east-west axis, are rectangular in shape and are of rammed earth about 2 metres in height.

Several thousand ancient bronzes of complex design and with fine decoration have been discovered at the Yin ruins. Among them is the largest, heaviest bronze to have been excavated in China, the famous Si Mu Wu *ding*, a cooking vessel 1.3 metres in height and weighing 875 kilograms.

Also discovered at the Yin ruins were a number of oracle bones which provide valuable information about life in the Shang dynasty more than three thousand years ago. The Shang people practised scapulimancy using tortoise shells or ox shoulder blades, namely, they practised divination by observing and interpreting the cracks which appeared on shells and blades after they had been drilled or burnt. They would then carve the divination records in the form of symbols or pictographic inscriptions on the bones. The imperial oracle bone inscriptions record all sorts of activities such as the offering of sacrifices to gods or ancestors, hunting, farming, war, and life in the imperial household, as well as information such as solar terms and astronomical phenomena. According to these records, agriculture and animal husbandry were fairly well developed during the Shang dynasty. The major crops were rice, corn, wheat and millet, and the most important domestic animals were oxen, sheep, pigs and dogs.

The large tomb in Wuguan village, excavated in 1950, was 14 metres long from north to south and 12 metres wide from east to west. Inside this tomb was a wooden coffin chamber. The occupant

Rubbing of oracle bone excavated from the Yin Ruins

of the tomb was a nobleman and slave owner, and 79 persons were killed and buried with him, including his concubines, bodyguards, charioteers and soldiers. The tomb also contained the remains of 27 horses, 11 dogs, 3 monkeys, 1 deer and 15 other animals. Bronze, jade and pottery artefacts were also found. Of particular interest is a stone chime with a tiger-skin motif; it is the earliest and most complete surviving large musical instrument.

Even more horrific was the scale of human sacrifice unearthed in a large pit in 1976: some 12,000 corpses and carcasses were found in a pit on the southern side of the tomb. These are the remains of people and animals killed to accompany the occupant of the tomb.

Another important discovery in 1976 was that of the tomb of Fu

The large tomb in Wuguan village

Hao with more than 1,600 artefacts. There are 750 beautifully carved jades in the form of human figures, dragons, phoenixes, tigers and oxen. A unique ivory cup, decorated with a *taotie* mask design and inlaid with turquoise, as well as two fragments from containers, were discovered. The tomb yielded more than 450 ritual bronzes and weapons, the largest store of such objects ever found in China. The most precious are an owl-shaped wine container, a double rectangular wine container, a three-compartment cooking vessel, and a mirror. There are also two large square cooking vessels, one of which, the Si Mu Xin *ding*, weighs 117.5 kilograms. Over 190 of the bronzes bear inscriptions, and from these it can be ascertained that the person buried in the tomb was Fu Hao, a consort of the Shang King Wu Ding. Fu Hao died *c.* 1200 BC. Many of her deeds were recorded in inscriptions on contemporaneous oracle bones. This is the only instance of a Shang dynasty tomb so far discovered where we are certain of the identity of the person interred and where we can relate the person to one mentioned in oracle bone inscriptions.

Location
The Yin ruins, with their centre in Xiaotun village, are situated on the banks of the meandering Huan river 5 kilometres northwest of Anyang, Henan province. They are accessible either by car or on foot.

THE LONGMEN CAVES
龙门石窟

History
The carving of the Longmen Caves, also known as the Yique or Gate of the Yi, was begun in AD 494 in the Northern Wei dynasty, when Emperor Xiaowen moved his capital from Datong to Luoyang. Over a period of more than one thousand years, from the Eastern Wei to the late Qing dynasty, caves and niches were hewn out of the cliff faces of the Longmen mountains along the Yishui river. The caves extend for approximately 1,000 metres from north to south. Together with the caves of Dunhuang and Yungang, the Longmen Caves are the most important Buddhist cave shrines in China.

Description
Today Longmen has 1,352 caves, 785 niches and over 40 pagodas. There are some 97,000 statues and 3,600 inscribed stelae.

The Longmen Caves

The majority of the caves are concentrated in the Longmen mountains. The most important are the Qianxi Temple (mid-seventh century), the Binyang Cave (built after the Northern Wei had moved its capital), the Ten Thousand Buddha Cave (completed in AD 680), the Lianhua Cave (late Northern Wei), the Guyang Cave (begun about AD 494), and the Fengxian Temple. Built in AD 675, the Fengxian Temple is the largest and most representative example from the Tang period. Its serene-faced seated statue of the Buddha, 17.1 metres high, is the largest at the Longmen Caves. Ancient records say that the Tang Empress Wu Zetian 'donated 2,000 strings of cash saved from her cosmetics budget to pay for its carving'. Flanking the Buddha are eleven disciples, bodhisattvas, divine generals and heavenly guards. Their powerful yet sensitive expressions are characteristic of Tang cave art.

The Guyang Cave, the earliest of the Longmen complex, is located at the southern end of the Longmen mountains. Of the twenty famous Wei inscriptions at Longmen with their simple yet vigorous calligraphy, nineteen are in this cave.

Head and torso of the seated Buddha in the Fengxian Temple

Facing the Longmen mountains, on the opposite bank of the Yishui river, is Fragrant mountain. On this hill is the Double Lotus Flower Temple, a cave temple which was built by the Tang Emperor Gaozong. Its ceiling is decorated with a lotus design and flying *apsara* in high relief, and the lower part of the four walls is carved with twenty-nine arhats, perhaps the finest sculptures at Longmen.

Another famous local site is the tomb of the great Tang poet Bai Juyi (AD 772–846) on the Pipa peak of Fragrant mountain. Bai Juyi spent his later years here and referred to himself as the Fragrant Mountain Hermit. In front of the tomb is a stone tablet inscribed with his name. The peak is covered with pine and cypress trees, and from the top there is a panoramic view of the site.

See Plate 25

Location
The Longmen Caves are situated 12 kilometres south of Luoyang, Henan province. They can be reached by buses 3 and 10 from the town.

THE SHAOLIN MONASTERY
少林寺

History
The Shaolin Monastery was begun during the Northern Wei dynasty in AD 495. In AD 527 the Indian monk Bodhidharma, regarded as the founder of Chan (Zen) Buddhism in China, preached at this temple, and Shaolin has been a major Chan temple over since. However, the monastery was destroyed during the persecution of Buddhism which took place in the Northern Zhou reign of Emperor Wudi (AD 561–77). It was restored and its name changed to the Zhihu Monastery during the reign of Emperor Jingdi (AD 579–80). In the Sui dynasty Emperor Wendi (AD 581–600), issued a decree restoring the original name, and the monastery was given 100 *qing* (6.7 square kilometres) of land. At the beginning of the Tang dynasty the monastery was rewarded by the emperor for its contribution to the establishment of the new regime. As a result, it flourished and was soon to house more than two thousand monks. It went into decline during the late Tang and the Five Dynasties periods but re-established itself in 1245. It was renovated in 1735. In 1928 the warlord Shi Yousan set fire to it, a fire which lasted for over forty days destroying the main buildings and ruining many works of art.

Description
Among the surviving structures at the Shaolin Monastery are the archway, the Guest Chamber, the Bodhidharma Pavilion, the White

The Shaolin Monastery

Drapery Hall, the Ksitigarbha Hall and the Thousand Buddha Hall.
The Thousand Buddha Hall contains a 300-square-metre mural
depicting five hundred Ming dynasty arhats paying homage to
Vairocana. The White Drapery Hall houses a collection of books
on Shaolin martial arts, as well as a wall painting depicting the rescue
of a Tang emperor by thirteen monks. The Bodhidharma Pavilion
is also known as the Standing in Snow Pavilion. This alludes to the
occasion when Huike, the Second Chan Patriarch, on a visit to
Bodhidharma, waited outside the pavilion in knee-deep snow during
a heavy snowfall.

To the west of the monastery is the Forest of Pagodas, a graveyard
for venerated monks, which now contains more than 220 brick
tombs dating from the Tang to the Qing dynasty. To the north-west
of the monastery is the Chuzu (First Patriarch) Hermitage which
was built in 1125. There is also the Bodhidharma Cave in which
Bodhidharma is said to have meditated for nine or ten years.
Near by are the Erzu (Second Patriarch) Hermitage, the Faru Pagoda,
the Tongguang Pagoda, the Five Dynasties Fahua Pagoda and the

The Forest of Pagodas

Yuangong Pagoda. The Hall of the Heavenly King and the Mahavira Hall have all collapsed and only vestiges of them remain today.

Scores of stelae, known as the Forest of Stelae, stand on each side of the main passage behind the archway and the two paths to the east and west. The best known of these include Wu Zetian's 'Poetry Tablet Erected by Imperial Decree', which was inscribed in AD 683

The Forest of Stelae

by Wang Zhijing, and 'The First Mountain' by the great Song dynasty artist Mi Fei. On the ruins of the Ciyun Chamber, formerly the residence of the temple's abbots, stand the 'Yu Gong Tablet' by the great Yuan calligrapher Zhao Mengfu and the 'Dao Gong Tablet' by the Ming artist Dong Qichang.

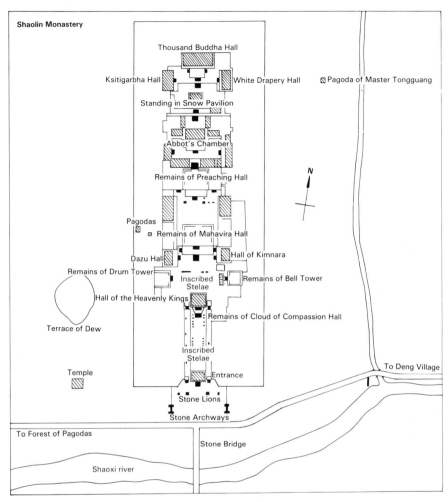

Shaolin Monastery

The Shaolin Monastery is famous not only as a Chan shrine but also for its tradition of martial arts. As a leading *gongfu* (*kung fu*, Chinese karate) school, it has played an important role in the development of Chinese martial arts. The many depressions in the floor of the Thousand Buddha Hall, each more than 2 metres wide, are said to be marks left by monks practising *gongfu*.

Location

The Shaolin Monastery lies at the foot of the Five-nipple peaks on the northern side of the Shaobao mountains in Dengfeng county, Henan province. Shaolin is accessible by bus from Zhengzhou.

The Songyue Temple Pagoda

THE SONGYUE TEMPLE PAGODA
嵩岳寺塔

History
Built in the sixth century AD, the Songyue Temple Pagoda is the earliest surviving brick pagoda in China. As such it is an important example of early Chinese architecture.

During the Northern Wei dynasty, the site was occupied by an imperial residence which was later converted into a temple. Northern Wei rulers were devout Buddhists and Emperor Xiaoming himself preached at the temple.

The main structures of the temple included the Fengyang Hall, the Baji Hall and the Xiaoyao Pavilion. During the late Sui or early Tang dynasty the temple adopted its present name. The buildings have been added to on several occasions throughout the history of the temple, and their arrangement in serried ranks now creates an imposing complex on the hillside. The Tang Empress Wu Zetian often stayed at the temple, and it was also used as an imperial palace. However, after the Tang dynasty it began to decline in importance. Today, as well as the pagoda, there remain the Entrance Gate, the Mahavira Hall, the Jialan Hall and the White Robe Hall. All are Qing structures with sloping roofs joined by a central ridge. Some scattered Tang stone tablets, a pair of stone lions and a stone box in the temple illustrate the fine stone carving of the period. The remaining stelae of the Song and Qing dynasties are also of great historical and artistic value. Tile ends, cylindrical tiles and floor slabs carved with flying *apsara*, bird, flower and animal-head motifs decorate the pagoda.

Description

The Songyue Temple Pagoda, 40 metres high, is a hollow twelve-sided structure, the only pagoda of its type to be found in China today. Its gently curving silhouette resembles that of a pine cone.

The pagoda stands on a simple plinth. On four of the lower façades are four fairly large openings, each of which has an arched top decorated with a lotus motif. Above the storey with the openings the pagoda is girdled by layers of corbelled bricks which divide the pagoda into two distinct sections. These corbelled bricks are repeated as overhanging eaves above each successive storey to the top of the pagoda. The lower section of the pagoda is quite plain while the upper section is ornately decorated. Half-buried octagonal shafts demarcate the corners of each storey, their tops carved with pearls encircled by flames or by inverted lotuses, and their bases shaped like an inverted plate. With the exception of the four entrance facades, each side has concave square niches. These have openings which lead to a rectangular interior, the walls of which are covered with polychrome images of the Buddha backed by flaming mandorlas. On the rear wall of the altar are two doors carved in bas relief and a pair of lions.

Detail of the Songyue Temple Pagoda

The upper section of the pagoda has fifteen overhanging eaves, made up of closely spaced layers of bricks. The facade of each storey is decorated with two bas-relief doors and one window. There are about five hundred such doors and windows, although only a few function as ventilation outlets. Traces of lime on the surface of the pagoda indicate that the structure was originally white-washed, and was repainted up until the Song dynasty. At the top of the pagoda is an inverted lotus with a Buddhist Wheel of the Law and an upturned lotus beneath, all carved from brick or stone.

See Plate 26

Location

The Songyue Temple Pagoda stands at the foot of the Song mountain, on the south side, 7 kilometres northwest of Dengfeng, Henan province. It is accessible by car from Luoyang or Zhengzhou.

THE YOUGUO TEMPLE PAGODA
祐国寺塔

History

The Youguo Temple Pagoda is also known as the Iron Pagoda because it is made of iron-coloured glazed bricks.

The pagoda was formerly in the compound of the Kaibao Temple. During the Northern Song this large and magnificent temple complex was divided into 280 sections which were grouped into twenty-four monasteries. It was here that imperial examinations were held to select *juren* (provincial-level scholars). Northern Song emperors often visited the temple, and so it came to be known as Kaibao, which was a Song reign title.

The Iron Pagoda was preceded by a wooden structure called the Inspiration Pagoda, said to have been built by the Song master craftsman Yu Hao. Octagonal in shape, it had thirteen storeys and was about 120 metres in height. According to historical records, 'When first completed, the pagoda leaned towards the northwest. Puzzled, people asked why. Hao replied, "The land around the capital is flat and has no mountains, and northwesterly winds are frequent. Within a hundred years, it should be vertical." ' It was one of the finest pagodas in Kaifeng until its destruction by lightning in 1044. It was later rebuilt by imperial decree, as today's Iron Pagoda. Its name was changed to the Youguo Temple Pagoda during the Ming. In 1841 the temple was levelled by floodwaters from the Yellow river and only the Iron Pagoda survived.

The pagoda's high, wide, carved stone base was entirely buried by the flooding. *The Gazetteer of Kaifeng Prefecture* states: 'There is an octagonal pond at the foot of the pagoda. To the north is a small bridge, which leads to the northern entrance.' Today, the ground floor of the pagoda has four gates: north, south, east and west. Inside the northern gate is a staircase winding up around a thick pagoda pillar to the top. The pagoda pillar and the outer wall are linked by the staircase, which together form a strong anti-earthquake system.

Description

The octagonal Youguo Temple Pagoda has thirteen storeys and is 55 metres high. The eaves, pillars, lintel and *dougong* brackets are made from twenty-eight different types of bricks all made to imitate wood. On each floor the eave corners are decorated with tiles with dragon or lotus motifs. On the hanging corners of all eight sides stand zoomorphic figures from whose mouths are suspended bronze bells which chime when the wind blows. The octagonal pinnacle is topped by an exquisite bronze vase. Many parts of the exterior of the pagoda, including the outer wall, doors and windows, are inlaid with glistening iron-coloured glazed bricks with over fifty different designs, including flying *apsara* holding peaches, roaring lions,

The Youguo Temple Pagoda

performing musicians and dancers, flowers and plants. Vivid and natural in style, they are masterpieces of brick carving.

Inside the Octagonal Pavilion to the south of the pagoda is a bronze statue of an ushering deity, which dates from the Song dynasty. The figure has a solemn expression, and the drapery, Buddhist swastika on the chest, and the mountain, water and cloud motif on the habit

22 Buddhist sculptures on Baodingshan, near Dazu, Sichuan province
(see p. 139)

23 The Zhuge Liang Memorial Hall, Chengdu, Sichuan province (see p. 141)

24 Du Fu's Cottage, Chengdu, Sichuan province (*see p. 144*)

25 The Longmen Caves, near Luoyang, Henan province (*see p. 166*)

26 The Songyue Temple Pagoda, near Dengfeng, Henan province (see p. 174)

27 The Yungang Caves, near Datong, Shanxi province (*see p. 185*)

28 The Dragon and Tiger Hall of the Yongle Palace, near Ruicheng, Shanxi province (see p. 206)

29 The Flying Rainbow Pagoda of the Guangsheng Temple, near Hongdong, Shanxi province *(see p. 210)*

are all exquisitely executed. Twelve tonnes in weight and 5.1 metres in height, the statue is one of the masterpieces of bronze casting of the period.

Location
The Youguo Temple Pagoda is located in northeast Kaifeng, Henan province. Visitors may take bus 3 to reach it.

THE WHITE HORSE TEMPLE
白马寺

History
The White Horse Temple, erected in AD 68 in the Eastern Han period, was the first Buddhist temple built with government funds after Buddhism had been introduced to China. It is therefore regarded as the fountainhead of Chinese Buddhism.

Historical records relate that the Han Emperor Mingdi once dreamed that he saw a golden figure with a halo flying above his palaces. When he asked his ministers for an explanation, a certain Fu Yi replied that this golden figure was a deity known in the western regions as the Buddha. The emperor then sent Cai Yin, Qin Jing and others to India in search of Buddhism and its scriptures. When they reached the state of Yuezhi they met two Indian monks named Kasyapa-matanga and Dharmaranga whom they invited to China. The Han emperor treated them with great respect and the following year ordered a temple to be built in Luoyang. It is said that two white horses carrying Buddhist scriptures came to China with the two monks, hence the temple's name.

Description
Today the Heavenly King Hall, the Great Buddha Hall, the Mahavira Hall, the Reception Hall, the Vairocana Pavilion and the Qiyun Pagoda are the major remaining structures. With the exception of the pagoda, all were rebuilt during the Ming dynasty.

The temple, rectangular in plan, occupies 40,000 square metres of land. Outside the entrance stand two Song dynasty stone horses facing each other. On a north-south axis are five structures with the Mahavira Hall as their centre, where religious services were held. It was rebuilt in the Ming dynasty with many of the original Eastern Han bricks.

The Vairocana Pavilion

Inside the hall is a clay statue of Sakyamuni, flanked by statues of Manjusri, Samantabhadra, one group of 18 arhats and another of 500 arhats. The bell inside the hall was cast in 1555 and weighs more than 1,000 kilograms.

To the rear of the temple lies the Cool and Refreshing Terrace. It was on this terrace that the Han Emperor Mingdi was said to have studied, and on which the two Indian monks lived and translated sutras. The monks were buried in two semicircular stone-laid mounds in the pine and cypress woods to the east and west just inside the entrance to the temple. Later Buddhist scriptures and images were kept on the Cool and Refreshing Terrace.

Among the temple's relics are many Song dynasty stelae. The best known of these are one with an unfinished inscription by Su Yijian and another with an inscription by the famous Yuan calligrapher Zhao Mengfu.

Slightly southeast of the temple stands a square multi-eaved brick pagoda. Rebuilt in 1175, it is known as the Qiyun Pagoda. It is one of the six celebrated sites at the temple, the others being the Cool and Refreshing Terrace, the monks' tombs, the stone stele bearing the unfinished inscription, the Scripture-burning Terrace and the Midnight Bell.

Location

The White Horse Temple lies 12 kilometres east of Luoyang, Henan province. It can be reached by bus 6 from the centre of the town.

THE GAOCHENG OBSERVATORY
观星台

History

The Gaocheng Observatory in Henan province is the oldest extant observatory in China. In the early years of the Yuan dynasty Kublai Khan set out to recalculate the calendar in an effort to improve agricultural production. To this end he appointed Guo Shoujing and Wang Xun the task of establishing twenty-seven astronomical observatories throughout the empire; the observatory at Gaocheng was regarded by early Chinese astronomers as 'the centre of the earth', and was the most important in the country.

Description

The observatory is made up of two principal structures, the tower and the adjacent long low wall known as the Sky Measuring Scale. The tower is built of bricks and stones, and is in the form of a truncated pyramid. The original tower is 9.5 metres in height, but

The Gaocheng Observatory

the addition of a Ming dynasty low-roofed building on top gives a total height of 12.6 metres. There are two external stairways enabling observers to climb to the top. The brick structure on the north side of the top of the platform is set over the vertical slot in the tower which once held the heliograph, the function of which was to cast a shadow on the Sky Measuring Scale.

The Sky Measuring Scale extends from the vertical slot in the tower 31.2 metres to the north, and is made of thirty-six blocks of dark-coloured stone. Its position corresponds with what is known today as the sun's meridian. The scale has two parallel troughs which extend its entire length, a water supply source at its northern extremity (in the tower) and a drain pool at its northern end. The scale is graded with markings to measure the end of the water. It was here that Guo Shoujing calculated the length of the year to be 365.2425 days by measuring the sun's shadow, findings which he published in the Shoushi Calendar of 1280. Guo's figure corresponds exactly with the Gregorian calendar, antedating the latter by three hundred years.

Location
The Gaocheng Observatory is located in Dengfeng county, Henan province, some 50 miles southeast of Luoyang. Gaocheng can be reached by bus from Luoyang or Zhengzhou.

Shanxi Province
山西省

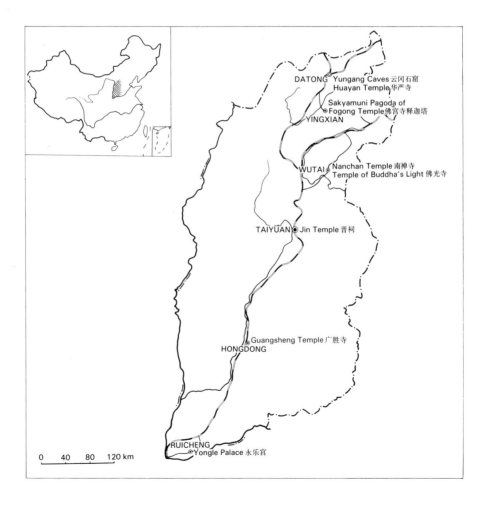

DATONG ⊙ Yungang Caves 云冈石窟
Huayan Temple 华严寺

Sakyamuni Pagoda of
⊙ Fogong Temple 佛宫寺释迦塔
YINGXIAN

WUTAI ⊙ Nanchan Temple 南禅寺
Temple of Buddha's Light 佛光寺

TAIYUAN ⊙ Jin Temple 晋祠

⊙ Guangsheng Temple 广胜寺
HONGDONG

RUICHENG
⊙ Yongle Palace 永乐宫

0   40   80   120 km

The Yungang Caves

THE YUNGANG CAVES
云冈石窟

History

The earliest of the Yungang Caves date from the year AD 453,
in the Northern Wei dynasty. The caves were begun by Emperor
Wencheng on his accession to the throne, as an act of self-aggran-
dizement through the creation of religious works of art. He assigned
the noted monk Tanyao as supervisor of the project. The Five
Caves of Tanyao (numbers 16–20) are both the earliest and the
most impressive of the caves at Yungang. Most of the caves in
the central section were completed between the years AD 462 and
495; caves 5 and 6 and the Five Elaborate Caves are the richest
in content and the most finely executed. Most of the groups of
caves in the eastern and western sections date from approximately
AD 495 to AD 524, while the individual caves in the western section
were completed after the capital was moved to Luoyang.

The initial major work on the caves was completed within a

period of sixty to seventy years. In succeeding dynasties many improvements and additions were made, and numerous Buddhist temples built, especially during the Liao and Jin dynasties. However, after 1,500 years of political turmoil and frequent wars, most of the ancient temples have disappeared, the oldest remaining building being no earlier than Qing in date. Only the caves have stood the test of time.

Description

The Yungang Caves are carved into the southern face of Wuzhou mountain in an area which stretches 1 kilometre from east to west. There are 53 extant caves, with a total of 1,100 niches containing some 51,000 carved images. The caves of each period exhibit their own special characteristics. The Five Caves of Tanyao are oval and contain images of human figures. The larger Buddha images in these caves are a minimum of 13 metres tall, and legend has it that the images were carved to represent the five founding emperors of the Northern Wei dynasty. The images are in both standing and seated positions, and each either occupies an entire cave to itself or is accompanied by bodhisattvas and disciples. Models of piety, solemnity and grandeur, these statues are expressions of the exalted status of the emperors of China. With the blurring of the distinction between man and god, worship of the Buddha became synonymous with paying homage to the Son of Heaven.

Most of the caves in the central section are rectangular and divided into a front and rear section. In addition to the large Buddha image in the centre of the cave, the four walls and the ceiling of each are decorated with relief carvings depicting Buddhist subjects. Caves 5 and 6 are the principal caves of the entire complex. The seated Buddhas of the Three Ages in the centre of cave 5 are 17 metres tall and the largest in the entire Yungang complex. Their sumptuous dress, with shoulder sashes and wide skirts, is that of the Han dynasty nobility and represents an advance from the earlier Gandhara style of Graeco-Roman drapery. These stylistic changes reflect the political and sartorial reforms carried out by Emperor Xiaowen. The four walls of the cave are covered with niches containing finely carved Buddhist images. A number of the caves are square, with square pagoda-shaped columns entirely covered with relief carvings set in the centre. Their four walls are also decorated with niches and Buddha images. In cave 6, for example, in addition to the square two-storey pagoda-shaped column is a series of relief carvings depicting the life of Sakyamuni on the

The seated figure of Sakyamuni in cave 20

lower part of the southern, western and eastern walls and on the four surfaces of the pagoda. These exquisite carvings display a level of skill and realism as high as any in the entire Yungang complex.

Among the Five Elaborate Caves, numbers 9 and 10 form a pair distinguished for their refined carvings of plants, and caves 11 and 13 form another pair. Cave 12, divided into front and rear sections, is the centrepiece of the five. This cave has three entrances and two

Buddha niches

pagoda-shaped columns, and is renowned for its carved ceiling which depicts a large number of figures holding musical instruments. Caves 1 to 4 in the eastern section all contain square pagoda-shaped columns with carvings of Buddha images and Buddhist tales. Most of the caves from number 20 to number 53 in the western section are either small or medium-sized and contain many small niches added in later dynasties. The seated image of Sakyamuni in cave 20, carved into the rock face of the mountain, is 13.7 metres tall. It is executed with its broad right shoulder exposed. Its sensuous face, with thin nose and lips, and its classical proportions make it the most representative sculpture of the Yungang Caves.

The stone carvings of Yungang are renowned throughout the world for their magnificence, attention to detail and richness of content. The height of the Buddha images ranges from 2 centimetres to 17 metres, and they are of great artistic interest. The images of bodhisattvas, arhats, guards and *apsara* are executed with superb realism. Of particular interest are the groups of *apsara* in the cupolas, the dragons, lions, tigers and gold-winged birds. In terms of style and technique, the sculpture shows the influence of the art of ancient India and other countries, as well as of the indigenous art of the Han dynasty. However, the resulting style is unmistakably that of the Northern Wei dynasty.

See Plate 27

Location
The Yungang Caves are located on the southern face of Wuzhou mountain, 16 kilometres to the west of Datong, Shanxi province. They can be reached by bus from Datong.

THE NANCHAN TEMPLE
南禅寺

History
It is difficult to ascertain the date of the founding of the Nanchan Temple; an ink inscription on one of the roof beams of the main hall suggests that it was rebuilt in the year AD 782. During the campaign to eradicate Buddhism carried out by Emperor Wuzong during the late Tang dynasty, most of the temples on Wutaishan were destroyed. Fortunately, the Nanchan Temple was spared, due possibly to its relative inaccessibility. The main hall of the Nanchan Temple is the oldest extant wooden building in China.

Description
The Nanchan Temple consists of a number of buildings laid out on a north-south central axis; these include the main entrance gate, the Hall of the Dragon Kings, the Hall of the Bodhisattvas,

General view of Wutaishan

The Nanchan Temple

One of the bodhisattva images in the Giant Buddha Hall

and the Giant Buddha Hall. The style is that of a typical Chinese courtyard house. The Giant Buddha Hall, which has a broad terrace in front of it, is three bays wide and three bays deep, and has a single-eaved gabled roof. Most of the weight of the roof is supported by columns rather than by the walls. The interior of the hall has neither columns nor a ceiling, contrary to the practice in most temple buildings. The columns of the hall are slightly inclined towards the centre of the hall, and the four corner ones are taller than the rest. These features reinforce the structural relationship between the beams, brackets and columns, giving the hall greater stability. The simplicity of the bracket system is characteristic of early Chinese architecture. The tops of the columns supporting the eaves are built up with numerous angled brackets and curved supports which set off the extended eaves and add a certain elegance to the overall contour of the hall.

Eighteen painted Buddha images are displayed in the hall on a platform. The main image of Sakyamuni is executed in the lotus posture, seated on a Sumeru base, with its hands making the flower-offering gesture of the Chan (Zen) sect. It is flanked by images of Manjusri and Samantabhadra, as well as a number of other disciples, Devaraja (Heavenly Kings) and attendants. With their sensuous faces, relaxed postures, well-proportioned bodies and flowing garments these images are fine examples of Tang dynasty sculpture, comparable to the Tang dynasty masterpieces in the Mogao Caves at Dunhuang.

The Dragon Hall was built in 1569, in the Ming dynasty, while the remaining buildings date from the Qing.

Location

The Nanchan Temple is located west of Lijiazhuang, 22 kilometres southwest of Wutai in Shanxi province. The temple can be reached by bus from Taiyuan.

THE TEMPLE OF BUDDHA'S LIGHT
佛光寺

History

According to early records the Temple of Buddha's Light was first built in the year AD 471, during the reign of Emperor Xiaowen of the Northern Wei dynasty. During the Sui and Tang dynasties its fame spread as far as Chang'an (present-day Xi'an), Dunhuang and even Japan, and descriptions of the temple appear in several early Buddhist works. In AD 845 it was destroyed following an edict by the Tang Emperor Wuzong proscribing Buddhism; it was rebuilt during the reign of the succeeding emperor, who reinstituted the faith. Major repairs were carried out in the Jin, Ming and Qing dynasties.

Group of Buddhist statues

Description

The Temple of Buddha's Light is one of the great treasure houses of Tang architecture, sculpture and mural painting, as well as of Northern Wei, Northern Qi and Tang stupas and stone carving.

The principal building in the original temple was the Hall of Maitreya, the laughing Buddha, which was approximately 32 metres high. But with the proscription of Buddhism under the Tang Emperor Wuzong, the hall was destroyed.

The largest structure in the temple today is the Hall of the Great Buddha, which dates from the year AD 857. The hall faces west, and is seven bays wide and four bays deep. Its wooden brackets, beams, eaves and tenons testify to the high level of architectural design attained during the Tang dynasty. The hall contains Tang painted statues and wall paintings. Thirty-five statues of various sizes, all images of Buddhas, bodhisattvas and guardians of the Buddhist faith, are arranged on the altar. The wall paintings depicting Buddhist subjects are painted with powerful, expressive strokes, and show

Statue of a bodhisattva

obvious resemblances to the wall paintings of the Mogao Caves near Dunhuang in Gansu province.

The Hall of Manjusri in the front courtyard was rebuilt in 1137. The hall faces north, and is similar in size to the Hall of the Great Buddha described above. To reduce the number of columns

30 Pottery figures and horses in pit near Qin Shihuang's mausoleum, near Xi'an, Shaanxi province (see p. 219)

31 The Small Wild Goose Pagoda, Xi'an, Shaanxi province (*see p. 231*)

32 The Ming City Walls of Xi'an, Shaanxi province (*see p. 236*)

33 The Imperial Palace, Shenyang, Liaoning province *(see p. 242)*

34 The Northern Mausoleum, Shenyang, Liaoning province *(see p. 246)*

35 Wall painting of musicians, Mogao Caves, near Dunhuang, Gansu province *(see p. 263)*

36 The Jiayu Pass, Gansu province *(see p. 271)*

37 The Ta'er Lamasery, near Xining, Qinghai province (see p. 276)

38 The ancient city of Gaochang, near Turpan, Xinjiang province (*see p. 279*)

39 The Potala Palace, Lhasa, Tibet (see p. 290)

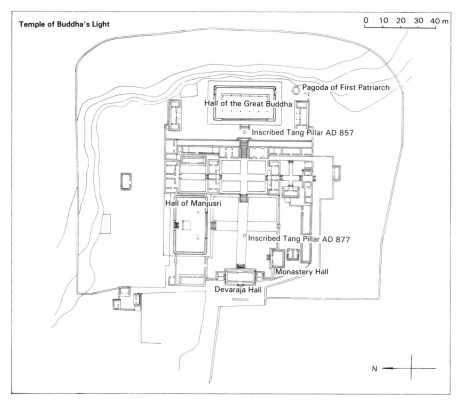

Temple of Buddha's Light

0 10 20 30 40 m

Pagoda of First Patriarch

Hall of the Great Buddha

Inscribed Tang Pillar AD 857

Hall of Manjusri

Inscribed Tang Pillar AD 877

Monastery Hall

Devaraja Hall

N

and increase the amount of unfettered space in the temple, inferior eaves which extend over a length of three bays are combined with rafters and crossbeams to create a single-arched roof structure. Such a roof design is unique amongst wooden structures in China. The other buildings include the main entrance gate (the Devaraja Hall), the Monastery Hall, the Hall of Myriad Virtues, the Tower of Fragrant Wind and Flowery Rain, as well as covered corridors and caves cut into the side of the mountain, all dating from the Ming and Qing dynasties.

The Temple of Buddha's Light also contains two Tang dynasty inscribed pillars. One is octagonal and stands before the Hall of the Great Buddha. Dated AD 857, its surface is carved with the *Dharam Sutra*, and an inscription at the end of the sutra reads 'Female Disciple and Abbess of the Temple Ning Gongyu'. Its similarity to the ink inscription in the Hall of the Great Buddha enables us to ascertain the date of the rebuilding of the hall. The other stone pillar, which was completed in the year AD 877, stands in the courtyard behind the main entrance gate.

To the left of the Hall of the Great Buddha is a hexagonal two-storey brick pagoda popularly known as the Pagoda of the First Patriarch. Its simple unusual design shows the influence of Indian architecture. Judging from the Wutaishan murals at Dunhuang, the pagoda would appear to date from the Northern Qi or Northern Wei dynasty. Six other Tang and Jin pagodas are situated within the vicinity of the Temple of Buddha's Light.

Location
The Temple of Buddha's Light is 32 kilometres southwest of Wutai, Shanxi province. It can be reached by car from Taiyuan.

THE JIN TEMPLE
晋祠

History
The precise date of the founding of the Jin Temple has not been determined. An entry in the *Annotated Classic of Rivers and Lakes* by Li Daoyuan of the Northern Wei dynasty describes the temple in this way: 'The Tang Shuyu Temple is surrounded by mountains and rivers. An outdoor pavilion stands by the spring, with its beams reaching out over the water.' From this we can imagine the beauty of the buildings and their surroundings, as well as deduce that the temple is at least 1,400 years old.

The name Tang Shuyu goes back to the Zhou dynasty. During the reign of King Wu (1066–1064 BC) Prince Shuyu was appointed ruler of the State of Tang, and so he came to be known as Prince Shuyu of Tang. Shuyu's son Xia renamed his kingdom Jin after the Jin river which flowed through his territory. In later times a memorial temple in honour of Shuyu was built at the source of the Jin river and this was called the Tang Shuyu Temple, or the Jin Temple.

In AD 550 in the Northern and Southern Dynasties period Gao Yang conquered the Eastern Wei and established the Northern Qi dynasty, making Jinyang the secondary capital. In the Tianbao period (AD 550–9) the temple was expanded, and in the first two decades of the Sui dynasty a pagoda containing the remains of monks was built to the southwest of the temple. In AD 646 Emperor Taizong visited the temple and left the inscription entitled 'Introduction and Essay on the Jin Temple' to commemorate his work of expansion. Between the years 976 and 983 Emperor Taizong

The Spring of Eternal Youth

of the Song dynasty made major improvements to the temple and left a stone inscription. In the years from 1023 to 1032 Emperor Renzong, having given Prince Shuyu of Tang the posthumous title of 'Prince of Eastern Fen', built the monumental Hall of the Saintly Mother in commemoration of Prince Shuyu's mother, Yi Jiang.

Some ladies-in-waiting to the Saintly Mother

Later other buildings such as the Bell Tower and the Drum Tower were added. These buildings were laid out along a central axis, with the Hall of the Saintly Mother in the central position, relegating the Temple of Prince Shuyu of Tang to a position of secondary importance alongside the new complex.

Description

The Jin Temple consists of almost one hundred halls, towers, pagodas, pavilions, gazebos, terraces and bridges. Not only are these fine examples of traditional architecture, but they are in a setting of great natural beauty at the foot of the Weng mountain near the source of the Jin river.

The buildings of the temple complex are laid out on a central axis which runs from east to west. The Lake Mirror Terrace, situated at the very front of the complex, was built in the Ming dynasty to serve as a stage for the performance of plays. Behind it are the Zhibo Channel, the Bridge of the Fairies, the Terrace of Golden Statues, the Gateway Facing Yue, the Drum Tower, the Bell Tower

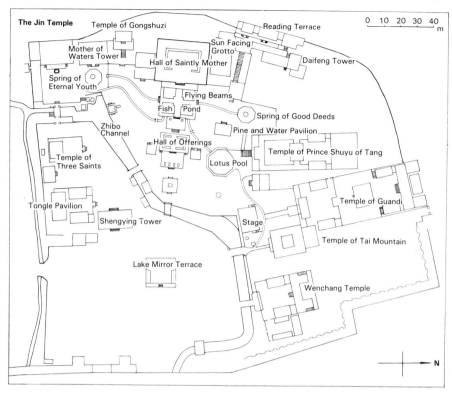

and the Hall of Offerings. On the Terrace of Golden Men are four cast-iron over life-sized human statues, dating from 1097, evidence of the high level of metallurgical skills attained in ancient China. To the west of the Hall of Offerings are the Fish Pond and the 'Flying Beams', both of which are connected directly to the Hall of the Saintly Mother. The square Fish Pond contains thirty-four octagonal stone piers supporting a bridge in the form of a cross made up of brackets and crossbeams, which are known as the 'Flying Beams'. Although this type of bridge was described in early texts, very few examples are to be found in China today.

The Hall of the Saintly Mother stands at the end of the central axis. Built between the years 1023 and 1032 in the Northern Song dynasty, the hall is a masterpiece of Song architecture. Nineteen metres high, seven bays wide and six bays deep, it is built in the 'reduced columns' style, with sixteen fewer columns in the interior and exterior than would normally be found in similar structures. The multi-eaved gabled roof is supported by columns in the corridors and under the eaves. The small number of columns makes the Hall of the Saintly Mother particularly broad and spacious. Inside the hall are forty-three realistic painted clay images, most of which date from the Song dynasty. The image of the Saintly Mother herself is displayed in an imposing central niche, and there are forty-two ladies-in-waiting to her left and right.

The buildings along the central axis of the temple complex combine with the Temple of Prince Shuyu of Tang, the Temple of the deity Hao Tian and the Wenchang Temple to the north, the Mother of Waters Tower, the Pavilion of the Spring of Eternal Youth, and the reliquary pagodas to the south to form a unique complex of religious architecture. The Spring of Eternal Youth and the Spring of Good Deeds flank the Hall of the Saintly Mother. By the Spring of Eternal Youth, the principal source of the Jin river, stands an octagonal pavilion with a pointed roof, dating from the Ming dynasty. The Spring of Eternal Youth, the Zhou cypress and Sui scholar tree, and the Song dynasty sculptures of ladies-in-waiting are regarded as the 'Three Treasures of the Jin Temple'.

Location
The Jin Temple is located 25 kilometres to the southwest of Taiyuan, Shanxi province. The temple can be reached by bus from Taiyuan.

THE HUAYAN TEMPLE
华严寺

History
The Huayan Temple is one of the principal temples of the Huayan (Avatamsa) Sect of Buddhism. The earliest structure in the temple, dating from 1038, is the Bhagawan Library, which serves as a repository for Buddhist scriptures. According to written records, during the reign of Daozong (1055–1100) the Huayan Temple contained stone and bronze images of the emperors, and so it may be regarded as the ancestral temple of the imperial clan. For a century during the mid-Liao dynasty, the temple flourished and the number of buildings increased. The Mahavira Hall was built in 1062. During the final years of the Liao, most of the buildings were destroyed by fire but the temple was rebuilt in 1140, in the Jin dynasty, and through the early Yuan dynasty remained one of the largest temples in northern China. In the early Ming dynasty the temple became the property of the government, and flourished once again in the Xuande (1426–35) and Jingtai (1450–6) periods following large-scale

The Buddhas of the Five Directions in the Mahavira Hall

construction. In the mid-Ming dynasty it was divided into two separate temples, each with its own main entrance gate. In the early Qing dynasty it was once again destroyed by fire, and after numerous rebuilding projects the temple finally attained its present dimensions. Today the Upper and Lower Huayan Temples are considered as parts of the one entity.

Description

The buildings in the Huayan Temple are arranged in two groups with the Bhagawan Library and Mahavira Hall as their respective centres. Because the Khitan people were sun worshippers, their major buildings face eastwards.

The Upper and Lower Huayan Temples are two closely related religious complexes. The Upper Temple is set on high ground and its buildings are more closely spaced than those of the Lower Temple. Its major structure is the Mahavira Hall.

The Mahavira Hall is nine bays wide and five bays deep. Its single-eaved overhanging roof has acroteria (roof ornaments) 4.5 metres high, that on the north of the roof dating from the Liao dynasty.

Statue of a bodhisattva in the Lower Huayan Temple

The hall stands on a platform and is designed in the 'reduced column' style, which means that there are twelve fewer columns in the interior than there would be in more conventional structures. For this reason there is a greater area of space in the hall, facilitating the display of a large number of Buddhist images and the performance of religious ceremonies. The principal statues in the hall are the

Buddhas of the Five Directions. They are flanked by twenty *deva* whose torsos lean at an angle of 15°, giving them a deferential air. The walls of the hall are decorated with 861 square metres of wall paintings dating from the Qing dynasty. On the ceiling of the hall are 973 square roof tiles decorated with dragons, phoenixes, flowers, plants and Sanskrit letters. Their complex patterns and brilliant colours enhance the setting for the Buddhist images and wall paintings.

The Lower Huayan Temple is located to the southeast of the Upper Temple. Its major structure is the Bhagawan Library, which stands on a tall platform. The library is five bays wide and four deep, and has a single-eaved roof with nine roof sections. The altar inside the hall is large enough to accommodate thirty-one Liao dynasty Buddhist images. In the centre there are three images of the Tathagata Buddha, in his manifestation as the Buddhas of the Three Ages (past, present and future) flanked by disciples, bodhisattvas and attendants. The sculptures are in sitting and standing positions, and display a wide variety of moods. The most lifelike is the image of a bodhisattva pressing its hands together and with its lips slightly parted. The bodhisattva's refined features, sensuous figure, and the natural flow of the garments make this an excellent example of Liao dynasty sculpture.

Location

The Huayan Temple is located in the western suburbs of Datong, Shanxi province. It can be reached either by bus or on foot.

THE SAKYAMUNI PAGODA OF THE FOGONG TEMPLE
佛宫寺释迦塔

History

The Sakyamuni Pagoda of the Fogong Temple was built in 1056, in the Liao dynasty, and is the tallest extant wooden building in China. Because it is constructed entirely of wood, it is popularly known as the Wooden Pagoda of Yingxian, after the administrative county in which it is located.

Description

The Sakyamuni Pagoda of the Fogong Temple is octagonal in shape, and has a double-eaved roof above its lowest level. From the outside

The Sakyamuni Pagoda of the Fogong Temple

the pagoda appears to have five storeys and six sets of eaves, although there are actually four invisible storeys between the five visible ones, making a total of nine. The pagoda is 67.1 metres high and has a diameter of 30 metres at its base. Throughout Chinese history the pagoda has served both as a centre for the dissemination of Buddhist teaching in times of peace as well as a point from which to observe and conduct battles in time of war.

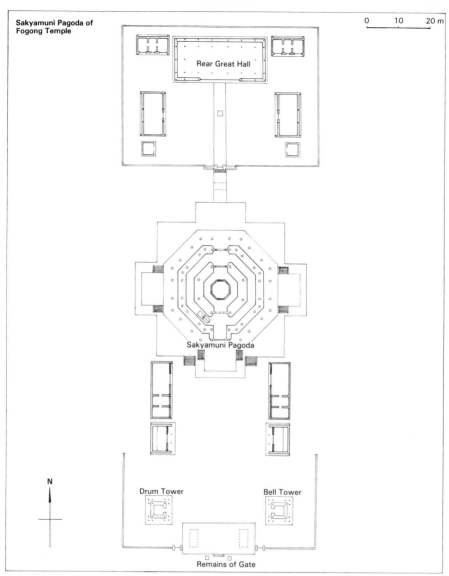

Sakyamuni Pagoda of Fogong Temple

0   10   20 m

Rear Great Hall

Sakyamuni Pagoda

N

Drum Tower

Bell Tower

Remains of Gate

The Sakyamuni Pagoda stands on the central axis of the Fogong Temple between the main entrance gate and the Great Hall, in the tradition of the Buddhist architecture of the Northern and Southern Dynasties period. The first storey of the pagoda is relatively tall, and is surrounded by a covered gallery, a mud wall and an earth wall 1 metre high. The upper portion of the pagoda is built entirely of wood. The external columns of each 'visible' storey rest atop the external columns of the storey beneath, though they are placed at a distance one-half the diameter of the columns towards the centre of the pagoda. Thus the pagoda narrows towards the top, giving it a tall and elegant appearance.

The pagoda makes use of more than sixty different types of brackets, covering the entire range of structural methods current in the Liao dynasty. From the simple to the complex, the gradual transformation offers a rich complement of variations which constitute a harmonious whole.

Large numbers of angled trusses are used between the visible and invisible storeys, reinforcing the entire internal structure of the pagoda. All the storeys are connected by a staircase which leads to the top. The roof is octagonal and rises to a pinnacle. It is capped by an iron spire which blends harmoniously with the rest of the pagoda.

In the original pagoda, each inner storey contained Buddhist images, but the only image which remains in good condition today is that of Sakyamuni on the first storey. The image is 11 metres tall and is in Liao dynasty style. A cache of precious relics was discovered recently in the pagoda when repairs were being carried out; these included hand-written and woodblock-printed Buddhist scriptures, paintings and Buddhist images printed on silk in several colours. These objects provide valuable material for the study of Liao politics, economics and culture. The wooden printing blocks filled a lacuna in the history of printing in China, while the Khitan sutras are of great interest to researchers in many fields. The coloured images on silk printed in red, yellow and blue water-based ink demonstrate the high level of printing attained in China more than ten centuries ago.

Location

The Sakyamuni Pagoda of the Fogong Temple is located in the northwestern suburbs of Yingxian, Shanxi province. Buses run from Datong to the pagoda.

THE YONGLE PALACE
永乐宫

History

Yonglegong (the Palace of Eternal Happiness) was originally called the Palace of Pure Sun and Longevity, and was one of the most important centres of the Northern Sect of Daoism, the Perfect Realization Sect.

According to stone inscriptions and early Daoist writings, the building evolved from a memorial temple to a Daoist monastery (*guan*) and finally to a palace (*gong*) during the late Tang dynasty. A memorial temple was built on the site of the former residence of Lü Dongbin, in the northwestern outskirts of Yongle township, and was known as the Temple of Master Lü. Towards the end of the Jin dynasty architectural improvements were made and the temple was enlarged into a monastery. In 1232 the monastery was elevated to the status of a palace and Pan Dechong, the abbot of the southern and northern sections of Hedong district, was appointed as supervisor. At that time the monastery was rebuilt as the Palace of Pure Sun and Longevity. From 1247 to 1262 three large statues were erected in the Hall of the Three Pure Ones, the Hall of Chunyang and the Zhongyang Hall (named after Wang Zhongyang, founder of the Perfect Realization Sect), and in 1294 the Dragon and Tiger Hall was completed; in 1325 the wall paintings in the Hall of the Three Pure Ones were completed, and in 1358 the wall paintings in the Chunyang Hall were finished. The Hall of Master Qiu, which originally stood to the rear of the Zhongyang Hall, was built to honour Qiu Changchun, a leader of the Perfect Realization Sect. Unfortunately it was destroyed centuries ago. The construction of the Yongle Palace Temple continued for a total of 110 years.

The Yongle Palace is located in an area which was flooded by the Sanmenxia Reservoir. From 1959 funds were made available by the state to move the temple from the town of Yongle to a less vulnerable site so that it might be preserved.

Description

The Yongle Palace is an imposing complex of buildings laid out in a rather spacious manner. Its major buildings, besides the palace gate, are the four halls: the Dragon and Tiger Hall, the Hall of the Three Pure Ones, the Chunyang Hall, and the Zhongyang Hall. These are arranged from south to north on a central axis, and are surrounded by a wall which delimits this long, narrow central section of the palace. The main building in the palace, the Hall of the Three Pure Ones, stands at the front of this group; this is very unusual, since in most temple complexes the largest hall stands to the rear. Such a layout is similar to that found in palace architecture. Even rarer are the Yuan dynasty wall paintings, of which there are 960 square metres in the palace.

A section of the wall painting

The Dragon and Tiger Hall stands on a platform. It is five bays wide and six rafters deep, with a single-eaved overhanging roof and a plaque above the central door inscribed 'Limitless Gate'. The wall paintings are to be found in the northeast and northwest corners of the hall. All the figures in the paintings are dressed for battle and hold swords or spears in their hands; these celebrated warriors are fine examples of early painting.

The Hall of the Three Pure Ones is built on a broad deep platform, is seven bays wide and four bays deep, and has a single-eaved overhanging roof. The name of the hall is derived from the three images displayed inside: the Great Pure One, the Jade Pure One and the Superior Pure One. The hall is windowless. The four interior walls are covered with paintings to a height of 4.3 metres and with a total length of 94.7 metres, covering a surface area of over 400 square metres. The title of these paintings is 'The Heavenly Court', and they depict the gods showing respect to the founding father of Daoism, 'The First Heavenly True One'. There are eight principal figures dressed in the garb of emperors and empresses and 290 other

A section of the wall painting

portraits arranged in rows. Each portrait has its own distinctive posture and facial expression, and each protects and addresses the Three Pure Ones in his or her appropriate manner. The principal figures are more than 3 metres tall, the subsidiary figures 2 metres tall. They are painted in a realistic manner and hold a variety of sacred and non-sacred objects. The large figures in the paintings in the Hall of the Three Pure Ones have a three-dimensional quality and are arranged in a spacious composition, with harmonious colours and flowing lines. The wall paintings owe much to the traditions of Tang and Song painting, but also show signs of Yuan dynasty developments in art. They are some of the finest extant wall paintings in China, and are a rich source for the study of costumes and artefacts.

The Chunyang Hall is five bays wide and three bays deep, has a single-eaved gabled roof, and is built on a platform the same height as that of the Hall of the Three Pure Ones. The hall contains a statue of Lü Dongbin, and takes its name from Lü's Daoist nickname, 'The Master of Chunyang'. The interior walls of this hall are decorated with a series of fifty-two wall paintings depicting the life of Lü Dongbin. This group of paintings is known as *The Transformations of His Highness Chunyang during his Mystical Journey.* Close attention is paid to the composition of each painting and a uniform background landscape of clouds and mist, trees and rocks maintains a sense of continuity from painting to painting. The content of the paintings provides a rich source for the study of life during the Song and Yuan dynasties. In addition to this, the painting entitled *Zhongli Quan and Lü Dongbin discuss the Dao*, which is behind the altar with the image of Lü Dongbin, captures the attitudes of master and disciple with a remarkable degree of realism. It is a fine example of early portraiture.

See Plate 28

Location

The Yongle Palace is located near Longquan village in Ruicheng county, Shanxi province. To reach the temple from Taiyuan, visitors should take the train to Yuncheng or Yongji and take a bus from there.

THE GUANGSHENG TEMPLE
广胜寺

History

The earliest Guangsheng Temple was built in AD 147, and was called the Pagoda Courtyard of King Asoka. It was rebuilt in AD 769 at the suggestion of the ruling official Guo Ziyi. After being destroyed

The Flying Rainbow Pagoda

several times by fire, it was rebuilt once again in 1305. It has since survived relatively intact despite two earthquakes, one in the Ming and the other in the Qing dynasty. The temple is noted for its Yuan dynasty wall paintings in the Hall of Prince Mingying which depict many aspects of Yuan drama.

Description

The Guangsheng Temple consists of three parts: the Upper and Lower Temples and the Temple of the Water God. The Upper and Lower Temples are located approximately half a kilometre from each other, while the Temple of the Water God is situated immediately to the west of the Lower Temple.

From south to north, the Upper Temple is composed of the following structures: the main gate, the Hall of Amitabha, the Mahavira Hall and the Vairocana Hall. The Flying Rainbow Pagoda is located in front of the Mahavira Hall on the central axis of the temple. A pagoda in such a position is a characteristic feature of early Chinese temple architecture. On both sides of the main axis there are wings and auxiliary halls.

Immediately inside the main gate is the pagoda courtyard with the Flying Rainbow Pagoda at its centre. The octagonal pagoda has thirteen storeys, and is built of brick and faced with yellow, green and blue glazed tiles. All the brackets, corner columns, panels and floral and animal decoration are extremely fine, giving the pagoda the appearance of a rainbow soaring into the sky. The present Flying Rainbow Pagoda, a fine example of Chinese glazed tile workmanship, was rebuilt between 1515 and 1527. The base of the pagoda is surrounded by a covered corridor, and inside the pagoda is a spiral staircase which ascends to the tenth storey. These are extremely rare features among China's extant pagodas.

The Hall of Amitabha is also called the Front Hall, and dates from the Ming. However, the statues of Amitabha and his two attendant bodhisattvas date from the Yuan.

The Mahavira Hall is also known as the Central Hall. It is five bays wide and has a single-eaved hipped roof. Inside the hall there are carved wooden altars containing images of Sakyamuni and the two bodhisattvas, Manjusri and Samantabhadra. Both the altar and the lifelike images are fine examples of early sculpture.

The Lower Temple stands to the north of the source of the Huo spring at the foot of the Huo mountain. Its three major statues, the main gate, and the front and rear halls are situated along a single axis. The Rear Hall, built in 1309 in the Yuan dynasty, is seven bays wide and has a single-eaved hipped roof. The upper part of the hall contains Yuan dynasty statues of the Buddhas of the Three Ages, and of Manjusri and Samantabhadra, all with finely executed drapery. The Yuan wall paintings were removed from the temple in 1928 and are now in the collection of the Nelson-Atkins Museum in Kansas City in the United States.

The Lower Temple

The Temple of the Water God is made up of the Main Gate, the Ritual Gate and the Hall of Prince Mingying on the central axis, with wings to each side. There are two courtyards; in the centre of the rear courtyard, is the Hall of Prince Mingying, the major building in the temple. According to legend, the Temple of the Water God was the site of worship of the god of the Huo spring. All four interior walls of the temple are decorated with wall paintings, the most famous being that depicting Yuan dynasty drama, on the eastern part of the southern wall. This painting was completed in 1324 and measures 4.1 by 3.1 metres. It depicts an entire theatrical troupe in the midst of performance, and shows the stage, scenery, props, actors and orchestra. Some of the eleven actors portray the traditional roles of older male (*sheng*), female (*dan*), painted face (*jing*) and young male (*mo*), and are shown wearing the appropriate make-up, beards, embroidered costumes and footwear. Props include swords, official plaques and fans, and among the musical instruments are the bamboo flute, drum and clapper for keeping time. The brick-paved stage is an indication that by the Yuan dynasty dramatic performances were held on permanent stages; there are also hanging curtains and finely executed scenery. The painting is of inestimable value in the study of the history and development of music and drama in China.

See Plate 29

Location

The Guangsheng Temple is located 8.5 kilometres to the northeast of Hongdong county, Shanxi province, to the north of the Huo mountain. It may be reached from Taiyuan by taking the train to Linfen, and from there by taking a bus to the temple.

Shaanxi Province
陕西省

YAN'AN

HUANGLING
Mausoleum of Yellow Emperor 黄帝陵

Qian Mausoleum 乾陵
BAOJI QIANXIAN
LINTONG Mausoleum of Qin Shihuang and its Auxiliary
Mao Mausoleum 茂陵 Pits of Pottery Figures 秦始皇陵及兵马俑丛葬坑
Tomb of Huo Qubing 霍去病墓 XI'AN Neolithic Village of Banpo 半坡遗址
Forest of Stelae 西安碑林
Large Wild Goose Pagoda 大雁塔
Small Wild Goose Pagoda 小雁塔
City Walls of Xi'an 西安城墙

0   50   100   150
km

The Mausoleum of the Yellow Emperor

THE MAUSOLEUM OF THE YELLOW EMPEROR
黃帝陵

History

The Yellow Emperor is said to be the earliest ancestor of the Han Chinese and a great leader. His family name was Gongsun and his given name Xuanyuan. Legend has it that some five thousand years ago he defeated Chi You and Yan Di and thus broke the strict boundaries between clan communes and encouraged the unity of hitherto disparate groups. Legend further asserts that it was during this period that sericulture, weaving, the written language, the compass and forms of transport were invented, and that Chinese civilization began to develop. The Yellow Emperor is traditionally considered as the 'Earliest Creator of Chinese Culture'.

It is said that he lived to the age of 111 and that after his death mausolea were built in his honour in Gansu, Hebei and Henan provinces and many other places.

The Xuanyuan Temple

Description

The Mausoleum of the Yellow Emperor is surrounded by lush cypress trees. In front of the mausoleum stands a stone tablet engraved: 'Qiaoling Long Yu' ('The Mausoleum of the Supreme Ruler at Qiaoling Hill'), written by a governor of Shaanxi in 1776.

On the southern side of the mausoleum stands another stele amidst cypress trees. On this tablet is engraved in the clerical script: 'Han Wu Xian Tai' ('The Sacred Altar of the Han Emperor Wudi'). Behind this are two high earthen terraces which are said to be altars where the Han Emperor Wudi offered sacrifices to the Yellow Emperor on his return from military campaigns.

As well as the tomb, the Xuanyuan Temple and the stone tablets, there is the famous Ancient Cypress of Qiaoling Hill in the mausoleum compound, believed to have been planted by the Yellow Emperor himself. Towering and magnificent, this tree is said to be over five thousand years old. It is one of the four of the original eight scenic spots in Huangling county, the other three being the

Moonlit Qiaoling Hill, the Northern Cliff Boulder, and the Sacred Altar of the Han Emperor Wudi.

Prior to 1949 the mausoleum was desolate and overgrown. It is now maintained by an administrative committee.

Location

The Mausoleum of the Yellow Emperor is situated on Qiaoling hill in northern Huangling county, 150 kilometres north of Xi'an. It can be reached by bus or taxi from Xi'an.

THE NEOLITHIC VILLAGE OF BANPO
半坡遗址

History

Banpo was typical of neolithic village settlements along the Yellow River some six thousand years ago, and was part of the matrilineal Yangshao culture. Covering nearly 50,000 square metres, the site consists of a dwelling area, a pottery centre and a graveyard. Excavations have so far uncovered the ruins of 45 dwellings, 2 stables, more than 200 storage pits, 6 kilns, 250 graves including 73 children's clay coffins, and as many as 10,000 fragments of tools and household utensils. Archaeologists have also found animal bones, fruit stones and millet.

Tools used in Banpo village were generally made of stone or bone. The stone tools included axes, adzes, chisels, knives, spades, rods, plates, arrowheads, net-weights and spinning wheels; the bone tools included knives, awls, chisels, needles, arrowheads, fish hooks and fishing spears. The sharply barbed fish hooks and needles with tiny eyes were exquisitely fashioned.

Household utensils were made mainly of clay. By composition, they can be grouped into refined clay pottery, coarse sandy pottery and refined sandy pottery. As types, they can be categorized into cooking vessels, bowls, basins, jars, pots and bottles. In terms of function, they can be classified as food, water, cooking and storage vessels. Most are red, but some are grey and black. Some earthenware vessels have impressed mat or cloth decoration at the bottom, evidence for early textile weaving. The painted pottery, which illustrates the high quality of neolithic art, is red with black geometric designs. The decoration includes images of animals such as open-mouthed fish and galloping deer, and plants. A clue to the sculpture of the period is indicated by the pottery handles, which are in the form of human heads, and the heads of birds and animals. Ornaments include bone hairpins, jade, animal teeth, stone beads, pottery rings and pendants. Some earthenware is incised with simple, neat signs which are believed to be a primitive script recording events and people.

Description

In 1958 a museum was built on the excavation site. Two types of home can be seen: one dug half-way into the ground, which belongs to the earlier period, and the other timber-framed and above ground which belongs to the later period. Some are square, others circular. All the doors faced south, and a fire pit occupied the middle of each house. The building materials were mainly earth, wood and straw. In the later period homes were fairly well constructed, and beside each was dug one or more storage pits which are thought to have fulfilled the function of public warehouses. The settlement is surrounded by a ditch, 300 metres long and between 5 and 6 metres deep. The pottery centre, the earliest of its kind excavated so far, lies to the east.

The museum displays a model showing the layout of the tombs, and the remains of corpses of the same sex which were buried in one grave. The graveyard lies to the north of the village. The burial objects were mainly utensils and ornaments.

The Banpo villagers discovered how to use steam for cooking and invented a type of distilling pot. They also discovered ways of drilling holes in stone axes, and of barbing fish hooks and spears. They made use of the law of gravity to manufacture bottles with pointed bases, and they knew enough about geometry to make simple calculations. As well as hunting and foraging they had begun to engage in agriculture and weaving.

Location

The Banpo Museum is on the eastern outskirts of Xi'an, accessible by buses 5, 31, 32, 33 and 37.

THE MAUSOLEUM OF QIN SHIHUANG AND ITS AUXILIARY PITS OF POTTERY FIGURES
秦始皇陵及兵马俑从葬坑

History

Qin Shihuang was the first emperor (221–210 BC) of the Qin dynasty, and a major figure in Chinese history. He annexed six ducal states and unified China, thus ending the Warring States period. Following this he established China's first centralized feudal monarchy.

Owing to the subsequent rapid development of the feudal economy, Qin Shihuang was able to amass a large fortune, a great deal of which he spent on monumental projects. One of these was his mausoleum. According to Sima Qian's *Records of the Historian*, 'As soon as the first emperor became king of Qin, excavations and building were begun at Mount Li and after he won his empire more than 700,000 conscripts from all over the country worked there. They dug through three subterranean streams and poured in molten copper to make the outer coffin. The tomb was filled with models of palaces, pavilions and offices, as well as fine bronze vessels and other precious objects. Any thief breaking in would be shot. The Yellow river, the Yangtze and other major waterways were reproduced in quicksilver and by some mechanical means made to flow into a miniature ocean. The heavenly constellations were shown above and the regions of the earth below. The candles were made of whale oil to ensure that they would burn for the longest possible time.' This description well illustrates the magnitude of the mausoleum and the sumptuousness of the burial objects. Construction continued throughout the ruler's thirty-five-year reign, first as king of the state of Qin, then as emperor of the Qin dynasty. Shortly after his burial, however, Xiang Yu captured the Qin capital and burnt down the mausoleum and the Afang Palace. The structures above ground were destroyed, and the tomb ransacked and looted of its countless treasures. For the following two thousand years the mausoleum remained in ruins.

A pit of pottery figures of warriors and horses, not mentioned in any historical records and unknown to the world, was unearthed in 1974 near the mausoleum when local peasants were sinking wells. Subsequent excavation revealed a pottery legion from Qin Shihuang's imperial army. The pit was opened as a museum in 1979 and has since attracted hundreds of thousands of tourists. It is regarded by many as the 'eighth wonder of the world'.

Description

Qin Shihuang's mausoleum is a mound of rammed earth, with a height of 76 metres and a circumference of over 2,000 metres. The original mound would have been much larger, but much of it has been eroded by the elements. It is nevertheless the largest such imperial mound known in China. After four years of surveying, from 1974 to 1978, it was established that the mausoleum was surrounded by two walls, an inner one 2,525 metres long and an outer one

The Qin Shihuang Mausoleum

The museum of pottery figures

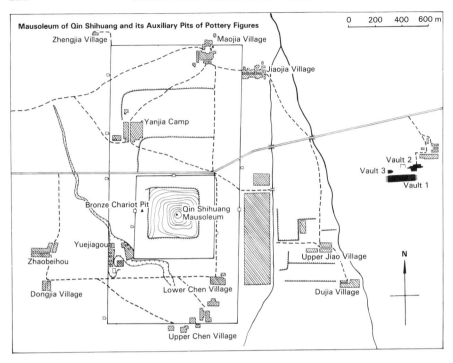

6,264 metres long. Within this area there are the remains of contemporaneous structures. In recent years three further pits of pottery figurines and pits containing bronze chariots have been discovered near by and about ten thousand artefacts have been excavated. In 1980, some 500 metres to the west of the mausoleum, were found a large number of graves in each of which there are two to four corpses in crouching positions. It is believed that these were slaves or artisans who worked on the building of the mausoleum.

Vault 1 lies 1,500 metres to the east of the mausoleum. So far four pits of this type have been discovered, of which this is the largest. It is 230 metres long from east to west, 62 metres from north to south and 5 metres deep. It contains six thousand life-size pottery warriors, chariots, and horses arranged in rectangular battle formation. Vault 2 contains formations of four different types of soldiers, while Vault 3 appears to be a military headquarters. Vault 4 has yet to be excavated. According to a preliminary survey, however, it contains figures of the imperial guards. There are about 10,000 pottery warriors and horses in all, which fall into four categories: infantrymen, archers, charioteers and cavalrymen. The soldiers all hold real weapons, such as arrows, bows, dagger-axes,

The bronze chariot

spears, halberds and hooks. Archers and cavalrymen all face east as though about to fight the ducal states which lay in that direction. The figures were originally coloured with polychromed pigments, their armour and colour illustrating their rank.

In 1980 two superbly cast bronze chariots were unearthed from a pit not far from the mausoleum. Each chariot is drawn by four horses and manned by a charioteer, the components of the assemblage being about half life size. Even the reins are forged of bronze, in the form of movable links which twist like leather.

See Plate 30

Location

The Qin Shihuang Mausoleum and the museum of pottery figures lie 30 kilometres east of Xi'an and are accessible by bus or car.

THE MAO MAUSOLEUM AND THE TOMB OF HUO QUBING
茂陵及霍去病墓

History

The Mao Mausoleum (Maoling) is that of the Han Emperor Wudi (140–87 BC). Han imperial tombs follow a fairly standard pattern:

The Mao Mausoleum

made of rammed earth, they are square in shape and have flat roofs. Emperor Wudi began building this tomb in 139 BC, shortly after ascending the throne. He reigned for fifty-four years, longer than any other Han emperor, and work on his tomb lasted for fifty-three years. Near by are the tombs of several of his high-ranking officials, including Huo Qubing, Wei Qing and Jin Richan.

Huo Qubing (140–117 BC) was a brilliant young general who began his career at the age of eighteen commanding troops in the Xilian mountain area when the Xiongnu were harassing northern borders. During his short life — he died at the age of twenty-four — he led six expeditions to the north to repulse the Xiongnu and won large areas of territory, thus making a remarkable contribution to the unification and consolidation of the Western Han empire. Emperor Wudi deeply mourned his death and ordered a grand funeral in his honour. He also ordered that a vast and magnificent tomb be built for Huo 1 kilometre from his own.

Description
The Mao Mausoleum, which is covered with a burial mound roughly square in shape, is the largest of the eleven Han imperial tombs.

The Tomb of Huo Qubing

To the east, west and north are the remains of three watchtowers. In recent years large numbers of rare and precious artefacts, such as fine jades, metalwork and decorated bricks and tiles, have been discovered near the Mao Mausoleum and neighbouring tombs.

To commemorate Huo Qubing's great victory in battle over the Xiongnu, Emperor Wudi ordered that the tomb be built in the shape of the Xilian mountain and that a number of imposing stone sculptures be placed in front of it. Carved to follow the natural shape of the stone, these sculptures depict a variety of subjects: a horse trampling a Xiongnu soldier, a mythical animal eating a sheep, a man struggling with a bear, as well as reclining horses and a bull, a wild boar, frogs and cicadas. Famous for their strength and simplicity of expression, these sculptures reflect the wealth, power and confidence of Western Han society, and are masterpieces of the art of the period. The best known of all the statues at the site, that of the horse trampling the Xiongnu soldier, symbolizes Huo Qubing's achievements in his expeditions against the northern invaders. The vigorous horse stands with its head thrown upwards while the soldier struggles beneath its hoof. The striking contrast of man and horse powerfully conveys the spirit and character of the two combatants.

Location

The Mao Mausoleum is located on the Weibei plateau in Xingping county, 50 kilometres west of Xi'an. It is accessible by train and bus.

THE FOREST OF STELAE
西安碑林

History

The important collection of historical stone stelae in Xi'an is the largest of its kind in China. Because they are as numerous as the trees in a forest, the collection has come to be known as the Forest of Stelae.

The Forest of Stelae was first established in the year 1090 in the reign of the Northern Song Emperor Zhezong to house a group of inscriptions on stone known as the Kaicheng Stone Canon. The collection continued to expand throughout ensuing dynasties. In 1555, in the reign of the Ming Emperor Jiajing, the Forest of Stelae was seriously damaged by an earthquake, but was rebuilt in the Wanli reign (1573–1620). The wooden buildings in which the stelae are displayed and the stone doors of these buildings date from this period, and the elaborately carved stone lintels are typical of Ming architectural style. Many new stelae were carved and added to the collection during the reign of Emperor Kangxi (1662–1722), and further additions were made in the Qianlong reign (1736–95). Following the founding of the People's Republic in 1949, the Forest of Stelae was refurbished in order to maintain the traditional style of the buildings and to emphasize the grandeur of the collection. At this time all the stone stelae were rearranged according to their date and content, while the buildings housing them were reinforced to prevent potential damage from earthquakes. In recent years a number of newly discovered stelae and tomb inscriptions have been added to the collection.

Description

The Forest of Stelae is composed of six large display rooms, six roofed corridors and a single pavilion housing a total of more than one thousand stelae and tomb inscriptions. There are examples of stone inscriptions from the Han, Northern Wei, Sui, Tang, Song, Yuan, Ming and Qing dynasties.

Included in the collection are some of the finest and best-known examples of Chinese calligraphy: examples of the seal

Entrance to the Forest of Stelae

script (*zhuanshu*) include stelae in the hands of Li Yangbing; examples of the clerical script (*lishu*) include the Cao Jin Stele and a Han dynasty rendering of the *Book of Changes*; examples

Some of the stelae

of the cursive script (*caoshu*) include several versions of the *Thousand Character Classic* by the monks Zhiyong and Huaisu and by Zhang Xu; and masterpieces of the regular script (*kaishu*) include essays and Buddhist texts by Ouyang Xun, Ouyang Tong, Chu Suiliang, Yan Zhenqing and Liu Gongquan. Many of the upper portions of the stelae are carved with elaborate relief sculptures, while the texts are often framed with panels of incised patterns, which enhance the elegant columns of calligraphy.

Many of the inscriptions on the stelae are unique historical documents in their own right. The Kaicheng Stone Canon, which dates from AD 837, comprises a total of 114 stelae inscribed with the text of a number of important classics: the *Book of Changes*, the *Shang Shu*, the *Book of Poems*, the *Zhou Rituals*, the *Book of Rites*, the *Zuo Zhuan*, the Gongyang and Gu Liang commentaries on the *Spring and Autumn Annals*, the *Classic of Filial Piety*, the *Analects of Confucius* and the *Er Ya*. These faultlessly carved texts consist of a total of more than 650,000 Chinese characters. Other stelae record early incidents of cultural exchange between China and the West, such as the Tang dynasty *Record of the Nestorian Christian Community at Chang'an* (present-day Xi'an) which dates from AD 781.

Among the stelae dating from the Northern Wei to the Tang and Song dynasties are several fine examples of decorative carving. The lifelike human figure and phoenixes embracing among the flowers found on the Tang dynasty Stele of the Zen Master Dazhi are the product of a rich artistic imagination.

Location
The Forest of Stelae is in the Shaanxi Provincial Museum in Xi'an.

THE LARGE WILD GOOSE PAGODA
大雁塔

History
The Large Wild Goose Pagoda (Dayanta) was formerly known as the Grace Monastery Pagoda (Ciensita). Built in AD 647 in honour of his mother by Li Zhi, the prince who three years later was to become the Tang emperor Gaozong, the monastery originally had thirteen courtyards surrounded by 1,897 rooms where some three hundred monks lived in seclusion. Among them was the celebrated Buddhist scholar Xuanzang (AD 602–64), also known as Monk Tripitaka, who journeyed to India and what is Pakistan today in the early Tang dynasty. He spent more than ten years studying Buddhist scriptures and introduced Chinese culture to India. In AD 645 he returned to China with 657 Buddhist scriptures and established an institute of translation in the Grace Monastery in Chang'an (present-day Xi'an). The first Large Wild Goose Pagoda was built on his recommendation in AD 652.

There are different versions of the origin of the name. *The Biography of Xuanzang of the Grace Monastery* tells how a flock of wild geese was flying over a monastery in the Indian kingdom of Magadha when one bird lost several feathers and fell dead. The monks, thinking it was a saint and greatly shocked, decided to bury it and build a pagoda.

The original structure was a square five-storey building made of rammed earth with a brick outer wall. It soon collapsed, however, and was rebuilt as a seven-storey brick structure during the reign of Chang'an (AD 701–4). During the reign of Dali (AD 766–79), three more storeys were built on, which were later destroyed. During the

The Large Wild Goose Pagoda

Ming dynasty a layer of bricks was added to strengthen the pagoda, and it is this structure which survives intact today.

Description

The Large Wild Goose Pagoda is 59.9 metres in height, and measures 25 metres on each side. Its simple square structure is well proportioned and imposing. A spiral staircase leads to each floor and arched windows give a view of the entire city.

During the Tang dynasty, successful candidates in the highest imperial examinations were expected to climb the pagoda and to write an inscription on the wall. Over hundreds of years many scholars have visited the Large Wild Goose Pagoda, leaving their poems and observations.

The pagoda houses many important examples of Tang calligraphy, painting and sculpture. Inset into the walls on the first storey are two stone tablets engraved by Chu Suiliang, a famous Tang calligrapher. The texts are taken from inscriptions by the Tang emperors Taizong and Gaozong and recount Xuanzang's journey to the West in search of Buddhist scriptures and his work translating them into Chinese. On the lintels above the four entrances are Tang Buddhist carvings.

Location

The Large Wild Goose Pagoda is situated within the compound of the Grace Monastery in the southern suburbs of Xi'an. Visitors can reach the pagoda by taking bus 5 or 19 from the city centre.

THE SMALL WILD GOOSE PAGODA
小雁塔

History

The Small Wild Goose Pagoda (Xiaoyanta) was built one hundred days after the death of Emperor Gaozong in AD 684. The emperor's relatives first built a temple, known as the Xianfu (Presenting Happiness) Temple, in honour of him; this was later renamed the Jianfu Temple.

A celebrated monk by the name of Yijing translated a large number of Buddhist scriptures at the Jianfu Monastery. Having travelled to India by sea in AD 671 and studied at a monastery in Nalanda, he spent several years on the Indonesian island of Sumatra on his return journey, and arrived home in AD 695 with some four hundred scriptures. These he translated into Chinese at the Foshouji and Fuxian monasteries in Luoyang, the Ximing Monastery in Chang'an, and finally at the Jianfu Temple, where he died in AD 713. Yijing was a learned and influential scholar who wrote the *Lives of Eminent Tang Monks Who Sought Buddhism in the Western Regions* and *A Record of Buddhist Discipline in the South Seas*, based on his own experiences. These are valuable records of early cultural exchanges between China and the countries of South and South-east Asia.

In AD 707 the pagoda was erected opposite the entrance to the temple. After the chaotic final years of the Tang dynasty, the Jianfu Temple was relocated inside the compound of the pagoda. Since the pagoda is smaller than that of the same name in the Grace Monastery, it is known as the Small Wild Goose Pagoda.

Description

Built entirely of brick, the pagoda was originally a square structure of fifteen storeys with multiple eaves. Several earthquakes caused extensive damage to the upper portion and now only thirteen storeys remain. Square at the base, the pagoda is 45 metres high and each side measures 11.4 metres. The building tapers towards the top and is more graceful than the Large Wild Goose Pagoda. On each storey arched doorways face south and north. Intaglio carvings of celestial figures and floral motifs adorn the lintels of the southern and northern entrances; these are fine examples of Tang art.

Since 1949 the Small Wild Goose Pagoda has been restored in its original architectural style. The foundations have been repaired and the arched doorways on the southern and northern façade have been renovated. The roof of the pagoda has been repaired, and drainage pipes and lightning rods installed. On the second, fifth, seventh, ninth and eleventh storeys steel bands now reinforce the structure. The Jianfu Temple houses a large bell cast in 1192 and precious stone stelae.

See Plate 31

Location

The Small Wild Goose Pagoda is situated within the compound of the Jianfu Temple, 1 kilometre south of Xi'an. Bus 4 goes directly to the pagoda. Alternatively, visitors can take bus 3, alight at Nanshaomen and walk 50 metres to the west.

The Small Wild Goose Pagoda

The three hills of the Qian Mausoleum

THE QIAN MAUSOLEUM
乾陵

History

The Qian Mausoleum (Qianling) was built for Li Zhi, the Tang Emperor Gaozong and his empress Wu Zetian.

Li Zhi, the ninth son of Emperor Taizong, was born in AD 628 and his mother was the Empress Dowager Chang Sun. Helped by his uncle, Li Zhi was chosen to succeed his father in AD 650, and he died in Luoyang in AD 683.

Wu Zetian (AD 624–705) was selected as an imperial concubine by Emperor Taizong and upon his death she became a Buddhist nun in the Ganye Temple. In AD 654 Emperor Gaozong, who had fallen in love with her, restored her to the court and gave her the title of Zhaoyi. In AD 655 he forced Empress Wang to abdicate and made Wu Zetian his empress. From AD 659 Wu began to exert an influence at court and her power grew steadily. After the death of Emperor Gaozong, she was proclaimed sole ruler in AD 690. She changed the dynastic title from Tang to Zhou and reigned for twenty-one years before handing over the throne to Zhongzong and moving

The Blank Tablet

to Luoyang with the honorary title of Supreme Ruler. She died there in AD 705 and was buried with Emperor Gaozong in the Qian Mausoleum.

Description
The Qian Mausoleum comprises three hills, of which the southern pair are artificial. The magnificent northern hill formed the main

part of the mausoleum. Historical records tell of 378 buildings on the site, which was originally surrounded by two walls.

The interior of the mausoleum has yet to be excavated. Archaeological surveys indicate that the grave passage runs from north to south on an incline fashioned from rectangular stones. There are thirty-nine layers of stone from the beginning of the passage to the entrance. Each layer was reinforced with iron plate and sealed with molten iron.

What can be seen at the site today consists primarily of stone stelae with inscriptions or images. These flank the path leading to the mausoleum. Outside the Red Sparrow Gate stand rows of huge stone statues, which include a pair of winged columns (huabiao), 2 winged horses, 2 red sparrows, 5 pairs of horses and 20 statues of court officials. The two realistic stone lions outside the Red Sparrow Gate date from the Qing dynasty.

One of the most prominent tablets is the Shu Sheng Ji Bei, which is fashioned in seven segments. The inscription, which is a eulogy of Emperor Gaozong's cultural and military attainments, was composed by Wu Zetian and the calligraphy was done by the Tang Emperor Zhongzong (AD 684 and 705–9). Another stone tablet to the east is known as the Blank Tablet, and on it Wu Zetian intended posterity to record its judgement of her merits and errors.

Sixty-one stone figures were erected in front of the mausoleum, carved at Wu Zetian's instruction to commemorate the attendance of foreign and local chieftains and envoys at Emperor Gaozong's funeral.

Since 1960 five neighbouring tombs have been excavated. These are the tombs of Princess Yongtai, Prince Yide, Prince Zhanghuai, the Chamberlain Xue Yuanchao and General Li Jin. From these tombs many wall paintings, three-coloured (sancai) pottery and stone carvings have been unearthed.

Location

The Qian Mausoleum is situated in Qianxian county, 85 kilometres from Xi'an. It is accessible by car, bus or coach.

THE CITY WALLS OF XI'AN
西安城墙

History

The size of the walled city of Xi'an was determined in the early Ming dynasty. After the founder of the Ming dynasty, Zhu

The Ming dynasty city walls of Xi'an

Yuanzhang, conquered Huizhou, a hermit named Zhu Sheng said to him: 'Build high walls, store a large quantity of grain and delay your ascent to the throne.' After the founding of the Ming dynasty city walls went up throughout the country. Xi'an was enlarged and its city walls date from the decade between 1370 and 1380. Although Xi'an was smaller than the Ming capitals of Nanjing and Beijing, it was a strategically important city and therefore required strong, high walls.

Description

On foundations of mixed lime, earth and glutinous rice, the walls were built of layers of rammed loess. Prominent terraces were constructed at the four corners of the city, all square in shape apart from the southwestern terrace which was circular. Four watchtowers were also built at the four corners and to the east of the southern entrance stood a building called the Guixinglou. The walls, designed primarily for defence, were surrounded by a deep, wide moat. In front of the city gate was a drawbridge.

The city is rectangular, and the perimeter of the wall measured 11.9 kilometres. The walls were 12 metres high, and the parapet was crenellated so that soldiers could observe or fire on the enemy through small square battlements. The inside of the parapet was ringed by a low protective wall. The only points of entry were four elaborate gates, one on each side of the city, each consisting of a citadel, an embrasured watchtower and an outpost. At the foot of each gate was a barbican where soldiers were stationed. Every 120 metres observation posts jutted out of the wall. As high as the wall itself, they were designed as places where soldiers could fire down on an enemy trying to climb the parapet. Half of the distance between each of these observation posts was within reach of an arrow. A watchtower was built on each of the ninety-eight terraces. Altogether there were 5,984 embrasures on the wall.

Still well preserved are the citadel, barbican and the embrasured watchtowers of the western and eastern gates, and the citadel and barbican of the southern gate.

See Plate 32

Location

Xi'an, Shaanxi province.

Liaoning Province
辽宁省

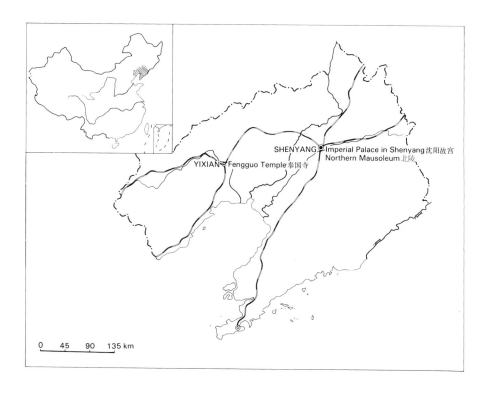

SHENYANG○Imperial Palace in Shenyang 沈阳故宫
Northern Mausoleum 北陵
YIXIAN○Fengguo Temple 奉国寺

0　45　90　135 km

A large hall in the Fengguo Temple

THE FENGGUO TEMPLE
奉国寺

History

The Fengguo Temple (Fengguosi), originally known as the Xianxi Temple, was built in 1020 and flourished during the Liao, Jin and Yuan dynasties. Because there are seven statues of the Buddha in the Mahavira Hall, the temple is more commonly known as the Temple of the Seven Buddhas or simply the Great Buddha Temple. The temple fell into decline after the Yuan dynasty and in the Ming and Qing dynasties the Mahavira Hall was the only Liao dynasty building remaining.

Description

The temple complex is narrow at the front and widens to the rear. Set along its central axis are the main gate, an archway, the Wuliang Hall and the Mahavira Hall.

One of the largest surviving examples of Liao dynasty wooden architecture, the Mahavira Hall is nine bays wide and five bays deep and is built on a vast brick platform. The building has three enormous doors at the front and one at the back. Inside, the square column bases are made of grey sandstone and are elaborately carved with peonies, lotuses and other floral motifs.

Clay figures

On a brick platform at the northern end of the hall are seven imposing polychrome statues of Buddhist deities, all outstanding examples of Liao sculpture. The largest statue is a figure of Vipasyin, 9.5 metres tall. This is flanked by two attendant bodhisattvas, and to the east and west are majestic images of the Heavenly Guardians.

Inside the hall the bracketed beams are decorated with brightly coloured Liao paintings of *apsara*, peonies and other floral motifs. The forty-two *apsara* on the roof beams are particularly fine. Holding offerings of either flowers or fruit, they have a graceful, ethereal quality in contrast to the static, solemn images of the Buddhist deities. Yuan and Ming images of the Buddha, bodhisattvas and arhats can be seen on the walls. In front of each Buddha is a set of twenty-one carved stone sacrificial vessels, and to either side of the platform are eleven stelae dating from the Jin, Yuan, Ming and Qing dynasties and recording the temple's rise and decline.

Location
The Fengguo Temple is located at the northern end of Dongjie Street in the Yixian, Liaoning province.

THE IMPERIAL PALACE IN SHENYANG
沈阳故宫

History
The palace in Shenyang of the Manchu rulers before their conquest of China was first known as the Shengjing Palace and then later as the Fengtian Palace after Manchu troops had entered central China.

In 1625 Nurhaci, whose consolidation of neighbouring tribes and astute military organization paved the way to the Manchu conquest of China, moved his capital from Liaoyang to Shenyang, and in that same year started building a central hall with eight curved roof corners and a bedchamber on a high platform. One year later he died. When his son Abahai took over he began in 1627 to build the Chongzheng Hall, also known as the throne room; it was completed in 1635. This formed the basis of the present-day imperial palace. In 1636 a grand celebration was held to mark the formal establishment of the Qing, and the name of their nationality was changed from Nüzhen to Manchu. The palace was renovated and enlarged under the succeeding Qing rulers Kangxi (1662–1722), Qianlong (1736–95) and Jiaqing (1796–1820).

Description
The imperial palace in Shenyang has more than seventy buildings with over three hundred rooms. Smaller in scale than the Forbidden City in Beijing, it is nevertheless an example of a complete imperial palace complex, enclosed by a high wall. The palace is comprised of three parts: the eastern, central and western parts. The eastern

The Imperial Palace in Shenyang

part consists primarily of the Dazheng Hall flanked by ten square pavilions. The central part includes the main Chongzheng Hall, the Great Qing Gate to the south and the Tranquillity Palace to the north, all on a north-south axis. This section also contains three courtyards. With the Wensuge Library as its centre, the western part includes a theatre, the Jiayin Chamber to the front and the Yangxi Study to rear.

The Dazheng Hall in the eastern part is where Emperor Shunzhi ascended the throne, where grand ceremonies were held and where ministers had audiences with the emperor. The hall is a wooden structure on a Sumeru base, surrounded by a stone balustrade. It is in the pavilion style with its eight sides faced with wood. Its double-tiered yellow tiled roofs have eight upturned curved eaves, and eight multi-coloured glazed tile ridges. The pinnacle consists of a 'precious vase' and a golden sphere. Inside, the caisson ceiling is decorated with dragon motifs and Sanskrit inscriptions. On either side of a central pathway in the front courtyard are distinctive pavilions, the Yiwang Pavilion and the Eight Banner Pavilion. Two

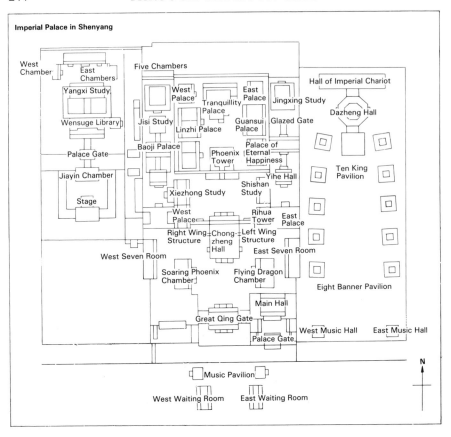

Imperial Palace in Shenyang

animated carved dragons decorate the pillars at the front gate. The Ten King Pavilion once served as administrative offices for the imperial princes and heads of the Eight Banners.

The Chongzheng Hall in the central part of the palace complex is where Abahai held meetings, and received foreign envoys and representatives of ethnic minorities from the border regions. Set on a wide platform, with stone-balustraded verandas to the front and rear, the hall is a five-bay structure with screens separating each room. It has a nine-purlin traditional sloping roof with four overhanging eaves at each corner, and is covered with yellow glazed tiles with a green tiled border. Between two pillars decorated with two golden carved dragons is a huge gold-inlaid screen and a throne. Flanking the Chongzheng Hall are the Flying Dragon Chamber and the Soaring Phoenix Chamber. Behind the hall is the central courtyard, to the east of which is the Shishan Study and to the west the Xiezhong Study and Xiaqi Chamber. Further north stands

The Phoenix Tower

the Inner Palace which is built on a platform and surrounded by a high wall.

The entrance to the Inner Palace is a triple-eaved hipped roofed building known as the Phoenix Tower. Surrounded on the outside by corridors, the tower, three bays wide and long, has a yellow glazed tile roof with a green tiled border. Its doorway leads directly to the Tranquillity Palace where Abahai used to rest or hold banquets. After the Manchu troops occupied central China this palace served as a repository for imperial documents and seals. This palace was the highest structure in Shenyang and was an ideal place from which to view the sunrise.

The Tranquillity Palace is a five-bay building with verandas to the front and rear and an eleven-purlin sloping roof covered with yellow glazed tiles and with a green border. The east wing of the palace once served as a bedchamber for Abahai and his wife and the west wing was where sorcerers conducted their ceremonies. In the southeast corner of the yard stands a pole with a tin bowl in which grain and meat were placed for feeding birds, a Manchu custom. To the east of the Tranquillity Palace stands the Guansui Palace and the Yongfu Palace, and to the west the Linzhi Palace and the Yanqing Palace, all of which served as bedrooms for the imperial concubines. Emperor Shunzhi was born in the Yongfu Palace (Palace of Eternal Happiness).

The Chongzheng Hall is flanked by two groups of buildings. The Jingdian Tower housed imperial family records, and the Chongmo Tower was a repository for the imperial archives. These towers were built between 1746 and 1748.

The Wensuge Library in the western part of the palace complex was built in 1782 to house the *Complete Library in Four Branches of Literature* (*Si ku quan shu*, a collection of 3,450 titles in the four divisions of Classics, History, Philosophy and *Belles-lettres*) compiled between 1773 and 1782. Architecturally it is an imitation of the Tianyige Library in Ningbo, Zhejiang province. It is a two-storey structure, six bays wide, with verandas to the front and rear. The triple-tiered sloping eave roof is covered with black glazed tiles and has a green border. To the east of the library is a pavilion containing a stone tablet with Chinese and Manchu inscriptions.

See Plate 33

Location

The Imperial Palace is situated in the centre of the old part of Shenyang, Liaoning province. It is accessible by bus or car.

THE NORTHERN MAUSOLEUM
北陵

History

The Northern Mausoleum (Beiling) is the final resting place of the Manchu ruler Abahai and his wife. By his military prowess and

The Northern Mausoleum

political acumen Abahai built on the foundation that had been laid by his father, his efforts culminating in the Manchu conquest of China which took place the year after his death in 1643. Originally called Zhaoling, the mausoleum is commonly referred to as the Northern Mausoleum. It is the largest and most elaborate of the three mausolea of pre-conquest Manchu rulers located in Liaoning province.

Construction of the mausoleum was begun in 1643 and completed in 1651, though further improvements were made during the reigns of the Kangxi (1662–1722) and Jiaqing (1796–1820) emperors. After the founding of the People's Republic in 1949 the site of the mausoleum was transformed into a spacious park planted with fine trees and provided with a man-made lake dotted with pavilions.

Description

Built on level ground, the mausoleum occupies an area of 180,000 square metres and is entirely enclosed by a wall. The main entrance to the south, a single-eaved gable-roofed structure pierced by three

The Northern Mausoleum

openings, is known as the Red Front Gate. To the sides are walls decorated with dragons made of coloured glazed tiles. In front of the gate stand stone lions, stone bridges, mounting stones, a stone memorial archway, a dressing pavilion and a sacrificial pavilion. The memorial archway, set directly in front of the gate, is carved out of black Liaoyang stone. With its four columns and three single-eaved gable roofs, it is a fine example of the stonemason's art.

The paved path which leads to the mausoleum from the gate is lined with two pairs of decorative columns, six pairs of stone animals and a pair of large observation pedestals. The two horses, known as 'Little Whitey' and 'Big Whitey', are said to be modelled after two of the emperor's favourite steeds. Further north is another memorial archway with a stone stele inscribed with a description of the mausoleum. To the east and west are buildings used for the preparation of tea and food and for bathing.

Even further north stands the square fortress-like enclosure which is the principal component of the mausoleum. In the centre of the enclosure is the Longen Hall. Built on an elegantly carved granite base, the hall is three bays wide, has four doors and eight windows, and a roof of yellow glazed tiles. The Longen Hall contains two alcoves: in the larger one is a 'precious bed' provided with curtains, pillows and quilts, while in the smaller are the spirit tablets of the deceased emperor and his wife. In front of the alcoves is a selection of palace furniture including 'dragon and phoenix' thrones, an offering table with candle holders and incense burners, and palace lanterns. The ceiling of the hall is finely carved and painted in brilliant colours. Auxiliary halls stand to the east and west of the Longen Hall. The square fortress is provided with four corner towers, and in addition to its southern entrance, the Longen Gate, there is a stele tower to the north which contains a stele inscribed with the name of the tomb's principal occupant. The domed tomb itself, under which lie the remains of Abahai and his wife, stands to the north of the fortress.

See Plate 34

Location

The Northern Mausoleum is located in the northern suburbs of Shenyang, Liaoning province.

Heilongjiang Province
黑龙江省

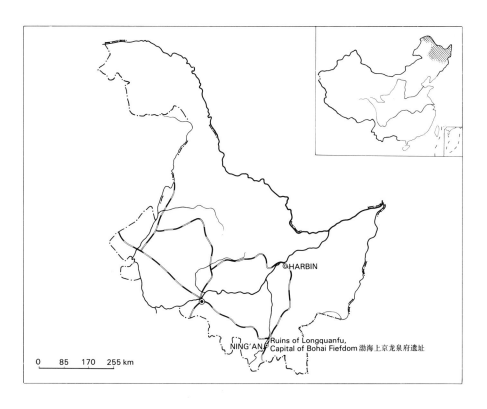

One of the palaces at Longquanfu

THE RUINS OF LONGQUANFU, CAPITAL OF THE BOHAI FIEFDOM

渤海上京龙泉府遗址

History

Bohai was a local fiefdom established in northeast China by the Sumo tribe of the Mohe people in the Tang dynasty. It was founded by Da Zuorong, chieftain of the tribe, in AD 698. In AD 713 the Tang emperor appointed him as governor of Huhan prefecture, Great General and Prince of Bohai. Thereafter, the Sumo area became a prefecture under Tang government rule, lasting for a period of 229 years, from the time of Da Zuorong to its last ruler Da Yinzhuan. It was destroyed eventually by the Khitans.

Longquanfu was twice the Bohai capital during the reigns of its third king Da Qingmo and of its fifth king Da Huayu, a total of more than 160 years. As such it was the largest and most enduring of the Bohai capitals. The city was built in the mid-eighth century by King Da Qingmo in imitation of the Tang capital Chang'an (present-day Xi'an). The scale of present-day Longquanfu was determined during the reign of Da Qingmo, while palaces and other buildings were actually constructed during the reign of the eleventh king. The town was destroyed when the Bohai state was conquered in AD 926.

Description

Longquanfu, rectangular in plan, may be divided into the outer town, the inner town, and the palace district which lay inside the inner town. The outer town, which had a perimeter of over 17 kilometres, was the residential area of the general populace. The city wall, built of rammed earth and stone, was over 2 metres high.

All that remains of the inner town today are a stone lamp and a stone statue of the Buddha. This walled town, which contained government offices and officials' dwellings, was rectangular with a perimeter of 4.5 kilometres. East of the palaces was the Forbidden, or Royal, Garden, in which there was once an oval pond flanked by rockeries.

The walled, rectangular palace district was the political centre as well as the home of the Bohai rulers. The Southern Gate was the main entrance to this district and a section of it still survives. There are ruins of five palaces, all on a central north-south axis. The first hall was the Throne Chamber, set on a foundation of rectangular stones, on which are forty large pillar plinths. Each main hall had two side halls, forming a separate complex, and five such complexes were linked by long corridors. To the east of the second hall was an octagonal well, known as the Eight Treasure Glazed Well.

The main finds from the ruins are building materials, mainly grey tiles with impressed textile designs. Also found were a number of small Buddhist images in iron, bronze or pottery, similar in style and technique to those of the Central Plains.

To the east of the ruins are groups of Sariputra stone reliquaries whose shape and decoration are similar to those found in Jingchuan county, Gansu province.

Location

The ruins of Longquanfu are located in the town of Dongjing in Ning'an county, Heilongjiang province.

Inner Mongolia
內蒙古

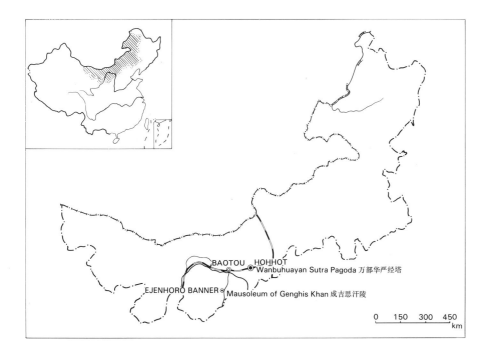

BAOTOU   HOHHOT

Wanbuhuayan Sutra Pagoda 万部华严经塔

EJENHORO BANNER◎   Mausoleum of Genghis Khan 成吉思汗陵

0   150   300   450
km

The Wanbuhuayan Sutra Pagoda

THE WANBUHUAYAN SUTRA PAGODA
万部华严经塔

History

Also known as the White Pagoda, the Wanbuhuayan Sutra Pagoda was built between AD 983 and 1031 and is one of the few relatively complete structures remaining from the old Liao city of Fengzhou. As such it is a valuable example of early Chinese architecture. A Yuan inscription verifies that it was once part of the Xuanjiao Temple.

According to historical records, the Wanbuhuayan Sutra Pagoda was renovated in 1162 on imperial instruction. Renovations and maintenance work were carried out during each succeeding dynasty, but the original design and structure remain unchanged.

Description

Constructed in brick and wood, the octagonal, seven-storey structure is built in the storeyed pavilion style. Above the south entrance on the first storey is carved 'Wanbuhuayan Sutra Pagoda'. Each storey has two round-arched doors as well as two false doors, the position of which alternates from storey to storey in order to create a sense of movement and balance. On the other four faces of the octagonal pagoda are the *zhiling* windows which were popular at the time. On the second storey there are images of the Buddha, bodhisattvas, Heavenly Kings and other deities, all executed in brick and considered to be masterpieces of Liao sculpture. Each storey of the pagoda is girdled by eaves and a railing.

Inside the pagoda a spiral staircase leads to the top. On the interior wall of the first storey are six stelae dating from the Jin dynasty and on the other walls are inscriptions by visitors from various dynasties. The majority are in Chinese but the presence of some in Mongolian, Tibetan, Khitan, Xixia and Nüzhen shows that the temple was visited by people of different nationalities and illustrates the close contact betweeen Han Chinese and other ethnic groups.

Location

The Wanbuhuayan Pagoda is located west of Baita village in the eastern suburbs of Hohhot, capital of Inner Mongolia. In the Liao dynasty the village site was part of the northwest section of the city of Fengzhou. The temple can be reached by bus from central Hohhot.

The Mausoleum of Genghis Khan

THE MAUSOLEUM OF GENGHIS KHAN
成吉思汗陵

History
Genghis Khan was the founder of the Yuan dynasty and is one of the most outstanding statesmen and strategists in Chinese history. He established the Mongol empire by uniting numerous Mongolian tribes, and in 1227, while leading his troops against the Xixia (Tangut), fell ill and died in Qingshui county, southeast of the Lupan mountain. In accordance with his last wishes, Genghis Khan was buried on the Ordos plateau, a site he is said to have chosen on one of his expeditions. So taken was he by its breathtaking beauty that his whip slipped from his fingers, and he asked to be buried at the spot where it fell. The place became known as Ejenhoro or the Master's Resting Place. Ever since his death, mass gatherings known as *suluding* have been held each spring to honour his memory. The word *suluding* means spear and symbolizes Genghis Khan's prowess as a strategist and warrior.

In order to prevent the mausoleum from being plundered during the anti-Japanese war, the coffin was moved in the summer of 1939 to Xinglongshan in Gansu province. In 1949 it was moved once again, this time to the Ta'er Lamasery in Qinghai province. It was later returned to its original site. In 1954 a special renovation fund was allocated by the central government and a monument, bearing Genghis Khan's name in gold lettering in both Mongolian and Chinese, was erected.

Description

The site of the mausoleum covers an area of 1,500 square metres and the main complex consists of three interconnecting halls in the shape of traditional Mongolian tents. The central hall has a multi-panelled dome with an exquisitely painted caisson ceiling; the two adjoining buildings, used as display halls, have single domes. All the buildings are octagonal. Their golden pinnacles are inlaid with blue glazed tiles in the shape of clouds, and their roof ridges are made of glazed tiles. In front of the memorial hall stand two flagpoles, between which is an incense burner. On an altar lies a sabre said to have belonged to Genghis Khan, and a statue of him stands in the centre of the hall. On either side of the statue are silver halberds and *suluding* with red tassels and yellow staffs. Contemporary paintings illustrating events in the life of Genghis Khan decorate the walls of the corridors. In the bedroom to the rear is a saddle believed to have been used by Genghis Khan, as well as the coffins of three of his wives and those of his grandson Kuyuk and his wife.

Location

Genghis Khan's mausoleum is located in Ejenhoro Banner on Gande'er hill, 15 kilometres southeast of Atensilen, Inner Mongolia. It can be reached by bus from Baotou.

Ningxia Province
宁夏省

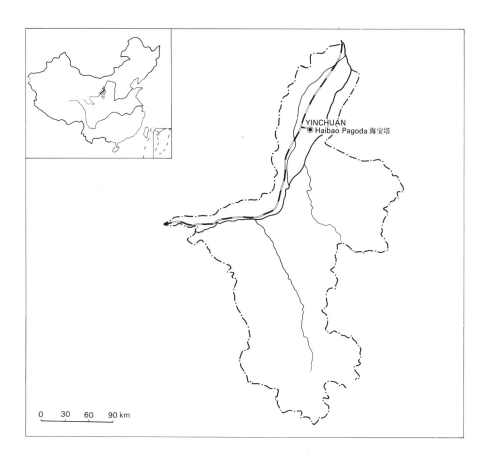

YINCHUAN
Haibao Pagoda 海宝塔

0   30   60   90 km

THE HAIBAO PAGODA
海宝塔

History

The Haibao Pagoda (Haibaota) was originally known as the Heibao Pagoda and according to the Ming dynasty *New Gazetteer of Ningxia*, 'It is situated three *li* north of the city and the original reasons for its construction are unknown.' *The Revised Records of the Haibao Pagoda*, compiled in the reign of the Qing Emperor Kangxi (1662–1722), says that it was renovated by the Xiongnu chieftain, Helian Bobo, and thus became known as the Helian Pagoda. Since there is a strong similarity between the three names, Haibao, Heibao and Helian Bobo, it is quite likely that the pagoda was named after Helian Bobo, whose kingdom of Xia (AD 407–31) was one of the Sixteen Kingdoms which ruled over west and north China during the period contemporaneous with the Eastern Jin in south China. A devout Buddhist, Helian Bobo rose to power by allying himself with King Yao Xing of the Later Qin. Having consolidated his power through military force, he established the Xia Kingdom. He founded twelve major cities, and it is probable that he also had temples and pagodas built in some of them.

The Qing *Gazetteer of Ningxia Prefecture*, which was compiled before the renovation of the pagoda in the reign of Kangxi, states that 'the Heibao Pagoda has thirteen storeys which rise up to the clouds. On the staircase leading upwards from the seventh storey, one hears on clear days the sighing of wind as though in a great void.' The exterior of the building underwent great changes during large-scale renovations in 1712. The spiral was moved inside the pagoda and the original thirteen storeys were reduced to the eleven which survive today.

Description

The eleven-storey brick pagoda, which rests on a square base, is 53.9 metres in height and is built in the pavilion style. A bridge to the rear connects the Weituo and Wofo Halls, both of which stand on the same base as the pagoda.

The pagoda itself is built in the form of a Maltese cross, a most unusual form for a pavilion-style pagoda in China. At the entrance to the first storey is a tiny devotion room at the rear of which is an arch facing an arhat niche. On each side of this are brick staircases leading to the top of the pagoda. There is an arch in the centre of each storey and false niches to each side of it. Above the arch and

The Haibao Pagoda

the niches of each floor are three rows of lozenge-shaped serrations. Beginning at the second storey there are an additional three layers of stepped stone slabs above these serrations, serving as the base for the arch and niches of the storey above.

The interior of the pagoda is also designed in the form of a Maltese cross. Beginning at the second storey, each storey is provided with wooden steps and wooden floorboards. In the centre of each storey is a square room, the width of which decreases by some 15 to 20 centimetres on each successive storey.

The form and construction of the top of the pagoda differ significantly from other Chinese pagodas. Made of green glazed tiles in the form of a four-sided pyramid, it has neither the standard decorative crown nor a precious jewel at its peak.

The Haibao Pagoda is unique among pagodas in China. From its upper storeys there is a most impressive view of the outskirts of Yinchuan, the Yellow river and the Jialan mountains.

Location

The Haibao Pagoda is located in the western suburbs of Yinchuan, the capital of Ningxia province.

Gansu Province
甘肃省

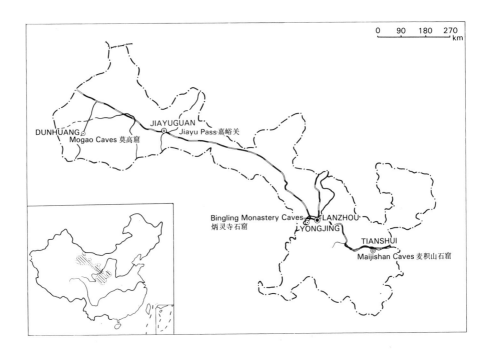

The Mogao Caves near Dunhuang

THE MOGAO CAVES NEAR DUNHUANG
莫高窟

History

The Mogao Caves near Dunhuang, also known as the Caves of the Thousand Buddhas, are one of the three most famous cave temple sites in China.

In the Han dynasty Dunhuang was a prefecture in Hexi, which lay west of the Yellow river in what are now Gansu and Qinghai provinces. It was an important staging post on the Silk Road. At the end of the Western Han Buddhism was introduced from India to China. By the end of the Eastern Han, Dunhuang was a flourishing town, one of the major Buddhist centres in China. History relates that one evening in AD 366 a monk named Lezun arrived at the foot of the Mingsha mountain near Dunhuang. In a vision he saw the Sanwei mountain, which lies opposite the Mingsha mountain, shining with a golden light, as from thousands of images of the Buddha, so he hollowed out the first cave from the cliff of the Mingsha mountain. Not long afterwards another monk, Faliang, dug a second cave beside the first. Over a period of almost one

The Buddha in Nirvana, Cave 158

thousand years, through the Western Liang, Northern Wei, Western Wei, Northern Zhou, Sui, Tang, Five Dynasties, Song, Western Xia and Yuan, row after row of caves were hollowed out of the cliff and together they formed the magnificent Caves of the Thousand Buddhas.

Description
The Mogao Caves, which stretch for 1,600 metres along the Mingsha mountain cliff near Dunhuang, can be divided into two groups: the southern and the northern group. The caves containing wall paintings and painted sculptures are concentrated on the southern side. On the northern side there are only four caves with wall paintings, and the remaining two to three hundred probably served to accommodate monks, priests, painters and sculptors. Today 492 caves survive with 2,100 statues and 45,000 square metres of wall paintings. There are, in addition, five wooden structures which were built during the Tang and Song dynasties.

The earliest of the 2,415 painted sculptures are statues carved during the Northern Wei dynasty. They are characterized by broad

Northern Wei statue of the Buddha

foreheads, elongated eyes and brows, a high nose bridge, thin lips, and wavy and coiled hair, and show the influence of Indian art. During the Sui dynasty a more sinicized style evolved: statues of the Buddha have full cheeks, a less pointed nose, ears with large lobes, and plump hands and feet. The Sui statues are outnumbered by those of the Tang dynasty, of which there are 670. The Tang statues are more lifelike, their faces suggestive of inner emotions. Most of the Buddha figures sit cross-legged and have a benign, graceful air. All the images of bodhisattvas have elongated eyes and brows, and gently smiling mouths, and they are bare chested and bare armed. It is the images of arhats which best display individual characteristics, examples being the sophisticated Ananda and the innocent Kasyapa. Also outstanding are the militant warriors of the Heavenly King. The Tang statues are the largest, and include the 33-metre statue in Cave 96 which was carved out of the cliff and then covered with clay.

The wall paintings of the Mogao Caves are the finest of all ancient Chinese murals. Thematically and stylistically rich, they depict the jataka stories of the life of the Buddha, stories of his previous incarnations, tales from Buddhist scriptures, as well as celestial beings and worshippers who donated money for the construction of the caves. Most of the wall paintings executed during the Northern and Western Wei dynasties show the Buddha preaching and also illustrate stories of his previous lives. Most of the Tang wall paintings illustrate the scriptures, mainly those of the Pure Land Sect which was the predominant Buddhist sect during the Tang dynasty.

In the wall paintings depicting the jataka stories and the scriptures, there are scenes of everyday life, of hunting, ploughing, tree felling and making pottery, and of weddings and funerals — all of these are extremely valuable for the study of Tang society. All the wall paintings are executed in gouache, except for those in one Yuan cave which are done in watercolours.

In 1900 more than 20,000 manuscripts dating from the fourth to the eleventh century were discovered in a pit in one of the Mogao Caves. These manuscripts are of great historical and literary value, as they provide information on religion, history, literature, art and daily life.

See Plate 35

Location

The Mogao Caves are located in the Mingsha mountain, 25 kilometres southeast of Dunhuang, Gansu province. From Beijing one may go by air to Lanzhou and change planes for Dunhuang, or one may go by train to Liuyuan and then by bus. The caves are accessible by bus, coach or car from the town of Dunhuang.

The colossal Tang dynasty seated Buddha in niche 171 at Bingling

THE BINGLING MONASTERY CAVES
炳灵寺石窟

History
The Bingling Monastery (Binglingsi) Caves, some of the best known in China, were begun during the Sixteen States period (AD 304–439). More caves were added by later generations.

Description
The majority of the Bingling Caves are spread along 2 kilometres of red cliff running from south to north at Dasigou. They are divided into three groups: the Upper Monastery, Donggou and the Lower Monastery. Today 195 niches dating from the Sixteen States period to the Qing dynasty survive. There are altogether 694 stone statues, 82 clay figures, more than 900 square metres of wall paintings and five stone or clay pagodas. The largest sculpture is over 30 metres in height and the smallest is only 20 centimetres.

Most of the niches and sculptures on the cliffs are made of stone. Of these, two-thirds date from the Tang. These full-bodied statues,

Tang dynasty standing Buddha and two bodhisattvas in niche 64

brimming with vitality, assume unique postures which are one of
the distinctive features of the sculpture of the Bingling Caves. The
Tang bodhisattva in Cave 50 is straight-legged but the upper part
of the torso turns slightly to the right in a supple, graceful pose.
The head inclines left, and the full face wears a lively expression.
The upper torso is rounded and robust, and the right hand holds
a bottle in upturned fingers while the left arm is bent upwards.
Although the posture is very difficult to imitate naturally, it does
not seem at all artificial. The damaged Tang statue of Avalokitesvara
in Cave 98 has an innocent and lively quality. The Tang seated
Buddha in the cliff at the Lower Monastery is over 30 metres high;
the lower portion is made of clay while the upper is carved from
the natural rock peak. The Northern Wei sculptures in Caves 126
and 128 are graceful and serene while the Western Qin carvings in
Cave 169 are vigorous, simple and sturdy. In the wall paintings in
Cave 169 the flowing sleeves of deities are particularly colourful.
An inscription on the wall, 'The first year of the reign of Emperor
Jianhong in the Western Qin dynasty' (AD 420), is the earliest
known cave inscription in China.

Location

The Bingling Monastery Caves are located in the Little Jishi mountains on the north bank of the Yellow river, 50 kilometres southwest of Yongjing in Gansu province.

THE MAIJISHAN CAVES
麦积山石窟

History

Maiji mountain (Maijishan), a solitary mountain with an almost perpendicular cliff face, is situated at the western end of the mountain range known as Qinling. The mountain is 130 metres high and shaped like a stack of wheat, hence the name Maiji (Wheat-stack) mountain.

Caves were first cut into the cliff and a monastery built at the foot of the mountain in the years AD 384–417 under the kingdom of Hou Qin, one of the sixteen kingdoms which held sway in west and north China during the period contemporaneous with the Eastern Jin dynasty in South China. Over three hundred monks were housed here during the early AD 420s under the noted abbots Tanhong and Xuangao. In AD 535 repairs to the cliff pavilion and the monastery were carried out, and from the Sui to the Qing more caves were dug. An earthquake split the mountain in AD 734 and divided the caves into eastern and western sections.

Description

The caves on Maijishan number 194 (54 to the east, 140 to the west), and they contain over 7,000 clay and stone statues of varying sizes and more than 1,300 square metres of wall paintings. The main caves and structures in the eastern section are the Nirvana cave, the Thousand Buddha Veranda, the Seven Buddha Pavilion above the Scattering Flowers Building, the Ox Chamber and the Central Seven Buddha Pavilion. The design of the caves and niches is in imitation of Chinese architecture in wood. Pillars were carved and then caves were hollowed out. In the western section are the famous Ten Thousand Buddha Chamber and the Paradise Cave. The carvings illustrate the evolution of sculpture over a period of more than 1,500 years.

The largest statue is 15 metres in height and the smallest is 20 centimetres. Cave 142 contains 81 statues. All the major images have emaciated features with topknots, thin necks and sunken chests,

Maijishan

The Ten Thousand Buddha Chamber

and are dressed in neat, symmetrical garments with high collars and long skirts. The robes and ornaments of the Buddha are richly coloured and have two streamers, characteristic of the Northern Wei dynasty. The Sui Buddha in Cave 13 is 15 metres high, and can be seen from the entrance to the Maiji mountain gorge. A statue of a deity at the entrance to Cave 133 is vivid and lifelike, the body slightly stooped, the head bowed, and the arms long and graceful with nimble fingers. The Song dynasty statue of the Buddha in Cave 156 has an elongated face, a calm expression, and wears simple garments. The robe folds and the apparent elasticity of the skin create contrasting textures quite unlike anything to be seen in the Song dynasty sculpture in the Mogao Caves near Dunhuang.

The Maijishan wall paintings are rich in variety, and are vividly painted with steady yet powerful brushstrokes. The best-known paintings are in the Seven Buddha Chamber above the Scattering Flowers Building in the eastern section.

Location

The Maijishan caves are 45 kilometres southeast of Tianshui, Gansu province. They can be reached by train from Xi'an or Lanzhou to Tianshui, and from there by coach.

THE JIAYU PASS
嘉峪关

History

During the Han and Tang dynasties the Jiayu Pass area was under the jurisdiction of Jiuquan, before becoming part of Suzhoulu in the Yuan dynasty. In 1372 it became a military pass with cavalry and munitions depots. A citadel was built in 1495. In 1506 more buildings, including the Eastern Building and the Western Building inside the town, the yamen and warehouses were constructed. In 1539 a wall, which was 50 kilometres long and passed right through the town, was built, thus forming a relatively comprehensive defence system.

Description

The Jiayu Pass was the western end of the Great Wall in the Ming dynasty. To the south is the Wenshu mountain, part of the Qilian range, and to the north is the Black mountain; between these two mountains is a level valley of 15 square kilometres. The Jiayu Pass

The Jiayu Pass

was built on a rocky mound in the valley, 1,625 metres above sea level. A particularly narrow section of the Hexi corridor, this valley has always been a place of strategic importance.

The settlement at Jiayu Pass comprises an outer town, an inner town, a barbican, a citadel and several auxiliary buildings. The entire tortoise-shaped complex was strongly fortified, and the outer town

The citadel

was surrounded by a wall 1,100 metres long. The western end of the outer town is called Luocheng and has a convex wall. This wall, made of rammed earth covered with bricks on a stone foundation, is 10.5 metres high. At the point where the wall juts out in the centre there is an arched gate with two iron-plated doors. This is the principal entrance, and on the lintel is inscribed 'Jiayu Pass'. On the crenellated wall there were observation holes, lamp niches and arrow chutes. There are tower corners at each end of both the southern and northern corners of the town.

The inner town, shaped like a trapezium with a wider eastern end, and with a wall of rammed loess and adobe, served as the pass headquarters. This inner town has two entrances, the Guanghua Gate in the east and the Ruoyuan Gate in the west. On top of each gate is an imposing three-storey tower with three sets of eaves, carved rafters, painted beams, painted walls, and upturned eave-corners. On the north, behind each gate, is a wide pathway leading to the top of the wall. At each of the four corners of the inner town is a square, two-storey tower with observation holes on all sides.

At the centre of both the southern and northern walls is a two-bay tower where soldiers on duty could rest and where weapons were stored. Outside the eastern and western gates are barbicans. On the lintel of the gate of the eastern barbican is carved 'Zhao Zong' ('Paying Homage to the Emperor') and of the western barbican 'Hui Ji' (Meeting the Supreme Lord').

See Plate 36

Location

The Jiayu Pass is on the western side of the Hexi corridor in Gansu province, more than 30 kilometres west of the city of Jiayuguan. It is accessible by train from Lanzhou.

Qinghai Province
青海省

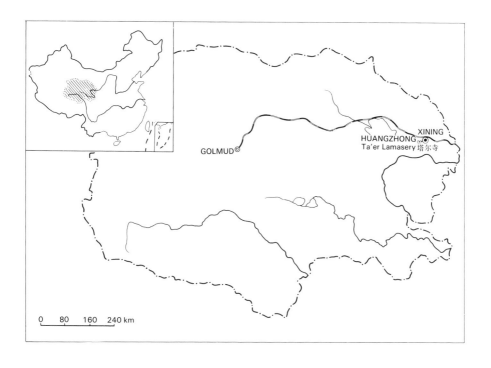

THE TA'ER LAMASERY
塔尔寺

History

The Ta'er Lamasery (Ta'ersi), one of the most famous Buddhist temples of the Yellow Hat Sect of Lamaism, was built in 1560. During its most prosperous era, the lamasery had 52 halls of various sizes and more than 9,300 chambers and dormitories which housed as many as 3,600 monks. It was the Buddhist centre of northwest China, known throughout the country and Southeast Asia.

Description

The Ta'er Lamasery occupies a site of about 40,000 square metres and is comprised of a number of halls, chambers, pagodas and dormitories built in a fusion of Han and Tibetan architectural styles.

The main structure, the Greater Golden Tile Hall, is a Han-style hall with three-tiered sloping eaves, built in 1561. In this lamasery stands a pagoda known as the Great Silver Pagoda. Legend has it that after the birth of Tsong-kha-pa, the founder of the Yellow Hat Sect, his mother buried the afterbirth on this spot. Later a bodhi tree grew up, and on its leaves appeared designs of roaring lions. His mother then had a small pagoda built on the site, and it was on this foundation that the Great Silver Pagoda was later constructed.

The Great Prayer Chamber, a typical Tibetan-style structure with a flat roof, was first built in 1606 and later enlarged several times. Today it is a large hall with 168 pillars, including 60 within the walls. Of the pillars, 108 are carved with exquisite designs, and bound by coloured fabric decorated with bright ribbons and streamers. In the hall hang colourful silk banners decorated with Buddhist symbols, and formerly there were a thousand hassocks used by pilgrims. Lamas from the lamasery's four schools, namely, the Xi'an School, the Esoteric School, the Shilun School (astronomy, almanacs and oracles) and the Medicine School, recited sutras and gave lectures in this hall.

The Nine-bay Hall was built in 1626. The three northern bays contain a statue of Tathagata, and in the three bays in the middle stand statues of Manjusri, Avalokitesvara and Vajrapani. In the three bays to the south is a statue of Tsong-kha-pa, flanked by statues of lamas wearing red or yellow hats. In front of this hall is a courtyard where lamas preached and performed their religious services. The Lesser Golden Tile Hall was built in 1631. It contains a number of grotesquely featured guardian figures.

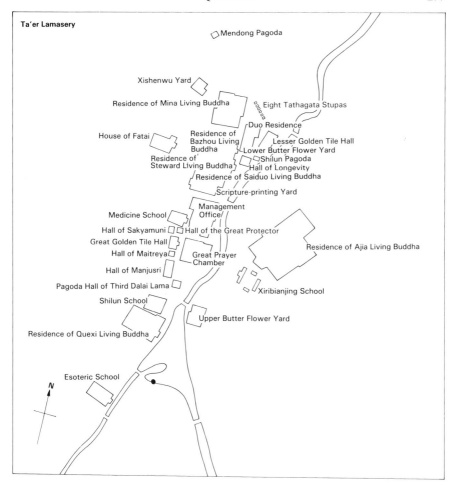

Ta'er Lamasery

Mendong Pagoda

Xishenwu Yard

Residence of Mina Living Buddha

Eight Tathagata Stupas

Duo Residence

House of Fatai

Residence of Bazhou Living Buddha

Lesser Golden Tile Hall

Lower Butter Flower Yard

Residence of Steward Living Buddha

Shilun Pagoda

Hall of Longevity

Residence of Saiduo Living Buddha

Scripture-printing Yard

Management Office

Medicine School

Hall of Sakyamuni

Hall of the Great Protector

Great Golden Tile Hall

Hall of Maitreya

Great Prayer Chamber

Residence of Ajia Living Buddha

Hall of Manjusri

Pagoda Hall of Third Dalai Lama

Xiribianjing School

Shilun School

Upper Butter Flower Yard

Residence of Quexi Living Buddha

Esoteric School

N

In front of the lamasery are the eight Tathagata Stupas, which serve as a symbol of the lamasery. They were built in 1776. All eight are white in colour and of similar size and shape, with a square base, a rounded upper portion and a pointed top. Another of the numerous pagodas at the Ta'er Lamasery is the Bodhi Pagoda, built in 1711, which contains 100,000 bricks, each carved with an image of the Buddha; the Ta'er Lamasery was consequently also known as the Temple of the One Hundred Thousand Buddhas.

See Plate 37

Location

The Ta'er Lamasery is situated in Huangzhong county, 25 kilometres from Xining, Qinghai province. It is accessible by bus, mini-bus or car from Xining.

Xinjiang Province
新疆省

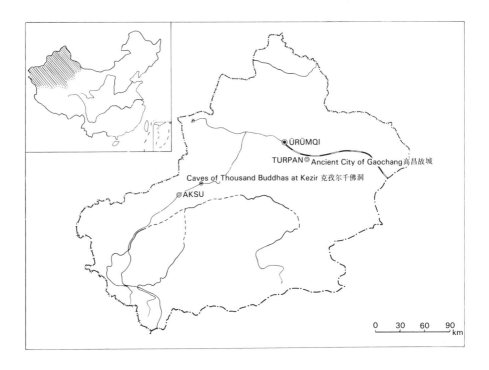

ÜRÜMQI

TURPAN ◎ Ancient City of Gaochang 高昌故城

Caves of Thousand Buddhas at Kezir 克孜尔千佛洞

◎ AKSU

0 30 60 90
km

Ruins of Gaochang

THE ANCIENT CITY OF GAOCHANG
高昌故城

History

Gaochang was a garrison town during the Han dynasty. In AD 327, during the suzerainty of the Former Liang Kingdom, the prefecture of Gaochang was established. Juqu Wuwei, brother of the Northern Liang ruler Juqu Maoqian, subsequently founded the kingdom of Gaochang. Following the downfall of the Northern Liang in AD 439, several kings ruled successively over the kingdom of Gaochang. In AD 640 Gaochang became part of the Tang empire and was renamed Xichang. After the Tang the area fell under Huihe, Western Liao and Yuan rule, and was ultimately abandoned during the early Ming after a history of some 1,500 years.

Description

The imposing scale of the ruined city of Gaochang reflects its former splendour. Built on loess, the city has a square wall made of rammed earth and with a perimeter of approximately 5 kilometres, containing an area of approximately 2 square kilometres. The city was divided into three sections: the outer, the inner and the royal sections, similar to the divisions of the Tang capital of Chang'an (present-day Xi'an). Battlements extend from the city wall. On the west side of the wall can be found two gates, one of which remains in a good state of repair, and from which can be had glimpses of the winding layout of the inner city. Ruins of two temples are to be seen at the south-east and south-west sides of the outer wall. The remains of the south-western temple are more extensive, covering an area of about 10,000 square metres. The temple's former glory can still be gauged from the crumbling main hall and the multi-storeyed pagoda with exquisitely painted niches. To the northeast and southeast of this ruined temple are the remains of workshops with numerous pottery shards, suggesting that these were artisans' dwellings.

At the centre of the inner city is a large round fort inside which is the Khan's Castle. At the centre of the blockhouse is a fifth-century stele, the oldest to have been found in Gaochang. It is believed that the fort may have been the site of a Buddhist temple in the kingdom of Northern Liang. In the far north of the city is the palace. The northern walls of the inner and outer city form the northern and southern walls of the royal area. In this section are the badly damaged remains of several residences.

See Plate 38

Location

Gaochang is located to the east of Astana, 40 kilometres southeast of Turpan, Xinjiang province.

THE CAVES OF THE THOUSAND BUDDHAS AT KEZIR
克孜尔千佛洞

History

The Ten Thousand Buddha Caves at Kezir may be compared with those of Dunhuang, Longmen and Yungang, China's most famous sites of early Buddhist art. The caves, which were begun around the third century AD and continued until the Tang dynasty, predate the earliest of the Mogao Caves near Dunhuang by fifty to one hundred years.

The Caves of the Thousand Buddhas

Description
The Caves of the Thousand Buddhas at Kezir are hollowed out of
the cliffs on the north bank of the Muzat river, and extend for a
distance of 2 kilometres. Of the 236 caves, 75 are well preserved
with a total of 10,000 square metres of wall paintings which, if judged
by their artistic merit, are second only to those of Dunhuang. Many
of the caves contain inscriptions in the Kuchean language, and
several contain remnants of sculpture. The remains of Buddhist

Wall painting in one of the caves

temples are visible on the peak above Cave 10 and in front of
Cave 220.

The Buddhist caves at Kezir served several different functions.
There were chapels for the worship of Buddhist images, places for
meditation and study, residences for Buddhist monks and nuns,
repositories for the ashes of the dead (arhat caves), and warehouses
for general storage. The fact that the caves served different functions
is a unique feature, for later cave complexes built to the east of

Yumenguan, such as Dunhuang, and in the Central Plains, such as Yungang and Longmen, were used mainly for worship, caves for meditation and study being very rare.

At Kezir most of the caves used for worship are rectangular and divided into two chambers. The outer chamber is generally tall and spacious, the wall which divides the caves being covered with niches designed to hold Buddhist images. The side walls are for the most part painted with subjects of an allegorical nature, while the ceiling is covered with a series of lozenge-shaped paintings depicting the jataka tales. Two passageways lead through the dividing wall to the main chamber. The ceilings of these passageways are also decorated with jataka tales, while on each side there are paintings of worshippers, bodhisattvas in attitudes of worship, and the eight heavenly dragons. The rear chamber is relatively narrow and poorly lit. The rear wall contains a niche with a sculpture of the Buddha attaining the state of Nirvana, and behind this, on the wall itself, is a painting of disciples and bodhisattvas in mourning. The front wall of the rear chamber is painted with scenes of the burning of coffins and the disposal of relic bones, above which are musicians playing celestial music, and hovering *apsara*. The various elements of these caves combine to form a striking artistic unity.

The wall paintings are the finest artistic treasures of Kezir. Among these, those illustrating the various Buddhist jataka tales are perhaps the most extraordinary. Cave 17, for example, contains thirty-eight of them, the finest at Kezir. At Dunhuang, such narrative wall paintings dating from the Northern Wei dynasty are in the 'comic-strip' format of sequential incidents, while at Kezir one entire story is arranged within a single lozenge. Notable examples are the Caitya jataka, in which a human sacrifice is carried out in order to feed a tiger, and the Monkey King jataka, in which the Monkey King transforms himself into a bridge in order to save the lives of the other monkeys. In these paintings the principal characters are depicted realistically, while the backgrounds are executed in a more decorative style, a technique which emphasizes the content of the story. In addition, a number of paintings provide details of everyday life.

Location

The Caves of the Thousand Buddhas at Kezir are located 7 kilometres to the southeast of the Kezir district of Baicheng, Xinjiang province.

Tibet
西藏

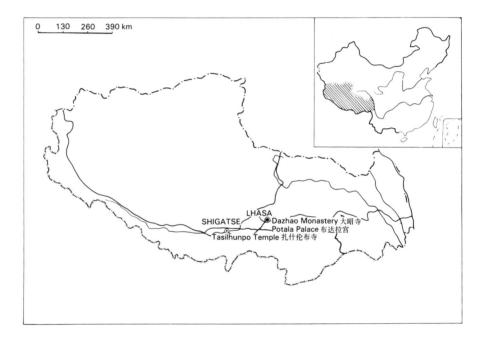

0   130   260   390 km

SHIGATSE   LHASA
Dazhao Monastery 大昭寺
Potala Palace 布达拉宫
Tasilhunpo Temple 扎什伦布寺

The Dazhao Monastery

THE DAZHAO MONASTERY
大昭寺

History

Srong-brtsan-sgam-po, the king who ruled Tibet from *c.* AD 630 to 650, had two consorts, the Nepalese Princess Chizun and the Chinese Princess Wencheng, a kinswoman of the Tang Emperor Taizong. Both consorts were devout Buddhists. The Dazhao Monastery (Dazhaosi) was designed by Princess Wencheng to harmonize with the surrounding terrain and was built by the Nepalese Princess Chizun. Having been restored several times, it underwent major renovations during the reign of the fifth Dalai Lama in the mid-seventeenth century. By then it had become a large complex of buildings occupying more than 21,000 square metres.

Description

Tibetan architecture is a subdivision of Chinese architecture, and the Dazhao Monastery displays not only Tibetan characteristics, but also architectural features from the Tang dynasty, and from Nepal and India. The monastery was built on an east-west axis with

The gilt-bronze statue of Sakyamuni

the main hall in the centre, surrounded by a sutra hall, a hall for Buddhist images and administrative offices. The buildings are so arranged that the spaces between them are of various shapes.

Most of the main buildings and courtyards are square or rectangular. The four-storey main hall is surmounted by a golden roof. In a niche inside the main hall is a life-sized gilt-bronze statue of the twelve-year-old Sakyamuni, said to have been brought from Chang'an (present-day Xi'an) by Princess Wencheng. In the side halls are statues of King Srong-brtsan-sgam-po, Princess Wencheng and Princess Chizun. Twenty wooden pillars in the main hall are decorated with superb high-relief carvings of human figures, swans and elephants. Beneath the eaves of the second and third floors are 108 sculptures of human-faced lions and other animals, a decorative arrangement rarely seen in Chinese architecture. However, the system of brackets inserted between the top of the column and the crossbeams and the roof of the main hall are typical of traditional architecture. The high level of gilding skills is indicated by the golden roof, its Wheel of the Law and the reclining deer.

An important feature of the monastery is the wall painting in the long corridor which covers an area of some 4,400 square metres. The 108 paintings depicting the jataka stories of the life of the Buddha illustrate the 108 merits of Sakyamuni. There are also many well-preserved historical artefacts dating from the Tang. In front of the monastery stands the 'Princess Willow' and a tablet in commemoration of the alliance between the Tang rulers and Tibet.

Location
The Dazhao Monastery is situated in the centre of Lhasa, capital of the Tibet Autonomous Region.

THE TASILHUNPO TEMPLE
扎什伦布寺

History
The Tasilhunpo (Zhashilunbo) Temple was founded in 1447 by dGe-'dun-grub-pa (1391–1475), who was a disciple of Tsong-kha-pa, the forefather of the Yellow Hat Sect, and who retrospectively became the first Dalai Lama. The temple was renovated and expanded by succeeding Dalai Lamas to become the structure it is today. In 1600 the fourth Panchen Lama was invited by the temple to be its head and after that it became the residence of all Panchen Lamas.

Description
The Tasilhunpo Temple is the fourth largest temple of the Yellow Hat Sect. It is divided into four Sutra Academies, namely the Toisamling, the Xarze, the Gyilkang and the Ngagba, and has ten principal halls. The temple originally housed more than three thousand lamas.

The earliest structure in the temple complex is the Zuoqin Hall, which was one of the principal gathering halls for lamas. Statues of Sakyamuni, Tsong-kha-pa and his pupils, as well as frescoes of Tsong-kha-pa, the four Heavenly Kings, the eighteen arhats and Maitreya can be found here.

The best known of Tasilhunpo's halls is the Tamkang (Maitreya)

The Tasilhunpo Temple

Hall. Construction began in 1914 under the ninth Panchen Lama, and the seven-storey hall took four years to complete. The Tamkang Hall houses the statue of Maitreya, which is 26.7 metres high and the largest and tallest gilded Buddha in China. According to historical records, between the statue's eyebrows are a walnut-sized diamond, thirty smaller diamonds, over three hundred pearls and a large quantity of coral, amber and turquoise. Approximately 279 kilograms of gold and 115,000 kilograms of copper were used to make the statue.

A funerary stupa for the fourth Panchen Lama was built in 1662. Set on a gold and silver foundation, the stupa is inlaid with diamonds and other precious stones. It took 4 years and 130 days to build and contains 85 kilograms of gold, over 15,000 kilograms of silver and countless treasures.

There is a reception chamber where the Panchen Lama received the envoys sent by each Qing emperor to inform him of imperial edicts and where he also saw ministers resident in Tibet. In the Western Buddha Hall is a portrait of Emperor Qianlong (1736–95) done in the Forbidden City in Beijing and also a Ten Thousand Year Tablet in honour of Emperor Daoguang (1821–50). After receiving imperial edicts the Panchen Lama would bow to these to show his gratitude.

The head of the gilded statue of Maitreya

In the northeast corner of Tasilhunpo is a massive platform built to celebrate the birth and enlightenment of Sakyamuni. From the fourteenth to the sixteenth day of the fourth month in the Tibetan calendar a huge portrait of Sakyamuni would be displayed on the platform to be worshipped by lamas and pilgrims.

Large quantities of precious objects are kept at Tasilhunpo, among which are seals and stamps made of gold and jade donated by Ming and Qing emperors, as well as imperial edicts and documents. The temple also contains Buddhist sculpture from the Sui and Tang dynasties, and early porcelain and textiles from the Yuan and Ming dynasties.

Location
The Tasilhunpo Temple is located at the foot of Niser mountain southeast of the town of Shigatse. It can be reached by bus or on foot from Shigatse.

THE POTALA PALACE
布达拉宫

History
The Potala Palace is the largest and most complete complex of palatial architecture in Tibet. It was first built in the seventh century by the thirty-second king of the Yarlung tribe, King Srong-brtsan-sgam-po, and its name in Tibetan means 'Sacred Place of Buddhism'.

Between the years AD 630 and 640 King Srong-brtsan-sgam-po led his armies north from southern Tibet to Lhasa, where he unified the tribes of the central plains and established the capital of the Tufan dynasty. It was here on Drnar-po ri (the Potala hill) that he built the huge Potala Palace, consisting of more than one thousand bays. During the middle period of the Tufan dynasty, the palace was destroyed by lightning, and at the end of the dynasty it was once again destroyed in a military uprising.

The present Potala Palace was built in the mid-seventeenth century during the reign of the fifth Dalai Lama. When work began on it in 1645, all the earlier Tufan buildings were razed with the exception of a meditation cave and the Hall of Guanyin from the Srong-brtsan-sgam-po period. It was these two sites which served as the centre of the White Palace. In 1652 the fifth Dalai Lama travelled to Beijing and was received by the Qing Emperor Shunzhi. The following year Shunzhi conferred a title upon the Dalai Lama, establishing him as the religious leader of Tibet. When the fifth Dalai Lama returned to Lhasa in 1653 he moved into the Potala from the nearby Zhefeng Monastery, and from that time on all major civil and religious ceremonies were held in the monumental palace. In 1690, eight years after the death of the Dalai Lama, the regent Sans-rgyas built a funerary pagoda to store his remains and began the construction of the Red Palace, a large complex of buildings located between the eastern and western wings of the

The great west gate

White Palace. During the reign of the thirteenth Dalai Lama in the first decades of the twentieth century, the heights of the eastern and western sections of the White Palace and the funerary pagoda halls of the Red Palace were increased to their present dimensions. The Potala served successively as the residence of nine high ministers and ten Dalai Lamas.

Description
The Potala Palace is built primarily of wood and stone. In typical Tibetan style, its thirteen storeys rise from the southern base of the Potala hill, following the contours of the hill to the peak. The Potala

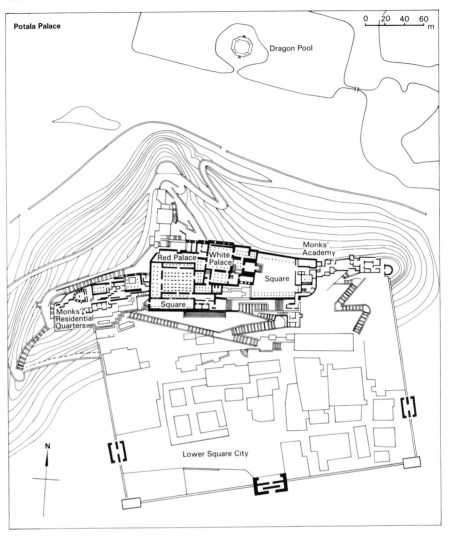

is composed of two major sections distinguished by the colour of their walls: the White Palace and the Red Palace. The western portion of the White Palace consisted principally of monks' residential quarters, while the eastern section served as the residence and official headquarters of the Dalai Lamas. The Red Palace, standing between these two sections, contained the funerary pagodas of the Dalai Lamas and other rooms serving religious functions.

The innumerable rooms of the Potala include palace halls, Buddhist chapels, scripture rooms, residential quarters, funerary pagodas and open courtyards. Some of the principal structures are:

the Great Eastern Hall, the largest hall within the White Palace, where important ceremonies such as the ordination of the Dalai Lama were held; the Great Western Hall, the principal structure in the Red Palace and the site of the fifth Dalai Lama's funerary pagoda; as well as the meditation cave of King Srong-brtsan-sgam-po and the Hall of Guanyin, two of the earliest sections of the Potala. Other rooms of interest include the scripture repository and the Hall of the Three Ages.

Most of the funerary pagodas in the Red Palace are decorated with pure gold. Of the eight extant pagodas (belonging to the fifth, and the seventh to the thirteenth Dalai Lamas), that of the fifth Dalai Lama is the largest. Standing 14.9 metres high, it consists of a base, body and crown, and has an outer shell of gold inlaid with pearls and precious stones. The embalmed corpse of the fifth Dalai Lama is preserved inside the pagoda. According to written records, the gold used in the pagoda weighs some 5,500 kilograms and more than 18,680 precious stones and pearls were used to decorate it. The pagoda also contains a number of valuable cultural relics.

The remaining seven pagodas are similar in design but vary in size, the pagoda of the thirteenth Dalai Lama being the largest after that of the fifth Dalai Lama. Built between 1934 and 1936, it is the most recent of the pagodas in the Red Palace.

In addition to the monumental architecture which characterizes the Potala, the palace contains a valuable collection of wall paintings, sculptures, Ming and Qing dynasty imperial documents, official seals and tribute gifts, as well as palm-leaf sutras and a large collection of Buddhist scriptures.

See Plate 39

Location
The Potala Palace is located within walking distance of central Lhasa.

Taiwan
台湾省

JILONG

TAIBEI

TAIZHONG

TAINAN — Anping Castle 安平古堡
Chikan Building 赤嵌楼
Temple of Prince Yanping 延平郡王祠
Temple of Confucius 孔庙

GAOXIONG

0   25   50   75   100 km

The Anping Castle (® The Stock House/Dan Rocovits)

THE ANPING CASTLE
安平古堡

History

The Anping Castle was built in 1630 by Dutch invaders. It has two
storeys, each with a protective wall. When Zheng Chenggong drove

away the Dutch invaders and Taiwan was recovered in February 1662, this castle served as Zheng's administrative centre. It was therefore also known as the Prince's City.

Description

Today only the ruined walls and the beacon, built in 1892, remain. From the top of the castle, is a panoramic view of the port and fishing boats in the distance. About 1 kilometre south of the castle is a battery which was built in 1875 by Shen Baozhen. Director General of the Arsenal from 1867 to 1874, Shen had been assigned to inspect conditions in Formosa in 1874. In May 1895 Liu Yongfu and his troops, then stationed in Tainan, used the battery and attacked a Japanese warship. After the Second World War only one large gun remained. The battery has been well preserved and is now open to the public.

Location

The Anping Castle is situated in the western outskirts of Tainan, southwest Taiwan.

THE CHIKAN BUILDING
赤嵌楼

History

The Chikan Building is also known as Foreigners' Town or the Red Hair Castle, because Dutch invaders were nicknamed Redheads. An anti-Dutch uprising led by Guo Huaiyi was suppressed in 1652, and one year later the Dutch built this castle in order to strengthen their control of Taiwan. In February 1662 Zheng Chenggong drove out the invaders and recovered Taiwan, and the building was used as a local government office. The original castle was destroyed by an earthquake in 1862. Two of its buildings, the Wenchang Library and the Sea God Temple, were built in 1879. In 1921 they became a museum known as the Chikan Building.

Description

Built in Chinese architectural style, the two-storey Chikan Building is well known in Tainan. Housed in the building are a three-dimensional map of Taiwan, models of ten large buildings, a map of the sea battles between Zheng and the Dutch, and a painting

The Chikan Building (® The Stock House/Steve Vidler)

of negotiations between the two sides. The stone lions in front of the building were made during the reign of the Qing Emperor Guangxu (1875–1908). There are also several stone stelae and nine huge stone tortoises which support a stele on which is carved an inscription by the Qing emperor on the suppression of Lin Shuangwen's revolt.

Location
The Chikan Building is in Nationality Road in Tainan, southwest Taiwan.

THE TEMPLE OF PRINCE YANPING
延平郡王祠

History
The Temple of Prince Yanping is also called the Zheng Chenggong Temple as a temple to Zheng Chenggong was built here in the early

Qing dynasty. The temple was renovated in 1845, and while on a mission in 1874 to inspect conditions in Formosa, Shen Baozhen, Director General of the Arsenal, asked the government to upgrade the state-level administration. The imperial court bestowed the title of Prince Yanping on Zheng Chenggong in 1875 and the temple was subsequently enlarged and renamed. A ceremony offering sacrifices to Zheng is held annually on the sixteenth day of the first month of the Chinese lunar calendar.

Description

In the central hall of the Temple of Prince Yanping stands a statue of Zheng Chenggong, flanked by his two generals, Gan Hui and Zhang Wanli. In the wings are fifty-seven statues of Zheng's subordinates and late Ming dynasty officers. The rooms for storing sacrificial and ceremonial implements have beautifully carved verandas and ceilings. The rear hall is devoted to Zheng's mother, a chamber to the right to Zheng's grandson, and one to the left to Zhu Shu, Prince Ningqing.

In the front courtyard are huge ancient trees and to the left a museum which contains a number of Zheng's possessions, a map of the port of Anping, a model of Tainan, and ancient robes. The plum tree behind the temple is said to have been planted by Zheng himself.

Location

The Temple of Prince Yanping is located in Kaishan Road, Tainan, southwest Taiwan.

THE TEMPLE OF CONFUCIUS IN TAINAN
台南孔庙

History

The Temple of Confucius, also known as Wenmiao (the Temple of Culture), was built with funds donated by Zheng Jing, son of Zheng Chenggong, the national hero who defeated Dutch invaders and recovered Taiwan in 1662, and by an official named Chen Yonghua. After renovation in 1685 it was named the Taiwan Institute of High Learning, and then the Tainan Institute of High Learning in 1888. It was repaired twelve times during the two hundred years from the reign of Emperor Kangxi (1662–1722) to that of Tongzhi (1862–73). Major renovations were begun in 1917 and lasted for three years.

Description

The temple is the largest temple of Confucius in Taiwan. Its main building is the Dacheng (Grand Accomplishment) Hall, in front of which is a terrace and an archway. To the east is the Memorial Chamber of Famous Officials and to the west the Jiexiao (Chastity and Filial Piety) Memorial Chamber, the Wenchang Pavilion and the Minglun Chamber. A little further to the east is the Pan Pond and the Li Gate. Horizontal boards with inscriptions written by Qing emperors hang from the beams of the hall. Some of the temple's numerous stelae record past renovations, while others are engraved with poems. On the altar inside the hall stand several wooden memorial tablets with the names of Confucius and his disciples on them, flanked by wooden memorial tablets for the ten sages and seventy-two followers of Confucius. To the rear of the main hall stand wooden memorial tablets to the parents of Confucius.

The northern part of the eastern side hall serves as a storage room for ritual instruments while on the western side is a room for musical instruments. These were used during the annual sacrifices to Confucius. There is a library containing ancient classics and records. The wall of the temple is very thick and has two archways. The eastern one is named the Dacheng Archway, and is inscribed 'Quan Tai Shou Xue' (the 'Primary Institute of Learning in All Taiwan'). To the left of this archway stands a stone tablet indicating the spot at which visitors should dismount.

Location

The Temple of Confucius is located in Wenmiao Street, Tainan, southwest Taiwan.

Glossary

Amitabha
: the Buddha who dwells in the Western Paradise; worshipped by followers of the Pure Land Sect

Ananda
: one of the chief disciples of the historical Buddha, said to have compiled the sutras. Dressed as a monk, he often appears with Kasyapa in support of the Buddha.

apsara
: Buddhist heavenly nymph, a celestial musician or dancer in attendance on the Buddha and bodhisattvas

arhat
: an enlightened, saintly man; the highest type of saint of Hinayana Buddhism. Arhat are called Lohan by the Chinese, who arranged them in groups of 16, 18 or 500.

Avalokitesvara
: Sanskrit name of the bodhisattva who is known in Chinese as Guanyin, first depicted as male, and by the Song dynasty usually as female and known as the Goddess of Mercy

bodhisattva
: a being who has achieved enlightenment but who defers entry into Nirvana in order to bring salvation to others. Bodhisattvas, generally crowned and bejewelled, appear alone or in pairs in support of a Buddha. Among the best-known bodhisattvas are Avalokitesvara, Manjusri and Samantabhadra.

Dalai Lama	the Grand Lama, spiritual head of Tibetan Buddhists
deva	a divine being in Buddhism
dougong bracket	a system of brackets inserted between the top of a column and a crossbeam in Chinese architecture
Eight Immortals	eight individuals, three of whom are historical and five imaginary, believed by Chinese of Daoist persuasion to have achieved immortality. They are depicted singly or in a group, each carrying his or her particular attribute.
Guanyin	*see* Avalokitesvara
huabiao	ornamental columns which were traditionally placed in front of palaces or tombs
jataka	any of some 550 'birth' stories or narratives of former incarnations of the Buddha in either animal or human form, collected in Buddhist sacred writings
Kasyapa	in Chinese Buddhism he is usually considered the chief disciple of the Buddha who became the first patriarch after the latter's death. He is shown as an elderly monk with a heavily lined face and often appears with Ananda in support of the Buddha, sometimes with two bodhisattvas.
Lokapala	the Guardian Kings of the Four Quarters, Guardians of the World and the Buddhist faith. Usually of fearsome aspect and armed, they stand at the entrance to a Buddhist hall.
Manjusri	the Bodhisattva of Wisdom, often shown riding a lion; Wenshu in Chinese
nan	an even-grained, yellowish fine wood used for furniture and pillars, commonly known as cedar

Panchen Lama	the lama next in rank to the Dalai Lama in Tibetan Buddhism
Puxian	*see* Samantabhadra
raja	one of the fierce spirits who are messengers and manifestations of Vairocana's wrath against evil spirits
Sakyamuni	The Holy One of the Sakyas, a title of the historical Buddha
Samantabhadra	the Bodhisattva of Universal Benevolence, often shown riding an elephant; Puxian in Chinese
Sumeru base	base, the silhouette of which resembles Mount Sumeru, the hourglass-shaped Buddhist world-mountain
sutra	a Buddhist sacred text, usually one attributed to the Buddha himself
Tripitaka	the canonical collection of Buddhist scriptures
Vajrapani	one of the Four Guardian Kings who wields the thunderbolt
Wheel of the Law	symbol of the Buddhist law, derived from an ancient solar symbol
Wenshu	*see* Manjusri

Index of Persons

Abahai, 242–6, 246–7, 249
Ahmed, 107
Ai, Duke, of the state of Lu, 60
Amitabha, 212, 300
Ananda, 44, 266, 300
Anigo, 9
Avalokitesvara, 276, 300

Bai Juyi, 96, 99, 169
Bai Qi, 154
Bodhidharma, 169–70

Cai Yin, 179
Chang Sun, 234
Chen Yonghua, 297
Chi You, 216
Chu Suiliang, 228, 231
Cixi, 28, 47
Confucius, 59–64, 298

Da Huayu, 251
Da Qingmo, 251–2
Da Yinzhuan, 251
Da Zuorong, 251
Dalai Lama, 301; the first, 287; the fifth,
    285, 290–3; the thirteenth, 291–3
Deng Wenzhuo, 71
Dharmaranga, 179
Dharmayasa, 113
Dong Qichang, 64, 172
Du Fu, 141, 144–7
Dutch, the, 295, 296, 298

Eight Immortals, 301

Facai, 114
Faliang, 263
Fan Guangwen, 92
Fan Mouzhu, 92
Fan Qin, 92
Fan Sheng, 155
Feng Huan, 133
Fenggan, 70
First emperor of the Han dynasty, 60, 66
First emperor of the Song dynasty, 40
First Heavenly True One, 208
French troops, 23
Fu Chai, 71
Fu Hao, 166
Fu Yi, 179

Gan Hui, 298
Gao Yang, 196

Gaozong, Tang dynasty Emperor, 168,
    231, 234–6
dGe-'dun-grub-pa, see Dalai Lama, the
    first
Geluofeng, 125
Genghis Khan, 256–7
German troops, 23
Gou Jian, 155
Gu Kaizhi, 64
Guan Yu, 144
Guanyin, 137, 138, 140, 301
Guo Huaiyi, 296
Guo Shoujin, 296
Guo Shoujin, 22, 181–3
Guo Ziyi, 210

Haitong, 135
Hanshan, 69–71
He Zhen, 64
Huaisu, 228
Huang, Tingjian, 147
Huike, 170
Huineng, 113
Huizong, Song dynasty Emperor, 60, 86
Huo Qubing, 224–5

Jin Richan, 224
Jingdi, 169
Juqu Maoqian, 279
Juqu Wuwei, 279

Kang Youwei, 71
Kangxi, Qing dynasty Emperor, 42, 46,
    50–1, 75
Kasyapa, 44, 266, 301
Kasyapa-matanga, 179
King Qingxiang, 154
King Wen of Chu, 154
King of Wu, 83
Kong Li, 64
Kong Zongyuan, 60
Kublai Khan, 181
Kuyuk, 257

Lady Cheng, 150
Lady Tang, 150
Lang, 58
Lezun, 263
Li Bai, 99–100
Li Bing, 131–3
Li Chun, 38
Li Daoyuan, 196
Li Jin, 236

Li Po, 120–1
Li Tianjing, 23
Li Yangbing, 227
Li Zhi, 229, 234
Liao empress dowager, 6
Lin Shuangwen, 297
Liu Bei, 142–4
Liu Fa, 150
Liu Gongquan, 228
Liu Gongchuo, 143
Liu Yongfu, 296
Lokapala, 301
Lu Jian, 142
Lu You, 71, 147
Luo Pin, 71
Lü Dongbin, 207–10

Ma Yuan, 120–1
Maitreya, 287, 301
Manjusri, 137, 180, 192, 212, 276
Marquis of Dai, 149–50
Mi Fei, 64, 172
Mingdi, 179–181

Ouyang Tong, 228
Ouyang Xun, 228

Pan Dechong, 207
Pan Geng, 163
Pan Yunduan, 85
Panchen Lama, 302; the fourth, 287–8;
    the ninth, 288
Pang Tong, 144
Pei Du, 142
Pei Wenzhong, 2
Prince Chai, 39
Prince Chun, 28
Prince Ningqing, 298
Prince of Eastern Fen, 197
Prince Yanping, 297, 298
Prince Yide, 236
Prince Zhanghuai, 236
Princess Chizun, 285–6
Princess Wencheng, 285–6
Princess Yongtai, 236
Pujing, 155
Puxian, 302

Qi Jiguang, 45, 66
Qian Chu, 90
Qianlong, Qing dynasty Emperor, 5, 10,
    15, 27, 42, 46–8, 50–1, 55, 81, 288
Qin Jing, 179
Qin Shihuang, 24, 66, 119, 219–20
Qin Changchun, 207

Renzong, Song dynasty Emperor, 60, 197

Saintly Mother, the, 200

Sakyamuni, 44, 105, 128, 141, 180, 186,
    192, 206, 212, 286–7, 287–9, 302
Samantabhadra, 137, 180, 192, 212, 302
Sans-rgyas, 290
Shen Baozhen, 296, 298
Shi Lu, 119–21
Shi Yousan, 169
Shi Zhengzhi, 77
Shide, 70–71
Shunzhi, Qing dynasty Emperor, 46,
    243–6, 290
Shuyu, 196
Sima Qian, 220
Song Zongyuan, 77
Srong-brtsan-sgam-po, 286, 290–3
Su Dongpo, 67, 96, 136
Su Yijian, 181
Sun Yu, 155

Taizong, 196, 231, 234, 285
Tang Yin, 71
Tanhong, 269
Tanyao, 185
Tathagata, 276
Tie Bao, 66
Tongzhi, 46
Tsong-kha-pa, 276, 287

Vajrapani, 276
Vipasyin, 241, 302

Wang, 234
Wang Shizhen, 71
Wang Xun, 22, 181
Wang Zhijing, 172
Wang Zhongyang, 207
Wanli, Ming dynasty Emperor, 18
Wei Gao, 135
Wei Junjing, 137
Wei Qing, 224
Wei Yingwu, 70–71
Wen Peng, 64
Wen Zhengming, 64, 71
Wencheng, Northern Wei Emperor, 185
Wendi, Northern Zhou Emperor, 169
Wenshu, 302
Wu Daozi, 64, 157
Wu Ding, 166
Wu Sangui, 128
Wu Zetian, 167, 175, 234–6
Wudi, Han dynasty Emperor, 28, 217,
    223–4
Wuzong, Tang dynasty Emperor, 189,
    192–3

Xianfeng, 46, 50
Xiang Yu, 220
Xiaoduan, 18

Xiaoming, 175
Xiaoqing, 18
Xiaowen, 166, 186
Xiaoxian, 45
Xie, 196
Xin Zhui, 149
Xu Da, 44
Xu Guangqi, 23
Xuangao, 269
Xuanzang, 229–31
Xue Yuanchao, 236

Yan Di, 216
Yan Zhenqing, 228
Yan Zhenzhi, 120
Yang Xianshu, 59
Yao Xing, 259
Yellow Emperor, the, 216–17
Yi Jiang, 197
Yijing, 231–3
Yongle, Ming dynasty Emperor, 18, 74,
    107, 158–9
Yongzhao Yunwu, 125
Yu Hao, 177
Yu Mengwei, 120–1
Yu Yue, 71
Yuan Jie, 122
Yue Fei, 71

Zhan Tianyou, 26
Zhang Ai, 84
Zhang Chuliao, 71
Zhang Fei, 144
Zhang Guolao, 39
Zhang Ji, 69–71
Zhang Jiuling, 157
Zhang Nanyang, 85
Zhang Wanli, 298
Zhang Xu, 228
Zhao Fan, 144
Zhao Lingjin, 110
Zhao Mengfu, 64, 172, 181
Zhao Yun, 144
Zhao Zhifeng, 139
Zhen Wu, 158
Zheng Banqiao, 64
Zheng Chenggong, 295, 296, 298
Zheng Jing, 298
Zhiyong, 228
Zhizhe, 155
Zhongzong, Tang dynasty Emperor,
    234–6
Zhou Guo, 155
Zhu Sheng, 237
Zhu Shu, 298
Zhu Yuanzhang, 73–6, 100, 236
Zhu Zhishan, 86
Zhuge Liang, 141–4

Index of Places

Afang Palace, 220
Altar of Heaven, 19–22
Amitabha Hall, 42
Ancient Cypress of Qiaoling Hill, 217
Ancient Observatory, 22–4
Angler's Terrace, 79–81
Anhai, 109
Anhui province, 98–102
Anji Bridge, 38–9, 44
Anping Bridge, 109–11
Anping Castle, 295–6
Anyang, 166
Appointment of Spring Hall, 86
Apricot Terrace, 60–1
Asia, South, 233; South-east, 233, 276;
   Western, 106
Astana, 280
Atensilen, 257
Autumn Moon on Calm Lake, 97
Auxiliary Pits of Pottery Figures, 219
Avalokitesvara Chamber, 88

Badaling, 24–6
Bai Causeway, 96–7
Baicheng, 283
Baita village, 255
Baji Hall, 175
Bamboo Rope Bridge, 133
Banpo Museum, 219
Banzhou Chamber, 157
Baoding mountains, Buddhist sculptures
   on, 139–41
Bao'en Guangxiao Temple, 113
Baotou, 26, 257
Beihai and Beihai Park, 6–9, 81
Beijing, 1–31, 36, 44, 46, 46–8, 65, 81,
   94–5, 100, 237, 266, 290
Beijing area, 4
Beijing Zoo, 31
Beijing's Western Hills, 26
Beiling mountains, 123
Beishan, 137–9
Beita Temple, 137
Beiwo, 65
Bell and Drum Tower, 88
Bell Tower, 71, 144, 159–60, 198
Bhagawan Library, 200–3
Bianliang, 7
Bingchuan, 128
Bingling Monastery Caves, 267–9
Binyang Cave, 167
Black mountain, 271
Bodhi Pagoda, 277
Bodhidharma Pavilion, 169

Bridge of the Fairies, 198
Brilliant Emperor lake, 96
Buddha Head peak, 125

Caishi village, 99
Caishiji, 99–100
Cangzhou, 44
Caves of the Thousand Buddhas, 263–4
Celestial Abstruseness Hall, 23–4
Central Lake, 7
Central Plains, 283
Central Seven Buddha Pavilion, 269
Chamber for Reading the Classics, 9
Chang'an, 28, 144, 192, 229, 233, 251,
   280, 286
Changling, 18
Changmen, 71, 73
Changping county, 16
Changrui mountain, 46
Changsha, 152
Changshan archipelago, 66
Changzhou, 137
Chen, 154
Chen Family Memorial Hall, 115–7
Chen Family School, 115
Chengde, 49–52, 55–6
Chengde Garden Resort, 49, 54, 56
Chengdu, 133, 137, 139, 141, 141–4,
   144–7
Chikan Building, 296–7
Chongqing, 139, 141
Chongzheng Hall, 242–6
Cishi Pavilion, 40
Ciyun Chamber, 172
Clepsydra Room, 23
Cold Mountain Temple, 69
Concealed Dragon Temple, 39–44
Cool and Refreshing Terrace, 181
Crow Ridge, 161
Cuixiu Chamber, 85

Da Yue Taihe Palace, 159
Dabie mountains, 79
Dacheng Archway, 299
Dacheng Hall, 299
Dadu river, 135–7
Dali, 125
Dali Kingdom, 127
Dangtu, 99
Dangyang, 158
Danjiang, 161
Danya mountain, 66–7
Dasigou, 267
Datong, 166, 189, 203, 206

Dazhao Monastery, 285–7
Dazheng Hall, 243
Dazhong Gate, 60
Dazu, 137–9, 139–41
Defend the Country Temple, 88
Dehua Tablet, 125
Dengfeng, 173, 176, 183
Deshengmen, 19
Dianchun Hall, 77
Dingling, 18–19
Dismount Arch, 74
Divine Kitchen, 21
Divine Warehouse, 20
Donggou, 267
Dongjing, 252
Double Lotus Flower Temple, 168
Dragon and Phoenix Gate, 18, 47
Dragon and Tiger Hall, 207–8
Dragon King Palace, 66
Dragon mountain, 137
Dragon Subduing Daoist Temple, 132–3
Drill Tower, 122
Drum Tower, 144, 160, 198
Du Fu Shrine, 146
Du Fu's Cottage, 144–7
Dunhuang, 25, 166; see also Mogao
    Caves
Du River Dyke, 131–3

Eastern Chamber, 157
Eastern Dyke, 31
Eastern Flowery Gate, 14
Eastern Iron Pagoda, 114–15
Eastern Palace, 51
Eastern Qing Mausolea, 46–8
Echo Wall, 22
Ejenhoro, 256–7
Emei station, 137
Entrance Gate, 175
Erhai lake, 125

Fahua Pagoda, 170
Fangcheng and Minglou, 47
Fangshan county, 4
Fangzhang, 66
Faru Pagoda, 170
Feng Huan Tower, 133–5
Fengguo Temple, 240–2
Fengmen, 78
Fengqiaozhen, 71
Fengtai, 5
Fengtian Altar, 107–9
Fengtian Palace, 242
Fengxian Temple, 167
Fengyang, 100–2
Fengyang Hall, 175
First Patriarch Hermitage, 170
Fish Mouth, 132
Fisherman's Garden, 76–8
Fishing Pond and the 'Flying Beams', 199

Five Dragon Pavilions, 9
Five Elaborate Caves, 185–7
Five Li Bridge, 109
Five Pavilion Bridge, 79–81
Five Peaks, 77
Five Phoenix Towers, 14
Flourishing Dragon Temple, 39
Flying Dragon Chamber, 244
Flying Rainbow Pagoda, 212
Fo'er cliff, 137
Fogong Temple, 205
Forbidden City in Beijing, 27, 101, 242,
    288
Forest of Pagodas, 170
Forest of Stelae, 171, 226–9
Foshouji Monastery, 233
Four Gate Pagoda, 58–9
Fragrant Hill, 28
Fragrant mountain, 168–9
Fuchengmennei Street, 11
Fujian province, 103–11
Funerary stupa, 288
Fuxian Monastery, 233
Fuzhou, 106, 109

Gande'er hill, 257
Ganlu Ordination Hall, 104–5
Gansu province, 144, 194, 216, 252, 257,
    263–74
Ganye Temple, 234
Gaochang, Ancient City of, 279–80
Gaocheng Observatory, 181–3
Garden of Joyful Spring, 27–8
Garden of Perfect Brightness, 27–8
Garden of Pure Ripples, 27–30
Garden of Repose and Brightness, 27–8
Garden of Repose and Ease, 27–8
Gate of Divine Prowess, 14
Gate of Great Achievement, 60–1
Gate of Heavenly Peace, 14
Gate of Heavenly Purity, 15
Gate to the Hall of Prayer for Good
    Harvests, 20
Gateway Facing Yue, 198
Giant Buddha Hall, 191
Giant Buddha Temple, 40
Gold Mountain Summer Palace, 26
Golden peak, 160
Gold Sea, 7
Golden Hall, 159, 160
Golden Hall of the Taihegong Temple,
    128
Golden Hall on Wudang mountain, 128
Grace Monastery, 229–31, 233
Grace Monastery Pagoda, 229
Great Buddha Bay, 140
Great Buddha Hall, 179
Great Buddha Temple, 33, 240
Great Eastern Hall, 293
Great Golden Gate, 74

Great Prayer Chamber, 276
Great Qing Gate, 243
Great Rainbow Bridge, 79
Great Red Gate, 17
Great Red Terrace, 56
Great Silver Pagoda, 276
Great Statue of Maitreya at Leshan, 135
Great Wall, 24–6, 44–5, 271
Great Western Hall, 293
Greater Golden Tile Hall, 276
Green Dragon mountain, 58–9
Green Shade Chamber, 80
Guangdong province, 112–17
Guanghua Gate, 273
Guangli Bridge, 4
Guangsheng Temple, 210–14
Guangxiao Temple, 113–15
Guangzhou, 44, 113–15
Guangxi province, 118–23
Guanxian, 133
Guanyin hill, 137
Guanyin Tower, 33–5
Guest Chamber, 169
Guilin, 122
Guixinglou, 237
Guyang Cave, 167
Gyilkang, 287

Haibao Pagoda, 259–61
Haidian district, 31
Haiyang river, 120
Hall of Amitabha, 212
Hall of Benevolent Tranquillity, 15
Hall of Chunyang, 207
Hall of Complete Harmony, 14–15
Hall of Culture, 15
Hall of Dragon Kongs, 189
Hall of Earthly Peace, 14–15
Hall of Fairy Scene of the Loka, 56
Hall of Great Achievement, 60–4
Hall of Guanyin, 290–3
Hall of Happiness and Longevity, 29
Hall of Healthy Longevity, 15
Hall of Heavenly Purity, 14–15
Hall of Humanity and Longevity, 29
Hall of Imperial Peace, 14
Hall of Jade Waves, 29
Hall of Luminous Virtue, 30
Hall of Maitreya, 193
Hall of Manjusri, 194
Hall of Martial Heroism, 15
Hall of Master Qiu, 207
Hall of Myriad Virtues, 195
Hall of Offerings, 199
Hall of Parting Clouds, 30
Hall of Peaceful Longevity, 15
Hall of Pleasing Eye, 30
Hall of Prayer for Good Harvests, 19–20
Hall of Preserving Harmony, 14–15
Hall of Prince Ming Ying, 211–13

Hall of Prince Wenxuan, 61
Hall of Repose, 60–4
Hall of Supreme Harmony, 14–15
Hall of the Boddhisattvas, 189
Hall of the Goddess of Mercy, 9
Hall of the Great Buddha, 195
Hall of the Heavenly Kings, 9, 10, 41, 54, 171
Hall of the Merciful Boat of Universal Salvation, 56
Hall of the Sage's Accomplishments, 60–4
Hall of the Saintly Mother, 198–200
Hall of the Seven Buddhas, 10
Hall of the Six Masters of Great Enlightenment, 41
Hall of the Six Transcendental Powers, 10–11
Hall of the Three Ages, 293
Hall of the Three Pure Ones, 207–10
Hall of Tranquil Longevity, 15
Hall of Vigorous Fertility, 14–15
Hall of Worship, 159–60
Hall to Receive Light, 7–9
Handan, 39
Hangzhou, 31, 79, 92, 96–7
Heavenly Emperor Hall, 19–20
Heavenly King Hall, 88, 104, 157, 179
Hebei province, 37–56, 216
Hefei, 100
Heibao Pagoda, 259
Heilongjiang province, 250–2
Henan province, 162–83, 216
Hexi, 263
Hexi corridor, 272–74
Hill of Long Life, 7
Hohhot, 255
Homage Court, 104
Hongdao Gate, 60
Hongdong county, 214
Hongshu Street, 115
Honouring the Classics Library, 95
Hovering Phoenix Chamber, 244
Huan river, 166
Huangjing Chamber, 160
Huangpu river, 86
Huangzhong county, 277
Huanhua Stream, 147
Huating, 83
Huayan Temple, 200–3
Hubei province, 128, 153–61
Huizhou, 237
Hunan province, 148–52
Huo mountain, 212–14
Huo Spring, 212–13

India, 113, 179, 229, 231, 263, 285
Inner Mongolia, 253–7
Imperial Garden, 15
Imperial Palace in Beijing, 7–9

Imperial Palace in Shenyang, 242
Imperial Vault of Heaven, 19–22
Inner lake, 97
Inspiration Pagoda, 177
Inverted Boat mountains, 156
Iron Mountain Garden, 64
Iron Pagoda, 155–7, 176–7

Jade Buddha Cave, 80
Jade Flowery Island, 7–9
Jade Islet, 6
Jade Ribbon Bridge, 31
Jade Spring, 97
Jade Spring Hill, 28–31
Jade Spring mountains, 158
Jade Spring Temple, 155–8
Japan, 71, 192
Jerusalem, 107
Ji mountain, 154
Ji'nan, 59
Ji'nancheng, 154–5
Jiangling, 155
Jiangsu province, 68–81
Jianguomen, 22
Jialan Hall, 175
Jialan mountains, 261
Jianfu Temple, 231–3
Jiayin Chamber, 243
Jiayu Pass, 25, 271–4
Jietai Temple, 105
Jiexiao Memorial Chamber, 299
Jiming Hill, 22
Jin river, 196–200
Jin Temple, 196–200
Jinding Temple, 128
Jingchuan county, 252
Jingong, 125
Jinjiang, 109–11
Jingshan, 7–9, 14
Jiuquan, 25, 271
Jixian, 36
Jixuzhai, 77
Jizu mountain, 128
Junxian county, 161

Kaibao Temple, 177
Kaifeng, 22, 86, 177–9
Kaishan Road, 298
Kaiyuan Monastery, 104–6
Kansas City, 212
Kezir, Caves of the Thousand Buddhas
    at, 280–3
Khan's Castle, 280
Kingdom of Changsha, 149
Ksitigarbha Hall, 170
Ksitigarbha Temple, 125–8
Kunming, 128
Kunming Lake, 28–31

Lake Balkash, 99

Lake Mirror Terrace, 198
Lake of Great Waters, 7
Lamaist dagobas, 54
Lamaist pagodas, 56
Langgong Temple, 58
Lanzhou, 266, 271, 274
Laoyingzhen, 161
Large Wild Goose Pagoda, 229–31, 233
Leshan, 137
Lesser Golden Tile Hall, 276
Lesser South Sea, 80
Lezhengmen, 51
Lhasa, 56, 287, 290–3
Li river, 119–20
Lianhua Cave, 167
Lianxing Temple, 81
Liao city of Fengzhou, 255
Liaoning province, 239–49
Liaoyang, 242
Library of Ten Thousand Volumes, 92
Licheng county, 59
Lijiazhuang, 192
Linfen, 214
Ling Canal, 119–22
Ling'an Hall, 18
Lingshan Temple, 88
Lingxin Gate, 60
Lingxing Archway, 75
Lingyan Temple in Shandong, 155
Lingyun mountain, 137
Listening to Orioles Pavilion, 80
Listening to Orioles Singing in the
    Willows, 97
Little Jishi mountains, 269
Little Lotus peak, 159–60
Liujiaodong river, 120
Liuyuan, 266
Long Dyke, 80–1
Long'en Hall, 47, 248–9
Longevity Hill, 28–31
Longmen Caves, 166–9, 280
Longmen mountains, 166
Longquan village, 210
Lotus Bridge, 81
Lotus Monastery, 104
Lugou Bridge, 4–5
Luoyang, 161, 166, 169, 176, 179–81,
    185, 233, 234
Luminous Pearl Hall, 40
Luoyang Bridge, 109
Lupan mountain, 256

Ma'an mountain, Zhejiang province, 90
Ma'anshan, Anhui province, 100
Magadha, Indian kingdom of, 229
Mahavira Hall, 54, 70, 88, 104–5, 113–
    14, 157, 171, 175, 179, 200–1, 212,
    240
Mahayana Pagoda, 54
Maijishan Caves, 269–71

Mansion of Confucius, 59–65
Mansion of the descendants of
    Confucius, 60
Mao Mausoleum, 223–6
Marco Polo Bridge, 4
Mausoleum of Genghis Khan, 256
Mausoleum of Qin Shihuang, 219
Mausoleum of the Yellow Emperor,
    216–18
Mawangdui, Western Han tombs at,
    149–52
Meditation cave of King Srong-btsan-
    sgam-po, 293
Memorial Chamber of Famous Officials,
    299
Meridian Gate, 13–14
Metropolitan Museum of Art in New
    York, 78
Mianzhou, 99
Miaoyan Chambers, 54
Miaoying Temple, 9–11
Mid–lake Pavilion, 97
Midnight Bell, 181
Min river, 132–3, 135–7
Mingfeng mountain, 128
Ming imperial mausoleum at Zhongdu,
    100
Ming Mausolea, 16–19
Minglun Chamber, 299
Mingsha mountain, 263–4
Mingshan Chamber, 107–8
Mingzhou Forest of Stelae, 95
Mogao Caves, 192, 263–6, 271, 280
Monastery Hall, 195
Mongol empire, 256
Moon Catching Pavilion, 100
Moon lake, 95
Moonlit Qiaoling Hill, 218
Mosque of Sacred Friends, 107
Mother of Waters Tower, 200
Mount Li, 220
Muzat river, 281

Nalanda, 231
Nan'an, 109–11
Nanjing, 22, 74–6, 100, 237
Nan Zhao Kingdom, 125
Nanchan Temple, 189–92
Nankou, 26
Nanning, 123
Nanshaomen, 233
Nanshi district, 86
Narrow West lake, 79–81
Nationality Road, 297
Nelson–Atkins Museum, 212
Neolithic village of Banpo, 218
Nepal, 285
Ngagba, 287
Nine–bay Hall, 276
Nine Dragon Screen, 9

Ning'an county, 252
Ningbo, 90, 92, 95, 246
Ningxia province, 258–61
Nirvana Cave, 269
Niser mountain, 290
Northern Cliff Boulder, 218
Northern Mausoleum, 246–9

Old Dragon Head, 45
Old Pillar Park, 128
Ordination Platform, 41
Ordos plateau, 256
Outer lake, 97
Outer town, 252, 272–3
Ox Chamber, 269

Pagoda Courtyard of King Asoka, 210
Pagoda of the First Patriarch, 196
Pakistan, 229
Palace Museum, 12–16
Palace of Eternal Happiness, 206
Palace of Pure Sun and Longevity, 206
Paradise Cave, 269
Patriarch Lü Hall, 66
Pavilion for Enjoying Springtime, 31
Pavilion for Watching the Waves, 67
Pavilion of Great Compassion, 40–2
Pavilion of Stelae, 56
Pavilion of the Constellation of Scholars,
    60
Pavilion of the Merciful Boat of
    Universal Salvation, 56
Pavilion of the Spring of Eternal Youth,
    200
Penglai, 65–7
Penglai county, 66–7
Penglai Pavilion, 66–7
People's Park, 123
Phoenix mountain, 102
Phoenix Tower, 245
Pine and Crane Study, 51
Pipa peak, 169
Plains of western Sichuan, 132
Ploughshair divide, 120
Potala hill, 290–1
Potala Palace, 55–6, 290–3
Precious Books Building, 92
Precious Bottle Neck, 132
Presenting Happiness Temple, 231
Prince's City, 296
Purity of Heart Hall, 10
Purple and Gold Hills, 76
Purple Cloud Hall, 105
Purple Forbidden City, 12
Purple Hills Observatory, 24
Putuozongsheng Temple, 55–6

Qian Mausoleum, 234–6
Qiantang river, 90–2
Qiantangmen, 96

Qianxi Temple, 167
Qianxian county, 236
Qiaoling Hill, 217–18
Qilian range, 271
Qin Dyke, 120
Qin, state of, 24
Qinghai province, 257, 275–7
Qingjing Mosque, 106–9
Qinglongqiao, 26
Qingshui county, 256
Qinghuangdao, 46
Qingyi river, 135–7
Qiyun Pagoda, 179–81
Quanhengsanjie Pavilion, 56
Queen Mother Palace, 66
Qunling, 269
Quanzhou, 106, 106–9, 111
Qufu, 65
Quxian county, 133

Reception Hall, 179
Reclining Buddha Hall, 114
Red Front Gate, 247
Red Hair Castle, 296
Red Palace, 290–3
Renshou Pagoda, 104
Revolving Scripture Library, 40
Rongwan, 122
Rongxian, 123
Round Alter, 19–22
Round City, 6–9
Ruan Yuan's Mound, 97
Ruicheng county, 210
Ruins of Longquanfu, 251–2
Ruoyuan Gate, 273
Russia, 55

Sacred Altar of the Han Emperor Wudi,
  217–18
Sacred Way, 47
Sacrificial Hall, 75
Sakyamuni Pagoda of the Fogong
  Temple, 203–6
Samgharama Hall, 114
Sand–flying Dyke, 132
Sanmenxia Reservoir, 207
Sanmoye Temple, 52
Sanqing Hall, 66
Sanwei mountain, 263
Sariputra Temple, 69
Sarira–stupa, 157
Scattering Flowers Building, 269–71
Scripture Explication Hall, 54
Scripture Repository, 157
Scripture repository, 293
Scripture–burning Terrace, 181
Sea God Temple, 296
Sea of Wisdom, 30
Second Patriarch Hermitage, 170
Seven Buddha Pavilion, 269

Seventeen–arch Bridge, 31
Shaanxi province, 215–38
Shandong province, 57–67
Shanghai, 65, 82–6
Shanhai Pass, 25, 44–6
Shanhaiwei, 44
Shanxi province, 184–214
Shaolin Monastery, 169–73
Shaoshi mountains, 173
Shengjing Palace, 242
Shengshi Gate, 60
Shentong Temple, 58
Shenyang, 242–6, 249
Shigatse, 290
Shijiazhuang, 44
Shiquan Street, 78
Shishan Study, 244
Sichuan province, 99, 130–47
Six Harmonies Pagoda, 90–2, 97
Six Points Pagoda, 90
Sixth Patriarch Hall, 114
Sky Pillar peak, 158–60
Small Golden Hill, 79–80
Small Southern lake, 97
Small Wild Goose Pagoda, 231–3
Solitary Hill, 97
Song mountain, 176
Songjiang, 83
Songjiang county, 84
Songyue Temple Pagoda, 174–6
Southern Heavenly Gate, 159
Spirit Way, 73–5
Square City, 74–6
Sramanera Temple, 66
Standing in Snow Pavilion, 170
Stelae Pavilion of Thirteen Emperors, 60
Stele Pagoda, 54
Stele Pavilion, 17, 47
Studio of the Calm Mind, 9
Su Dyke, 30, 96–7
Sumatra, Indonesian island of, 231
Summer Palace, 26–31
Sundial Hall, 24
Sutra Chamber, 88
Sutra Repository, 71, 105
Suzhou, 71, 73, 78
Suzhoulu, 271
Syria, 107

Ta'er Lamasery, 257, 276–7
Tablet Pavilion, 75
Tai'an, 59
Taibai Memorial Hall, 99–100
Taihe, 125
Taihe Palace, 158–61
Tainan, 296, 297, 298
Tainan Institute of High Learning, 298
Taiwan, 294–9
Taiwan Institute of High Learning, 298
Taiyuan, 192, 196, 200, 210, 214

Tamkang Hall, 287
Tang Shuyu Temple, 196
Tangshan, 10
Tanyao, Five Caves of, 185
Tasilhunpo Temple, 287–90
Tathagata Stupas, 277
Temple of Buddha's Light, 192–6
Temple of Confucius, 59–65, 95, 298–9
Temple of Confucius in Tainan, 298
Temple of Culture, 298
Temple of Eternal Peace, 7–9
Temple of Explaining Happiness, 9
Temple of Gratitude and Longevity, 28
Temple of Great Compassion, 40
Temple of Liu Bei, 142
Temple of Master Lü, 207
Temple of Prince Yanping, 297–8
Temple of Singular Happiness, 33
Temple of the deity Hao Tian, 200
Temple of the Dragon King, 31
Temple of the Four Sages, 120
Temple of the Great Buddha, 193–6
Temple of the One Hundred Thousand
    Buddhas, 277
Temple of the Soul's Retreat, 97
Temple of the Unity of the Myriad
    Truths, 56
Temple of Universal Peace, 52
Temple of Water God, 212–3
Ten King Pavilion, 244
Ten Thousand Buddha Cave, 167
Ten Thousand Buddha Chamber, 160,
    269
Ten Thousand Buddha Tower, 9
Ten Thousand Volume Chamber, 76
Terrace of Golden Men, 199
Terrace of Golden Statues, 198
Thousand Buddha Hall, 170–3
Thousand Buddha Veranda, 269
Three Pools Mirroring the Moon, 97
Throne Chamber, 252
Tianjin, 32–6
Tianshou Hill, 16–18
Tianshui, 271
Tiantai Temple in Zhejiang, 155
Tianyi Pool, 95
Tianyige Library, 92–5, 246
Tibet, 52, 55, 284–93
Tiger Hill, 71–3
Tiger Hill Pagoda, 71–3
Tiny Wave valley, 79
Toisamling, 287
Tomb of Huo Qubing, 223
Tombs of the Three Generals, 120
Tongguang Pagoda, 170
Tongwen Gate, 60
Toudong Road, 128
Tower of Buddha Fragrance, 30
Tower of Fragrant Wind and Flowery
    Rain, 195
Town of Rams, 113

Town of Sujab, 99
Tranquility Chamber, 243
Treasure City, 75–6
Tumen Street, 109
Turpan, 280
Two Princes Temple, 132–3

United States, 212

Vairocana Hall, 42, 157, 179, 212
Vairocana Pavilion, 179
Viewing Fish at Flower Harbour, 97
Volga river, 55

Wanbuhuayan Sutra Pagoda, 255
Wangshi Lane, 77
Water City of Penglai, 65
Wave Calming Bridge, 132–3
Weibei plateau, 226
Weituo Hall, 259
Wenchang Library, 296
Wenchang Pavilion, 299
Wenchang Temple, 200
Weng mountain, 198
Wenhuige Library in Yangzhou, 95
Wenjinge Library in Chengde, 94
Wenlange Library in Hangzhou, 94
Wenmiao Street, 299
Wenshu mountain, 271
Wensuge Library in Shenyang, 94–5, 244,
    246
Wenyuange Library in the Forbidden
    City, 94–5
Wenyuange Library in the Old Summer
    Palace, 95
Wenzongge Library on Jinshan, 95
West Garden, 7
West Lake, 30, 79, 95–7
Western Buddha Hall, 288
Western Chamber, 157
Western Dyke, 30–1
Western Flowery Gate, 14
Western Iron Pagoda, 114–15
Western Mongols, 55
White Dagoba, 9, 9–11, 79–81
White Dagoba in Miaoyingsi, 9
White Dagoba Temple, 10
White Drapery Hall, 169
White Horse Temple, 179–81
White Pagoda, 255
White Palace, 290–3
White Robe Hall, 175
Wind Pavilion, 80
Wofo Hall, 259
Wooden Pagoda of Yingxian, 203
Wu Gate, 101
Wudang mountains, 158
Wuguan village, 163
Wuhan, 155, 158, 161
Wukang, 85
Wuliang Hall, 240

Wulin lake, 95
Wulipai, 152
Wusong river, 84
Wutai, 192, 196
Wutaishan, 189, 196
Wuzhou mountain, 186–9

Xarze, 287
Xiamen, 106, 109
Xi'an, 218, 219, 223, 226, 226–9, 231,
   233, 236, 236–8, 271; city walls of,
   236–8
Xiang river, 119–21
Xianxi Temple, 240
Xiao Mausoleum, 73–76
Xiaoling, 46–7
Xiaoshui river, 39
Xiaotun village, 166
Xiaoyao Pavilion, 175
Xiaqi Chamber, 244
Xichang, 279
Xiezhong Study
Xiguan Street, 36
Xihua Gate, 101
Xijie Street, 106
Xili lake, 97
Xilian mountain, 224
Xillin Epigraphy Society, 97
Ximing Monastery, 233
Xing'an, 120
Xing'an Canal, 119
Xing'an county, 122
Xinglongshan, 257
Xingping county, 226
Xingshengjiao Temple Pagoda, 83–4
Xining, 277
Xinjiang province, 52, 278–83
Xiu river, 123
Xixia, 256
Xixia Temple in Nanjing, 155
Xu Garden, 79
Xuanjiao Temple, 255

Yalu river, 45
Yan, state of, 24
Yandun and Tiantai mountains, 46
Yangqing county, 26
Yangshan Pavilion, 86
Yangtze river, 73, 80, 119
Yangxi Study, 243
Yangzhou, 79–81
Yantai, 67
Yanzhou, 65
Yellow river, 177, 219, 261, 263, 269
Yi county, 242
Yinchuan, 261
Yingdu, 154
Yingpan hill, 137
Yingxian, 206

Yingzhou, 44, 66
Yin Ruins, 163–6
Yique, 166
Yishui river, 166–8
Yongchang Fort, 137
Yongding river, 4–5
Yongji, 210
Yongjing, 269
Yongle township, 207
Youguo Temple Pagoda, 176–9
Youtingpu, 139, 141
Yu Garden, 85–6
Yue Fei's Tomb and Temple, 97
Yuangong Pagoda, 171
Yue lake, 97
Yuelun hill, 92
Yuezhi, state of, 179
Yuhua Chamber, 86
Yulei mountain, 133
Yulin, 123
Yuling, 48
Yumenguan, 283
Yuncheng, 210
Yungang, 280
Yungang Caves, 166, 185–9
Yunnan province, 124–9

Zhangjiakou, 26
Zhangming, 99
Zhao, state of, 24
Zhaojiaping village, 135
Zhaoling, 247
Zhaoqing Temple in Hangzhou, 105
Zhaoxian, 39
Zhaozhou Bridge, 38
Zhaozhou Great Stone Bridge, 38
Zhefeng Monastery, 290
Zhejiang province, 85, 87–97, 246
Zheng Chenggong Temple, 297
Zhending prefecture, 7
Zhengding, 40–4
Zhenguo Pagoda, 104
Zhengzhou, 173, 176, 183
Zhenjiang, 80, 95
Zhenwu Pavilion, 122–123
Zhenyang Gate, 66
Zhibo Channel, 198
Zhihu Monastery, 169
Zhongdu, 100–2
Zhongshanbalu, 117
Zhongshanliulu, 115
Zhongyang Hall, 207
Zhoukoudian, 2–4
Zhu river, 119
Zhuge Liang Memorial Hall, 141–144
Zhungar, 52
Zhusheng Pavilion, 109
Zi Xiao Palace, 161
Zuoqin Hall, 287
Zunhua county, 48